THINGS THAT
MATTER

THREE DECADES OF PASSIONS,
PASTIMES AND POLITICS

CHARLES

KRAUTHAMMER

CROWN
FORUM
NEW YORK

Published in the United States by Crown Forum,
an imprint of the Crown Publishing Group,
a division of Penguin Random House LLC, New York.
www.crownpublishing.com

CROWN FORUM with colophon is a registered trademark
of Penguin Random House LLC.

Originally published in hardcover in slightly different
form in the United States by Crown Forum,
an imprint of the Crown Publishing Group,
a division of Penguin Random House LLC,
New York, in 2013.

The following originally appeared in *The New Republic*:
"The Tirana Index" (December 13, 1982);
and "On Ethics of Embryonic Research"
as "Crossing Lines" (April 29, 2002).

Library of Congress Cataloging-in-Publication Data
is available upon request.

ISBN 978-0-385-34919-2
eBook ISBN 978-0-385-34918-5

Printed in the United States of America

Cover design by Michael Nagin
Cover photograph by Frank Longhitano

2 4 6 8 10 9 7 5 3 1

First Paperback Edition

For Robyn and Daniel

CONTENTS

PART TWO: POLITICAL / 131

Part Three: HISTORICAL / 239

PART FOUR: GLOBAL / 319

EPILOGUE (2015) / 367

THINGS THAT MATTER

INTRODUCTION

I. THE BOOK

What matters? Lives of the good and the great, the innocence of dogs, the cunning of cats, the elegance of nature, the wonders of space, the perfectly thrown outfield assist, the difference between historical guilt and historical responsibility, homage and sacrilege in monumental architecture, fashions and follies and the finer uses of the F-word.

What matters? Manners and habits, curiosities and conundrums social and ethical: Is a doctor ever permitted to kill a patient wishing to die? Why in the age of feminism do we still use the phrase "women and children"? How many lies is one allowed to tell to advance stem cell research?

What matters? Occam's razor, Fermat's last theorem, the Fermi paradox in which the great man asks: With so many habitable planets out there, why in God's name have we never heard a word from a single one of them?

These are the things that most engage me. They fill my days, some trouble my nights. They give me pause, pleasure, wonder. They make me grateful for the gift of consciousness. And for three decades they have occupied my mind and commanded my pen.

I don't claim these things matter to everyone. Nor should they. I have my eccentricities. I've driven from Washington to New York to watch a chess match. Twice. I've read Stephen Hawking's *A Brief History of Time*. Also twice, though here as a public service—to reassure my readers that this most unread bestseller is indeed as inscrutable as they thought. And perhaps most eccentric of all, I left a life in medicine for a life in journalism devoted mostly to politics, while firmly believing that what really matters, what moves the spirit, what elevates the mind, what fires the imagination, what makes us fully human are all of these endeavors, disciplines, confusions and amusements that lie outside politics.

Accordingly, this book was originally going to be a collection of my writings about everything but politics. Things beautiful, mysterious, profound or just odd. Working title: *There's More to Life than Politics.*

But in the end I couldn't. For a simple reason, the same reason I left psychiatry for journalism. While science, medicine, art, poetry, architecture, chess, space, sports, number theory and all things hard and beautiful promise purity, elegance and sometimes even transcendence, they are fundamentally subordinate. In the end, they must bow to the sovereignty of politics.

Politics, the crooked timber of our communal lives, dominates everything because, in the end, everything—high and low and, most especially, high—lives or dies by politics. You can have the most advanced and efflorescent of cultures. Get your politics wrong, however, and everything stands to be swept away. This is not ancient history. This is Germany 1933.

"Beauty is truth, truth beauty,—that is all / Ye know on earth, and all ye need to know," every schoolchild is fed. But even Keats— poet, romantic, early 19th-century man oblivious to the horrors of the century to come—kept quotational distance from such blissful innocence. Turns out we need to know one more thing on earth: politics— because of its capacity, when benign, to allow all around it to flourish, and its capacity, when malign, to make all around it wither.

This is no abstraction. We see it in North Korea, whose deranged Stalinist politics has created a land of stunning desolation and ugliness, both spiritual and material. We saw it in China's Cultural Revolution, a sustained act of national self-immolation, designed to dethrone, debase and destroy the highest achievements of five millennia of Chinese culture. We saw it in Taliban Afghanistan, which, just months before 9/11, marched its cadres into the Bamiyan Valley and with tanks, artillery and dynamite destroyed its magnificent cliff-carved 1,700-year-old Buddhas lest they—like kite flying and music and other things lovely—disturb the scorched-earth purity of their nihilism.

Politics is the moat, the walls, beyond which lie the barbarians. Fail to keep them at bay, and everything burns. The entire 20th century with its mass political enthusiasms is a lesson in the supreme power of politics to produce ever-expanding circles of ruin. World War I not only killed more people than any previous war. The psychological shock of Europe's senseless self-inflicted devastation forever changed Western sensibilities, practically overthrowing the classical arts, virtues and modes of thought. The Russian Revolution and its imitators (Chinese, Cuban, Vietnamese, Cambodian) tried to atomize society so thoroughly—to war against the mediating structures that stand between the individual and the state—that the most basic bonds of family, faith, fellowship and conscience came to near dissolution. Of course, the greatest demonstration of the finality of politics is the Holocaust, which in less than a decade destroyed a millennium-old civilization, sweeping away not only 6 million souls but the institutions, the culture, the very tongue of the now-vanished world of European Jewry.

The only power comparably destructive belongs to God. Or nature. Or, if like Jefferson you cannot quite decide, Nature's God. Santorini was a thriving island civilization in the Mediterranean until, one morning 3,500 years ago, it simply fell into the sea. An earthquake. A volcanic eruption. The end.

And yet even God cannot match the cruelty of his creation. For every Santorini, there are a hundred massacres of innocents. And that is the work of man—more particularly, the work of politics, of groups of men organized to gain and exercise power.

Which in its day-to-day conduct tends not to be the most elevated of human enterprises. Machiavelli gave it an air of grandeur and glory, but Disraeli's mordant exultation "I have climbed to the top of the greasy pole," best captured its quotidian essence—grubby, grasping, manipulative, demagogic, cynical.

The most considered and balanced statement of politics' place in the hierarchy of human disciplines came, naturally, from an American. "I must study politics and war," wrote John Adams, "that my sons may have the liberty to study mathematics and philosophy, geography, natural history, and naval architecture, navigation, commerce, and agriculture, in order to give their children a right to study painting, poetry, music, architecture, statuary, tapestry and porcelain."

Adams saw clearly that politics is the indispensable foundation for things elegant and beautiful. First and above all else, you must secure life, liberty and the right to pursue your own happiness. That's politics done right, hard-earned, often by war. And yet the glories yielded by such a successful politics lie outside itself. Its deepest purpose is to create the conditions for the cultivation of the finer things, beginning with philosophy and science, and ascending to the ever more delicate and refined arts. Note Adams' double reference to architecture: The second generation must study naval architecture—a hybrid discipline of war, commerce and science—before the third can freely and securely study architecture for its own sake.

The most optimistic implication of Adams' dictum is that once the first generation gets the political essentials right, they remain intact to nurture the future. Yet he himself once said that "there never was a democracy yet that did not commit suicide." Jefferson was even less sanguine about the durability of liberty. He wrote that a constitutional revolution might be needed every 20 years. Indeed, the lesson of our history is that the task of merely maintaining strong and sturdy the structures of a constitutional order is unending, the continuing and ceaseless work of every generation.

To which I have devoted much of my life. And which I do not disdain by any means. Indeed, I intend to write a book on foreign policy and, if nature (or God or Nature's God) gives me leave, to write yet one more on domestic policy. But this book is intended at least as much for other things. Things that for me, as for Adams, shine most brightly.

Biologist and philosopher Lewis Thomas was once asked what one artifact we should send out into space as evidence of human achievement. "I would vote for Bach, all of Bach, streamed out into space, over and over again," he suggested. Then added ruefully, "We would be bragging, of course."

Not a single State of the Union address, I'd venture. Not one version of the Nuclear Non-Proliferation Treaty. Nor, God help us, what we actually did send out into space when we first got the chance. The interstellar Voyagers 1 and 2 carry, among other artifacts, the first audio greetings from our species. Who is it that, on behalf of all humanity that has ever lived, speaks to some unknown alien race across the infinity of space? Whose voice will survive into eternity long after Earth has turned to a cinder? Why, the head of the one political institution that represents all mankind, the then UN Secretary-General Kurt Waldheim. Later discovered to be . . . a Nazi. A minor one, mind you. Just a small willing cog in the machine. Makes you wish that we'd immediately sent out a Voyager 3 beeping frantically: Please disregard all previous messages.

Thomas was right about Bach. Though I do concede that beaming out a digital copy of the Magna Carta or the Declaration of Independence would have made a fine second choice. But here I draw a distinction. While political practice deserves grudging respect for its power, political philosophy commands reverence for its capacity for grandeur and depth, as exemplified in the sublime texts of the American founding. Accordingly, I have weighted much of the politically oriented writings in this volume toward those dealing with constitutional issues and general principles. I've skipped over much of the partisan contention that characterizes the daily life of a democracy— the tentative, incremental, ever-improvised back-and-forth that occupies much of the attention of a political columnist. I've tried to give as little space as possible to campaigns and elections, to personalities and peccadilloes, to things that come and go.

These contingencies are not ignored, of course. They cannot be. That's not how actual political life is lived. But because these more transient, more partisan, more pole-climbing events tend to mundanity and redundancy, they lose their interest over time. They fade from memory, and deservedly so. I've tried to filter most of that out. I've tried to stick to what matters.

II. THE AUTHOR

That's how this book was put together. For those readers interested in how the author was, let me offer a brief account of my writing career. It is a measure of its improbability that until age 30, I had not the faintest idea or expectation of becoming a writer. I had a brief accidental stint in college, then quite casually left it behind for a decade, only to return to it by the sheerest serendipity.

My first published article was a short, pompous editorial in the *McGill Daily* titled "End of the Monolith." I got to write the equally pompous headline because I happened to be my own editor. It was a month into my senior year at McGill and my first day on the job as editor in chief. A week earlier, the student council had fired the previous editor on the grounds that the paper's mindless, humorless Maoism had rendered it unreadable. (Yes, Maoism—Stalinism being too moderate and lacking in romance. This was, after all, the '60s.) A search was launched for someone not loony-left. The roulette wheel spun my way.

By today's standards, I would have been considered a centrist, but on a 1969 campus that was considered a fairly exotic, somewhat reactionary political orientation. So I decided to issue a manifesto clarifying the new management's creed. It was simple. The paper was now open to all points of view. "The Daily is under the present editorship because it is committed to publish a pluralist paper," I wrote. Not only would "dissenting and critical analyses be actively solicited," but henceforth newsworthiness would be determined by no single ideological standard. Or, as I phrased it, by "no one histori-cal paradigm"—Thomas Kuhn having made the notion of "paradigm shift" too voguish for any self-respecting 19-year-old to resist.

Pluralism was not the most fashionable flag to fly those days, but unlike most of my contemporaries, I never had a Marxist phase. And if I did, it would have lasted no more than a weekend—undoubtedly a good one, I suspect, because I don't remember a minute of it.

This devotion to pluralism reflected my aversion to the politics of certainty, so prevalent at the time, and in particular to the politics of the extreme. I had learned that lesson early. At McGill, I wit-nessed a mass rally to turn the university, then considered by the left a bastion of Anglo imperialism, into a French-speaking school for the local proletariat. At the head of the march, linked arm-in-arm, were two men: McGill's most radical Marxist professor and the leader of a neo-fascist, anti-immigrant popular front.

It was for me a seminal moment: visual, tangible evidence of the ultimate convergence of left and right, an object lesson in the virtues of ideological moderation, and my good-bye, if there ever was a hello, to political romanticism. It set my own political course toward philo-sophical skepticism and political tolerance. That didn't mean splitting differences or straddling some ideological midpoint. It meant view-ing certainty with suspicion and acknowledging, with both regret and resolve, the imperfectibility of man, the fallibility of institutions and the tragic—rather than redemptive—nature of history.

When my senior year was up, I went on to pour myself into politi-cal philosophy at Oxford. It is there that I discovered my muse for this prudential view of the possibilities of politics: John Stuart Mill, whose *On Liberty* is the foundational document of classical liberal-ism. To this day it is the first thing I recommend to any young per-son seeking political guidance, to be followed by Isaiah Berlin's *Four Essays on Liberty*, perhaps the finest, and surely the most accessible, 20th-century elaboration of that tradition.

I say Mill's liberalism, invoking the 19th-century understanding of the word. Today that political orientation is the essence of conservatism. In the 20th century, liberalism became more ambitious. It outgrew the classical individualism of the Millian tradition and fell in thrall to the romantic progressivism of the age. Mill held that truth emerges from an unfettered competition of ideas and that individual character is most improved when allowed to find its own way uncoerced. That vision was insufficient for 20th-century American liberalism. Mill lacked sweep and glory. Modern liberalism's perfectionist ambitions—reflected in its progenitor (and current euphemism), progressivism—seeks to harness the power of government, the mystique of science and the rule of experts to shape both society and citizen and bring them both, willing or not, to a higher state of being.

It was natural, therefore, that I would in time turn to conservatism. But that proved to be years away, largely because I then abruptly left the field and abandoned my studies. Mill had his crisis of conscience at 20. I had mine at 21. I had become increasingly uncomfortable with a life of theory. I began to regard it as something of an intellectual self-indulgence, increasingly divorced from reality and from duty. One morning that August, I called the registrar at Harvard Medical School, where I'd previously been accepted, to ask for immediate admission. Quite by chance, a student had just dropped out—a week before the beginning of the term. If I was there by Monday, the spot was mine.

I didn't pack. I left immediately to take up what I was sure would be my life's work: the practical, the real, the indisputably worthy work of medicine. There I spent the next seven years, a nice biblical sum, four as a medical student, three as a psychiatric resident at Massachusetts General Hospital.

Medicine had not been my first choice. I had long preferred the graceful lines of physics to the ragged edges of biology. But at 16, I'd come to the realization that I didn't have what it took to do important work in theoretical physics, namely genius. A friend in my Special Relativity class, who had come to the same awful conclusion about his own intellectual capacities, told me that he was changing his major because he didn't want to end up testing steel for General

Motors. (The great physicist Max Planck did once tell John Maynard Keynes that he had thought of studying economics but decided it was too difficult. That I take as an exercise in either humor or good manners.)

Not thirsting to test steel, I chose medicine. I have no regrets. It was challenging and enlarging. I absorbed more knowledge in those seven years than at any other time in my life. Although it did turn out that I wasn't quite the perfect fit for psychiatry either. In my first year at Mass General, I discovered that all freshmen residents were required to attend a weekly group-therapy session. Seeing this as pointless, I refused. This did not go over well with management. Around week seven, I was called into the department chairman's office. He asked me why I had not been attending.

"Because I came here to give therapy, not get it," I said.

"You're just in denial," he protested loudly.

"Of course I am, sir. It's the best defense mechanism ever invented. Why, I'm a master of denial. I should be a professor—I could give a course in denial."

I was enjoying the riff, but the chief was not. He cut me short: Attend the sessions or leave the program. Having few marketable skills and fewer prospects, I attended. But for the remaining 20 or so weeks, I said nary a word in the group. I was occasionally asked why. "I'm in denial," I explained.

Don't get me wrong. This was something of an aberration. I had gone to Mass General because it was the most biologically (and least psychoanalytically) oriented of all the psychiatric programs in the Boston area. Remarkably and brilliantly so. Their pharmacological treatments were superb. They pioneered a new method of (unilateral) electric shock therapy that was astonishingly successful in curing the most profound and recalcitrant depressions. And they even used hypnosis, which I learned to administer to in-patient burn victims in order to block the excruciating pain that accompanies bandage changes—thus sparing them the need for potentially addictive narcotics.

It was a noble life. I remain forever respectful of the work carried on by my colleagues and grateful for my own seven years there. Medicine—and particularly hospital medicine, which lives in a sea of human suffering—has a way of beating callowness out of even the most self-possessed youth. Its other invaluable residue is best described by Arthur Conan Doyle, himself a physician: "The moral training to keep a confidence inviolate, to act promptly on a sudden call, to keep your head in critical moments, to be kind yet strong— where can you, outside medicine, get such a training as that?"

Nonetheless, my life as a doctor felt constricted. It was conducted entirely within the four walls of the hospital. Outside, there was a history unfolding to which I felt impelled to contribute—but saw no way to. How to get from here to there? Having moved from New York to Montreal when I was five (prudently bringing my parents with me) and having not resided again in the United States until medical school, I had few contacts outside Boston, and none in politics or journalism.

And then, pure blind luck. With only a few months left in my residency, a professor with whom I'd written a couple of papers on manic-depressive disease was appointed out of the blue by President Carter to head a newly created federal superagency overseeing the National Institute of Mental Health (NIMH). At my suggestion, he took me to Washington to help shape national research on a new diagnostic system designed to move psychiatry from its anecdotal Freudian origins to a more empirical and scientific foundation.

It was my "Go West, young man" moment. Although I knew no one in Washington, I figured it was there that I would find my way back to my long-dormant interest in public affairs.

This is no place for an extended biography, so I'll be brief about the unfolding. While working at the NIMH, I began writing articles for *The New Republic* and was then offered a speechwriting job for Vice President Walter Mondale. It was spring 1980. Six months of that and our side lost, badly. Such was my political career. At which point, *The New Republic* offered me a job as a writer and editor. I began my new life in journalism on the day Ronald Reagan was sworn in, January 20, 1981.

Some of the articles in this book are from those early years at *The New Republic*. Others are from the monthly back-page essay I began writing for *Time* magazine in 1983. Most of the pieces in this book, however, are from the weekly column I have been writing for the *Washington Post* since 1984.

These quite fantastic twists and turns have given me a profound respect for serendipity and a rather skeptical view about how much one really is master of one's fate. A long-forgotten, utterly trivial student council fight brought me to journalism. A moment of adolescent angst led to the impulsive decision to quit political studies and enroll in medical school. A decade later, a random presidential appointment having nothing to do with me brought me to a place where my writing and public career could begin. When a young journalist asks me today, "How do I get to be a nationally syndicated columnist?" I have my answer: "First, go to medical school."

These turns in my career path were a matter of fate. But there was one other transformation that was not, and it needs a word of explanation. It was deliberate, gradual and self-driven: my ideological evolution.

I'm often asked: "How do you go from Walter Mondale to Fox News?" To which the short answer is: "I was young once." The long answer begins by noting that this is hardly a novel passage. The path is well trodden, most famously by Ronald Reagan, himself once a New Deal Democrat, and more recently by a generation of neoconservatives, led by Irving Kristol and Norman Podhoretz. Every story has its idiosyncrasies. These are mine.

I'd been a lifelong Democrat, and in my youth a Great Society liberal. But I had always identified with the party's Cold War liberals, uncompromising Truman-Kennedy anti-communists led by the likes of Henry Jackson, Hubert Humphrey and Pat Moynihan. Given my social-democratic political orientation, it was natural for me to work for Democrats, handing out leaflets for Henry Jackson in the 1976

Massachusetts primary (Jackson won; I handed out a lot of leaflets) and working for Mondale four years later.

After Reagan took office in 1981, however, Democratic foreign policy changed dramatically. Some, of course, had begun their slide toward isolationism years earlier with George McGovern's "Come Home, America" campaign. But the responsibility of governance imposes discipline. When the Soviets provocatively moved intermediate-range nuclear forces (INF) into Eastern Europe, President Carter and German chancellor Helmut Schmidt got NATO to approve the counter-deployment of American INFs in Western Europe.

However, as soon as they lost power in 1981, the Democrats did an about-face. They fell in the thrall of the "nuclear freeze," an idea of unmatched strategic vacuity, which would have canceled the American INF deployment while freezing the Soviet force in place. The result would have been a major strategic setback, undermining the nuclear guarantee that underwrote the NATO alliance.

Years later, leading European social democrats repented their youthful part in the anti-nuclear movement of the early '80s. But the Democratic Party never did. It went even further left. It reflexively opposed every element of the Reagan foreign policy that ultimately brought total victory in the Cold War: the defense buildup, the resistance to Soviet gains in Central America and the blunt "evil empire" rhetoric that gave hope and succor to dissidents in the gulag. Democrats denounced such talk as provocative and naïve—the pronouncements of "an amiable dunce," to quote Clark Clifford's famous phrase disdaining Reagan.

And most relevant now, Democrats became implacable foes of missile defense, in large part because the idea originated with Reagan. The resistance was militant and nearly theological. It lasted 30 years—until, well, today, when a Democratic administration, facing North Korean nuclear threats, frantically puts in place (on Guam, in Alaska, in California and off the Korean coast) the few missile-defense systems that had survived decades of Democratic opposition and defunding.

I wrote most of the *New Republic* editorials opposing the Democratic Party's foreign policy of retreat, drawing fierce resistance from and occasioning public debate with my more traditionally liberal *TNR* colleagues. My attack on the nuclear freeze, announced the publisher rather ruefully at the next editorial meeting, produced more canceled subscriptions than any other article in the magazine's history. At that time, I still saw myself as trying to save the soul of the Democratic Party, which to me meant keeping alive the activist anti-communist tradition of Truman and Kennedy. But few other Democrats followed. By the mid-1980s, Humphrey and Jackson were dead and Moynihan had declined to pick up their mantle. The Cold War contingent of the Democratic Party essentially disappeared. As someone who had never had any illusions about either communism or Soviet power, I gave up on the Democrats.

On foreign policy, as the cliché goes, I didn't leave the Democratic Party. It left me.

Not so on domestic policy. The Democratic Party remained true to itself. I changed. The origin of that evolution is simple: I'm open to empirical evidence. The results of the Great Society experiments started coming in and began showing that, for all its good intentions, the War on Poverty was causing irreparable damage to the very communities it was designed to help. Charles Murray's *Losing Ground* was one turning point. Another, more theoretical but equally powerful, was Mancur Olson's *The Rise and Decline of Nations*, which opened my eyes to the inexorable "institutional sclerosis" that corrodes and corrupts the ever-enlarging welfare state. The '80s and '90s saw the further accumulation of a vast body of social science evidence—produced by two generations of critics, from James Q. Wilson to Heather Mac Donald, writing in *The Public Interest, City Journal* and elsewhere—on the limits and failures of the ever-expanding Leviathan state.

As I became convinced of the practical and theoretical defects of the social-democratic tendencies of my youth, it was but a short distance to a philosophy of restrained, free-market governance that gave more space and place to the individual and to the civil society that stands between citizen and state. In a kind of full-circle return, I found my eventual political home in a vision of limited government that, while providing for the helpless, is committed above all to guaranteeing individual liberty and the pursuit of one's own Millian "ends of life."

Such has been my trajectory. Given my checkered past, I've offered this brief personal history for those interested in what forces, internal and external, led me to change direction both vocationally and ideologically. I've elaborated it here because I believe that while everyone has the right to change views, one does at least owe others an explanation. The above is mine. This book represents the product of that journey.

III. A WORD ON ORGANIZATION AND METHOD

The body of this book is made up of newspaper columns and shorter magazine pieces grouped by theme in 16 chapters. I have included, however, five longer essays on subjects of enough complexity to have required more extensive treatment. The first of these is on the ethics of embryonic research, originally published by the President's Council on Bioethics, of which I was then a member. It is included as the last entry in chapter 9, "Body and Soul." The second essay is a meditation on Jewish destiny, first published in the late 1990s and included here at the end of chapter 12, "The Jewish Question, Again." And finally, the book's last chapter, "Three Essays on America and the World," is based on three speeches on U.S. foreign policy delivered over two decades about the structure and demands of the post–Cold War international system.

Every article in this book, long or short, is reproduced in its original form, except for three considerations. First, I have rewritten some of the headlines. Generally speaking, columnists and essayists don't write their own headlines. Many times have I been dismayed by the editor's ultimate choice, which was often dictated by the space requirements of the laid-out page.

That constraint doesn't exist in a book. I am finally released from the tyranny of the one- or two-column head. It's my chance to get it right. I do, however, include the location and exact date of publication of each article, to enable those readers enjoying far too much leisure time to consult the original headline if they wish.

Second, I altered some punctuation and usage, largely for the sake of uniformity. The different publications in which I appear follow different style books. (For example, regarding serial commas: whether you write a, b, and c rather than a, b and c.) My syndicated columns adhere to the Associated Press style book. The version appearing in the *Washington Post* follows the *Post*'s own style. Same with *Time*. As for the others, God knows what they use. To keep the chaos to a minimum, I have tried to impose a consistency in style and usage. This has the welcome subsidiary benefit of allowing me to exercise my petty punctuational prejudices, most importantly, my war on commas. They are a pestilence. They must be stopped. This book is a continuation of that campaign.

Finally, I have corrected typographical errors and on rare occasions edited a line or two of text for reasons of opacity, redundancy or obsolescence, the last encompassing references so historically obscure today as to have otherwise required cluttering up with explanatory footnotes. Altogether, these are perhaps a dozen. They change no meaning.

The rest, alas, remains untouched. It stands as it was on the day it was first published: imperfect, unimproved, unapologetically mine.

Washington, D.C., August 12, 2013

PART ONE

PERSONAL

Tatjana Ebner

CHAPTER 1

THE GOOD AND THE GREAT

MARCEL, MY BROTHER

PLACE: Los Angeles area emergency room.

TIME: Various times over the last 18 years.

SCENE: White male, around 50, brought in by ambulance, pale, short of breath, in distress.

Intern: *You're going to be alright, sir. I'm replacing your fluids, and your blood studies and electrolytes should be back from the lab in just a few minutes.*

Patient: *Son, you wait for my electrolytes to come back and I'll be dead in 10 minutes. I ran the ICU here for 10 years. I'm pan-hypopit and in (circulatory) shock. I need 300 mg of hydrocortisone right now. In a bolus. RIGHT NOW. After that, I'll tell you what to run into my IV, and what lab tests to run. Got it?*

Intern: *Yes sir.*

This scene played itself at least half a dozen times. The patient was my brother Marcel. He'd later call to regale me with the whole play-by-play, punctuated with innumerable, incredulous can-you-believe-its. We laughed. I loved hearing that mixture of pride and defiance in his voice as he told me how he had yet again thought and talked his way past death.

Amazingly, he always got it right. True, he was a brilliant doctor, a UCLA professor of medicine and a pulmonologist of unusual skill. But these diagnostic feats were performed lying flat on his back, near delirious and on the edge of circulatory collapse. Marcel instantly knew why. It was his cancer returning—the rare tumor he'd been carrying since 1988—suddenly popping up in some new life-threatening anatomical location. By the time he got to the ER and was looking up at the raw young intern, he'd figured out where it was and what to do.

I loved hearing these tales, in part because it brought out the old bravado in him—the same courage that, in the 1980s, when AIDS was largely unknown and invariably fatal, led Marcel to bronchoscope patients with active disease. At the time, not every doctor was willing to risk being on the receiving end of the coughing and spitting up. "Be careful, Marce," I would tell him. He'd laugh.

Friends and colleagues knew this part of Marcel—the headstrong cowboy—far better than I did. We hadn't lived in the same city since he went off to medical school when I was 17. What I knew that they didn't, however, was the Marcel of before, the golden youth of our childhood together.

He was four years older and a magnificent athlete: good ballplayer, great sailor and the most elegant skier I'd ever seen. But he was generous with his gifts. He taught me most everything I ever learned about every sport I ever played. He taught me how to throw a football, hit a backhand, grip a nine-iron, field a grounder, dock a sailboat in a tailwind.

He was even more generous still. Whenever I think back to my childhood friends—Morgie, Fiedler, Klipper, the Beller boys—I realize they were not my contemporaries but his. And when you're young, four years is a chasm. But everyone knew Marcel's rule: "Charlie plays." The corollary was understood: If Charlie doesn't play, Marcel doesn't play.

I played. From the youngest age he taught me to go one-on-one with the big boys, a rare and priceless gift.

And how we played. Spring came late where we grew up in Canada, but every year our father would take us out of school early to have a full three months of summer at our little cottage in the seaside town of Long Beach, New York. For those three months of endless summer, Marcel and I were inseparable—vagabond brothers shuttling endlessly on our Schwinns from beach to beach, ballgame to ballgame. Day and night we played every sport ever invented, and some games, like three-step stoopball and sidewalk Spaldeen, we just made up ourselves. For a couple of summers we even wangled ourselves jobs teaching sailing at Treasure Island, the aptly named day camp nearby. It was paradise.

There is a black-and-white photograph of us, two boys alone. He's maybe 11, I'm 7. We're sitting on a jetty, those jutting piles of rock that little beach towns throw down at half-mile intervals to hold back the sea. In the photo, nothing but sand, sea and sky, the pure elements of our summers together. We are both thin as rails, tanned to blackness and dressed in our summer finest: bathing suits and buzz cuts. Marcel's left arm is draped around my neck with that effortless natural easefulness—and touch of protectiveness—that only older brothers know.

Whenever I look at that picture, I know what we were thinking at the moment it was taken: It will forever be thus. Ever brothers. Ever young. Ever summer.

My brother Marcel died on Tuesday, January 17. It was winter. He was 59.

The Washington Post, January 27, 2006

WINSTON CHURCHILL:
THE INDISPENSABLE MAN

I t is just a parlor game, but since it only plays once every hundred years, it is hard to resist. Person of the Century? *Time* magazine offered Albert Einstein, an interesting and solid choice. Unfortunately, it is wrong. The only possible answer is Winston Churchill.

Why? Because only Churchill carries that absolutely required criterion: indispensability. Without Churchill the world today would be unrecognizable—dark, impoverished, tortured.

Without Einstein? Einstein was certainly the best mind of the century. His 1905 trifecta—a total unknown publishing three papers (on Brownian motion, the photoelectric effect and the special theory of relativity), each of which revolutionized its field—is probably the single most concentrated display of genius since the invention of the axle. (The wheel was easy, the axle hard.)

Einstein also had a deeply humane and philosophical soul. I would nominate him as most admirable man of the century. But most important? If Einstein hadn't lived, the ideas he produced might have been delayed. But they would certainly have arisen without him.

Indeed, by the time he'd published his paper on special relativity, Lorentz and Fitzgerald had already described how, at velocities approaching the speed of light, time dilates, length contracts and mass increases.

True, they misunderstood why. It took Einstein to draw the grand implications that constitute the special theory of relativity. But the groundwork was there.

And true, his general theory of relativity in 1916 is prodigiously original. But considering the concentration of genius in the physics community of the first half of the 20th century, it is hard to believe that the general theory would not have come in due course too.

Take away Churchill in 1940, on the other hand, and Britain would have settled with Hitler—or worse. Nazism would have prevailed. Hitler would have achieved what no other tyrant, not even Napoleon, had ever achieved: mastery of Europe. Civilization would have descended into a darkness the likes of which it had never known.

The great movements that underlie history—the development of science, industry, culture, social and political structures—are undeniably powerful, almost determinant. Yet every once in a while, a single person arises without whom everything would be different. Such a man was Churchill.

After having single-handedly saved Western civilization from Nazi barbarism—Churchill was, of course, not sufficient in bringing victory, but he was uniquely necessary—he then immediately rose to warn prophetically against its sister barbarism, Soviet communism.

Churchill is now disparaged for not sharing our multicultural late 20th-century sensibilities. His disrespect for the suffrage movement, his disdain for Gandhi, his resistance to decolonization are undeniable. But that kind of criticism is akin to dethroning Lincoln as the greatest of 19th-century Americans because he shared many of his era's appalling prejudices about black people.

In essence, the rap on Churchill is that he was a 19th-century man parachuted into the 20th.

But is that not precisely the point? It took a 19th-century man—traditional in habit, rational in thought, conservative in temper——to save the 20th century from itself. The story of the 20th century is a story of revolution wrought by thoroughly modern men: Hitler, Stalin, Mao and above all Lenin, who invented totalitarianism out of Marx's cryptic and inchoate communism (and thus earns his place as runner-up to Churchill for Person of the Century).

And it is the story of the modern intellectual, from Ezra Pound to Jean-Paul Sartre, seduced by these modern men of politics and, grotesquely, serving them.

The uniqueness of the 20th century lies not in its science but in its politics. The 20th century was no more scientifically gifted than the 19th, with its Gauss, Darwin, Pasteur, Maxwell and Mendel—all plowing, by the way, less-broken scientific ground than the 20th.

No. The originality of the 20th surely lay in its politics. It invented the police state and the command economy, mass mobilization and mass propaganda, mechanized murder and routinized terror—a breathtaking catalog of political creativity.

And the 20th is a single story because history saw fit to lodge the entire episode in a single century. Totalitarianism turned out to be a cul-de-sac. It came and went. It has a beginning and an end, 1917 and 1991, a run of 75 years neatly nestled into this century. That is our story.

And who is the hero of that story? Who slew the dragon? Yes, it was the ordinary man, the taxpayer, the grunt who fought and won the wars. Yes, it was America and its allies. Yes, it was the great leaders: FDR, de Gaulle, Adenauer, Truman, John Paul II, Thatcher, Reagan. But above all, victory required one man without whom the fight would have been lost at the beginning. It required Winston Churchill.

The Washington Post, December 31, 1999

PAUL ERDOS: SWEET GENIUS

One of the most extraordinary minds of our time has "left." *Left* is the word Paul Erdos, a prodigiously gifted and productive mathematician, used for "died." *Died* is the word he used to signify "stopped doing math." Erdos never "died." He continued doing math, notoriously a young person's field, right until the day he died last Friday. He was 83.

It wasn't just his vocabulary that was eccentric. Erdos' whole life was so improbable no novelist could have invented him. As chronicled by Paul Hoffman a decade ago in *The Atlantic Monthly*, Erdos had no home, no family, no possessions, no address. He went from math conference to math conference, from university to university, knocking on the doors of mathematicians throughout the world, declaring, "My brain is open" and moving in. His colleagues, grateful for a few days' collaboration with Erdos—his mathematical breadth was as impressive as his depth—took him in.

Erdos traveled with two suitcases, each half-full. One had a few clothes, the other mathematical papers. He owned nothing else. Nothing. His friends took care of the affairs of everyday life for him—checkbook, tax returns, food. He did numbers.

He seemed sentenced to a life of solitariness from birth, on the day of which his two sisters, ages three and five, died of scarlet fever, leaving him an only child, doted upon and kept at home by a fretful mother. Hitler disposed of nearly all the rest of his Hungarian Jewish family. And Erdos never married. His *Washington Post* obituary ends with this abrupt and rather painful line: "He leaves no immediate survivors."

But in reality he did: hundreds of scientific collaborators and 1,500 mathematical papers produced with them. An astonishing legacy in a field where a lifetime product of 50 papers is considered quite extraordinary.

Mathematicians tend to bloom early and die early. The great Indian genius Srinivasa Ramanujan died at 32. The great French mathematician Evariste Galois died at 21. (In a duel. The night before, it is said, he stayed up all night writing down everything he knew. Premonition?) And those who don't literally die young, die young in Erdos' sense. By 30, they've lost it.

Erdos didn't. He began his work early. At 20 he discovered a proof for a classic theorem of number theory (that between any number and its double must lie a prime—i.e., indivisible, number). He remained fecund till his death. Indeed, his friend and benefactor, Dr. (of math, of course) Ron Graham, estimates that perhaps 50 new Erdos papers are still to appear, reflecting work he and collaborators were doing at the time of his death.

Erdos was unusual in yet one other respect. The notion of the itinerant, eccentric genius, totally absorbed in his own world of thought, is a cliché that almost always attaches to the adjective *antisocial*. From Bobby Fischer to Howard Hughes, obsession and misanthropy seem to go together.

Not so Erdos. He was gentle, open and generous with others. He believed in making mathematics a social activity. Indeed, he was the most prolifically collaborative mathematician in history. Hundreds of colleagues who have published with him or been advised by him can trace some breakthrough or insight to an evening with Erdos, brain open.

That sociability sets him apart from other mathematical geniuses. Andrew Wiles, for example, recently achieved fame for having solved math's Holy Grail, Fermat's Last Theorem—after having worked on it for seven years in his attic! He then sprang the proof on the world as a surprise.

Erdos didn't just share his genius. He shared his money. It seems comical to say so because he had so little. But, in fact, it is rather touching. He had so little because he gave away everything he earned. He was a soft touch for whatever charitable or hard-luck cause came his way. In India, he once gave away the proceeds from a few lectures he had delivered there to Ramanujan's impoverished widow.

A few years ago, Graham tells me, Erdos heard of a promising young mathematician who wanted to go to Harvard but was short the money needed. Erdos arranged to see him and lent him $1,000. (The sum total of the money Erdos carried around at any one time was about $30.) He told the young man he could pay it back when he was able to. Recently, the young man called Graham to say that he had gone through Harvard and now was teaching at Michigan and could finally pay the money back. What should he do?

Graham consulted Erdos. Erdos said, "Tell him to do with the $1,000 what I did."

No survivors, indeed.

The Washington Post, September 27, 1996

RICK ANKIEL: RETURN OF THE NATURAL

In the fable, the farm boy phenom makes his way to the big city to amaze the world with his arm. At a stop at a fair on the train ride to Chicago, he strikes out the Babe Ruth of his time on three blazing pitches. Enter the Dark Lady. Before he can reach the stadium for his tryout, she shoots him and leaves him for dead.

It is 16 years later and Roy Hobbs returns, but now as a hitter and outfielder. (He can never pitch again because of the wound.) He leads his team to improbable glory, ending the tale with a titanic home run that, in the now-iconic movie image, explodes the stadium lights in a dazzling cascade of white.

In real life, the kid doesn't look like Robert Redford, but he throws like Roy Hobbs: unhittable, unstoppable. In his rookie year, appropriately the millennial year 2000, he throws it by everyone. He pitches the St. Louis Cardinals to a division title, playing so well that his manager anoints him starter for the opening game of the playoffs, a position of honor and—for 21-year-old Rick Ankiel—fatal exposure.

His collapse is epic. He can't find the plate. In the third inning he walks four batters and throws five wild pitches (something not seen since 1890) before Manager Tony La Russa mercifully takes him out of the game.

The kid is never the same. He never recovers his control. Five miserable years in the minors trying to come back. Injuries. Operations. In 2005, he gives up pitching forever.

Then, last week, on Aug. 9, 2007, he is called up from Triple-A. Same team. Same manager. Rick Ankiel is introduced to a roaring Busch Stadium crowd as the Cardinals' starting *right fielder*.

In the seventh inning, with two outs, he hits a three-run home run to seal the game for the Cardinals. Two days later, he hits two home runs and makes one of the great catches of the year—over the shoulder, back to the plate, full speed.

But the play is more than spectacular. It is poignant. It was an amateur's catch. Ankiel ran a slightly incorrect route to the ball. A veteran outfielder would have seen the ball tailing to the right. But pitchers aren't trained to track down screaming line drives over their heads. Ankiel was running away from home plate but slightly to his *left*. Realizing at the last second that he had run up the wrong prong of a Y, he veered sharply to the right, falling and sliding into the wall as he reached for the ball over the wrong shoulder.

He made the catch. The crowd, already delirious over the two home runs, came to its feet. If this had been a fable, Ankiel would have picked himself up and walked out of the stadium into the waiting arms of the lady in white—Glenn Close in a halo of light—never to return.

But this is real life. Ankiel is only 28 and will continue to play. The magic cannot continue. If he is lucky, he'll have the career of an average right fielder. But it doesn't matter. His return after seven years—if only three days long—is the stuff of legend. Made even more perfect by the timing: Just two days after Barry Bonds sets a synthetic home run record in San Francisco, the Natural returns to St. Louis.

Right after that first game, La Russa called Ankiel's return the Cardinals' greatest joy in baseball "short of winning the World Series." This, from a manager not given to happy talk. La Russa is the ultimate baseball logician, driven by numbers and stats. He may be more machine than man, but he confessed at the postgame news conference: "I'm fighting my butt off to keep it together."

Translation: I'm trying like hell to keep from bursting into tears at the resurrection of a young man who seven years ago dissolved in front of my eyes. La Russa was required to "keep it together" because, as codified most succinctly by Tom Hanks in *A League of Their Own*, "There's no crying in baseball."

But there can be redemption. And a touch of glory.

Ronald Reagan, I was once told, said he liked *The Natural* except that he didn't understand why the Dark Lady shoots Roy Hobbs.

Reagan, the preternatural optimist, may have had difficulty fathoming tragedy, but *no one* knows why Hobbs is shot. It is fate, destiny, nemesis. Perhaps the dawning of knowledge, the coming of sin. Or more prosaically, the catastrophe that awaits everyone from a single false move, wrong turn, fatal encounter. Every life has such a moment. What distinguishes us is whether—and how—we ever come back.

The Washington Post, August 17, 2007

CHRISTOPHER COLUMBUS:

DEAD WHITE MALE

The 500th anniversary of 1492 is approaching. Remember 1492? "In Fourteen Hundred Ninety-Two / Columbus sailed the ocean blue." Discovery and exploration. Bolívar and Jefferson. Liberty and democracy. The last best hope for man.

The left is not amused.

In Madrid, the Association of Indian Cultures announces that it will mark the occasion with acts of "sabotage." In the U.S., the Columbus in Context Coalition declares that the coming event provides "progressives" with their best political opening "since the Vietnam War." The National Council of Churches (NCC) condemns the "discovery" as "an invasion and colonization with legalized occupation, genocide, economic exploitation and a deep level of institutional racism and moral decadence." One of its leaders calls for "a year of repentance and reflection rather than a year of celebration."

For the left, the year comes just in time. The revolutions of 1989 having put a dent in the case for the degeneracy of the West, 1992 offers a welcome new point of attack. The point is the Origin. The villain is Columbus. The crime is the discovery—the rape—of America.

The attack does, however, present the left with some rather exquisite problems of political correctness. After all, Columbus was an agent of Spain, and his most direct legacy is Hispanic America. The denunciation of the Spanish legacy as one of cruelty and greed has moved one Hispanic leader to call the NCC's resolution "a racist depreciation of the heritages of most of today's American peoples, especially Hispanics."

That same resolution opened an even more ancient debate between Protestants and Catholics over the colonization of the Americas. For Catholics like historian James Muldoon, the (Protestant) attack on

Columbus and on the subsequent missionary work of the (Catholic) church in the Americas is little more than a resurrection, a few centuries late, of the Black Legend that was a staple of anti-Catholic propaganda during the Reformation.

The crusade continues nonetheless. Kirkpatrick Sale kicked off the anti-celebration with his anti-Columbus tome, *The Conquest of Paradise*. The group Encounter plans to celebrate 1992 by sailing three ships full of Indians to "discover" Spain. Similar merriment is to be expected wherever a quorum gathers to honor 1492.

The attack on 1492 has two parts. First, establishing the villainy of Columbus and his progeny (i.e., us). Columbus is "the deadest whitest male now offered for our detestation," writes Garry Wills. "If any historical figure can appropriately be loaded up with all the heresies of our time—Eurocentrism, phallocentrism, imperialism, elitism and all-bad-things-generally-ism—Columbus is the man."

Therefore, good-bye Columbus? Balzac once suggested that all great fortunes are founded on a crime. So too all great civilizations. The European conquest of the Americas, like the conquest of other civilizations, was indeed accompanied by great cruelty. But that is to say nothing more than that the European conquest of America was, in this way, much like the rise of Islam, the Norman conquest of Britain and the widespread American Indian tradition of raiding, depopulating and appropriating neighboring lands.

The real question is, What eventually grew on this bloodied soil? The answer is, The great modern civilizations of the Americas—a new world of individual rights, an ever-expanding circle of liberty and, twice in this century, a savior of the world from totalitarian barbarism.

If we are to judge civilizations like individuals, they should all be hanged, because with individuals it takes but one murder to merit a hanging. But if one judges civilizations by what they have taken from and what they have given the world, a non-jaundiced observer—say, one of the millions in Central Europe and Asia whose eyes are turned with hope toward America—would surely bless the day Columbus set sail.

Thus Part I of the anti-'92 crusade is calumny for Columbus and his legacy. Part II is hagiography, singing of the saintedness of the Indians in their pre-Columbian Eden, a land of virtue, empathy and ecological harmony. With Columbus, writes Sale, Europe "implanted its diseased and dangerous seeds in the soils of the continents that represented the last best hope for humankind—and destroyed them."

Last best hope? No doubt, some Indian tribes—the Hopis, for example—were tree-hugging pacifists. But the notion that pre-Columbian America was a hemisphere of noble savages is an adolescent fantasy (rather lushly, if ludicrously, animated in *Dances with Wolves*).

Take the Incas. Inca civilization, writes Peruvian novelist Mario Vargas Llosa, was a "pyramidal and theocratic society" of "totalitarian structure" in which "the individual had no importance and virtually no existence." Its foundation? "A state religion that took away the individual's free will and crowned the authority's decision with the aura of a divine mandate turned the Tawantinsuyu [Incan empire] into a beehive."

True, the beehive was wantonly destroyed by "semiliterate, implacable and greedy swordsmen." But they in turn represented a culture in which "a social space of human activities had evolved that was neither legislated nor controlled by those in power." In other words, a culture of liberty that endowed the individual human being with dignity and sovereignty.

Is it Eurocentric to believe the life of liberty is superior to the life of the beehive? That belief does not justify the cruelty of the conquest. But it does allow us to say that after 500 years the Columbian legacy has created a civilization that we ought not, in all humble piety and cultural relativism, declare to be no better or worse than that of the Incas. It turned out better.

And mankind is the better for it. Infinitely better. Reason enough to honor Columbus and bless 1492.

HERMANN LISCO: MAN FOR ALL SEASONS

ermann Lisco, a gifted scientist and legendary teacher, died last week. He was a quiet man from an unquiet place. German-born, he received his medical degree from the University of Berlin in 1936, came to the United States to teach pathology at Johns Hopkins University and was recruited to the Manhattan Project. In secret, he worked with a team of scientists at the University of Chicago studying the biological effects of a strange new human creation: plutonium.

Later, he was flown to Los Alamos to study the first person to be killed by acute radiation poisoning. Lisco performed the autopsy and, later, those of eight other victims of accidents at Los Alamos. His findings were a scientific milestone, the first published account of the effects of acute radiation exposure on the human organism.

A decade later, he was instrumental in producing a landmark United Nations report on the effects of radiation on humans and on the environment. But Dr. Lisco was more than a scientist. At Harvard Medical School, where he subsequently became a professor, he was the most beloved and influential mentor of an entire generation of students.

His home was always alive with the sound of students. He and his wife, Lisa (a formidable intellect in her own right and daughter of James Franck, winner of the 1926 Nobel Prize in physics), ran a combination halfway house and salon.

Medical school is not hard, but it is all-consuming. As our world got narrower, Hermann's goal was to keep us human, in touch with a larger world and larger possibilities.

He did so, in part, by example. He was a rare specimen of what used to be called a humanist: His mastery of science was comple-mented by deep knowledge of the humanities. With his supple and sophisticated mind, he discoursed easily on art, literature, politics, history.

His belief in broad horizons was more than theoretical. He was instrumental in setting up a traveling scholarship for students to take a year off and see the world. He arranged for Michael Crichton to be given the freedom as a fourth-year medical student to research and write books.

As for me, well, he made my career possible. Toward the end of my freshman year, I was paralyzed in a serious accident. Hermann, then associate dean of students, came to see me in intensive care. He asked what he could do for me. I told him that, to keep disaster from turning into ruin, I had decided to stay in school and with my class.

If Hermann had doubts—I would not have blamed him: No one with my injury had ever gone through medical school—he never showed it. He told me he would do everything possible to make it happen.

He did. Within a few days, a hematology professor, fresh from lecturing to my classmates on campus, showed up at my bedside and proceeded to give me the lecture, while projecting his slides on the ceiling above me. (I was flat on my back in traction, but I'm sure Hermann had instructed everybody to carry on as if such teaching techniques were entirely normal.)

He then went to work behind the scenes: persuading professors to let me take their tests orally with a recording secretary (I did not learn to handwrite for another three years); getting me transferred for my 12 months of inpatient rehab to a Harvard teaching hospital so that I could catch up at night with my class' second-year studies and rejoin it in third year; persuading (ordering?) skeptical attending physicians to allow their patients to be cared for by the student in the wheelchair with the exotic medical instruments (the extra-long stethoscope Hermann had made for me was a thing of beauty).

Hermann did all this quietly, without fanfare. At graduation, he took not only pride but a kind of mischievous delight in our unspoken conspiracy. We broke no rules, but we bent a few, especially the stupid ones. I'm sure he liked that.

That was Hermann's great gift: He was a man of orderly habits and orderly mind, but he never flinched from challenging the orderly. In Germany, he had seen order turned into malevolence. Mild mannered as he was—I never once heard him raise his voice—he was good at defiance. In Nazi Germany, Hermann married a Jew, the daughter of an early, very prominent anti-Nazi. Defiance ran in the family. Hermann's father was fired as head of Göttingen's elite high school for his opposition to the regime.

Hermann did not much respect nature's strictures, either. At age 70, he was still climbing mountains in his beloved Adirondacks. At 80, he was still taking miles-long walks in the woods.

And now, just short of 90, he is gone. Those who were touched by this man, so wise and gracious and goodly, mourn him. I mourn a man who saved my life.

The Washington Post, August 25, 2000

Chapter 2

MANNERS

No Dancing in the End Zone

Rounds: The ritual whereby a senior doctor goes from bed to
bed seeing patients, trailed by a gaggle of students.

Roundsmanship: The art of distinguishing oneself from the
gaggle with relentless displays of erudition.

The roundsman is the guy who, with the class huddled at the
bed of a patient who has developed a rash after taking penicil-
lin, raises his hand to ask the professor—obnoxious ingratiation is best expressed in the form of a question—whether this might
not instead be a case of Schmendrick's Syndrome reported in the latest issue of the *Journal of Ridiculously Obscure Tropical Diseases*.

None of the rest of us gathered around the bed has ever heard
of Schmendrick's. But that's the point. The point is for the prof to
remember this hyper-motivated stiff who stays up nights reading
journals in preparation for rounds. That's the upside. The downside,
which the roundsman—let's call him Oswald—ignores at his peril,
is that this apple polishing does not endear him to his colleagues, a
slovenly lot mostly hung over from a terrific night at the Blue Parrot.

The general feeling among the rest of us is that we should have
Oswald killed. A physiology major suggests a simple potassium injection that would stop his heart and leave no trace. We agree this is a

splendid idea and entirely just. But it would not solve the problem. Kill him, and another Oswald will arise in his place.

There's always an Oswald. There's always the husband who takes his wife to Paris for Valentine's Day. Valentine's Day? The rest of us schlubs can barely remember to come home with a single long-stemmed rose. What *does* he think he's doing? And love is no defense. We don't care how much you love her—you don't do Paris. It's bad for the team.

Baseball has its own way of taking care of those who commit the capital offense of showing up another player. Drop your bat to admire the trajectory of your home run and, chances are, the next time up the unappreciative pitcher tries to take your head off with high cheese that whistles *behind* your skull.

Now, you might take this the wrong way and think that I am making the case for mediocrity—what Australians call "the tall poppy syndrome" of unspoken bias against achievement, lest one presume to be elevated above one's mates. No. There is a distinction between show and substance. It is the ostentation that rankles, not the achievement. I'm talking about dancing in the end zone. Find a cure for cancer and you deserve whatever honors and riches come your way. But the check-writer who wears blinding bling to the Cancer Ball is quite another matter.

Americans abroad have long been accused of such blinging arrogance and display. I find the charge generally unfair. Arrogance is incorrectly ascribed to what is really the cultural clumsiness of an insular (if continental) people less exposed to foreign ways and languages than most other people on Earth.

True, America as a nation is not very good at humility. But it would be completely unnatural for the dominant military, cultural and technological power on the planet to adopt the demeanor of, say, Liechtenstein. The ensuing criticism is particularly grating when it comes from the likes of the French, British, Spanish, Dutch (there are many others) who just yesterday claimed dominion over every land and people their Captain Cooks ever stumbled upon.

My beef with American arrogance is not that we act like a traditional great power, occasionally knocking off foreign bad guys who richly deserve it. My problem is that we don't know where to stop—the trivial victories we insist on having in arenas that are quite superfluous. Like that women's hockey game in the 2002 Winter Olympics. Did the U.S. team really have to beat China 12–1? Can't we get the coaches—there's gotta be some provision in the Patriot Act authorizing the CIA to engineer this—to throw a game or two, or at least make it close? We're trying to contain China. Why, then, gratuitously crush them in something Americans don't even care about? Why not throw them a bone?

I say we keep the big ones for ourselves—laser-guided munitions, Google, Warren Buffett—and let the rest of the world have ice hockey, ballroom dancing and every Nobel Peace Prize. And throw in the Ryder Cup. I always root for the Europeans in that one. They lost entire empires, for God's sake; let them have golf supremacy *for one weekend*. No one likes an Oswald.

The Washington Post, December 22, 2006

"Women and Children." Still?

You're on the *Titanic II*. It has just hit an iceberg and is sinking. And, as last time, there are not enough lifeboats. The captain shouts, "Women and children first!" But this time, another voice is heard: "Why women?"

Why, indeed? Part of the charm of the cosmically successful movie *Titanic* is the period costume, period extravagance, period class prejudice. An audience can enjoy these at a distance. Oddly, however, of all the period mores in the film, the old maritime tradition of "women and children first" enjoys total acceptance by modern audiences. Listen to the booing and hissing at the on-screen heavies who try to sneak on with—or ahead of—the ladies.

But is not grouping women with children a raging anachronism? Should not any self-respecting modern person, let alone feminist, object to it as patronizing and demeaning to women? Yet its usage is as common today as it was in 1912. Consider these examples taken almost at random from recent newspapers:

Dateline Mexico: "Members of a paramilitary group gunned down the Indians, most of them women and children."

Dateline Burundi: "As many as 200 civilians, most of them women and children, were killed."

Dateline Croatia: "Kupreskic was named in an open indictment . . . for the massacre in Ahmici in which 103 Muslims, including 33 women and children, were killed."

At a time when women fly combat aircraft, how can one not wince when adult women are routinely classed with children? In Ahmici, it seems, 70 adult men were killed. Adult women? Not clear. When things get serious, when blood starts to flow or ships start to sink, you'll find them with the children.

Now, children are entitled to special consideration for two reasons: helplessness and innocence. They have not yet acquired either the faculty of reason or the wisdom of experience. Consequently, they are defenseless (incapable of fending for themselves) and blameless (incapable of real sin).

That is why we grant them special protection. In an emergency, it is our duty to save them first because they, helpless, have put their lives in our hands. And in wartime, they are supposed to enjoy special immunity because they, blameless, can have threatened or offended no one.

"Women and children" attributes to women the same pitiable dependence and moral simplicity we find in five-year-olds. Such an attitude made sense perhaps in an era of male suffrage and "Help Wanted: Female" classifieds. Given the disabilities attached to womanhood in 1912, it was only fair and right that a new standard of gender equality not suddenly be proclaimed just as lifeboat seats were being handed out. That deference—a somewhat more urgent variant of giving up your seat on the bus to a woman—complemented and perhaps compensated for the legal and social constraints placed on women at the time.

But in this day of the most extensive societal restructuring to grant women equality in education, in employment, in government, in athletics, in citizenship writ large, what entitles women to the privileges—and reduces them to the status—of children?

The evolutionary psychologists might say that ladies-to-the-lifeboats is an instinct that developed to perpetuate the species: Women are indispensable child bearers. You can repopulate a village if the women survive and only a few of the men, but you cannot repopulate a village if the men survive and only a few of the women. Women being more precious, biologically speaking, than men, evolution has conditioned us to give them the kind of life-protecting deference we give to that other seed of the future, kids.

The problem with this kind of logic, however, is its depressing reductionism. It recapitulates in all seriousness the geneticist's old witticism that a chicken is just an egg's way of making another egg.

But humans are more than just egg layers. And chivalrous traditions are more than just disguised survival strategies. So why do we say "women and children"? Perhaps it's really "women for children." The most basic parental bond is maternal. Equal parenting is great—it has forced men to get off their duffs—but women, from breast to cradle to cuddle, can nurture in ways that men cannot. And thus, because we value children—who would deny them first crack at the lifeboats?—women should go second. The children need them.

But kiddie-centrism gets you only so far. What if there are no children on board? You are on the *Titanic III,* a singles cruise. No kids, no moms, no dads. Now: Iceberg! Lifeboats! Action!

Here's my scenario. The men, out of sheer irrational gallantry, should let the women go first. And the women, out of sheer feminist self-respect, should refuse.

Result? Stalemate. How does this movie end? How should it end? Hurry, the ship's going down.

Time, March 30, 1998

DON'T TOUCH MY JUNK

Ah, the airport, where modern folk heroes are made. The airport, where that inspired flight attendant did what everyone who's ever been in the spam–in–a–can crush of a flying aluminum tube—where we collectively pretend that a clutch of peanuts is a meal and a seat cushion is a "flotation device"—has always dreamed of doing: Pull the lever, blow the door, explode the chute, grab a beer, slide to the tarmac and walk through the gates to the sanity that lies beyond. Not since Rick and Louis disappeared into the Casablanca fog headed for the Free French garrison in Brazzaville has a stroll on the tarmac thrilled so many.

Who cares that the crazed steward got arrested, pleaded guilty to sundry charges and probably was a rude, unpleasant SOB to begin with? Bonnie and Clyde were *psychopaths,* yet what child of the '60s did not fall in love with Faye Dunaway and Warren Beatty?

And now three months later, the newest airport hero arrives. His genius was not innovation in getting out, but in deconstructing the entire process of getting in. John Tyner, cleverly armed with an iPhone to give YouTube immortality to the encounter, took exception to the TSA guard about to give him the benefit of Homeland Security's newest brainstorm—the upgraded, full-palm, up the groin, all-body pat-down. In a stroke, the young man ascended to myth, or at least the next edition of *Bartlett's,* warning the agent not to "touch my junk."

Not quite the 18th-century elegance of "Don't Tread on Me," but the age of Twitter has a different cadence from the age of the musket. What the modern battle cry lacks in archaic charm it makes up for in full-body syllabic punch.

Don't touch my junk is the anthem of the modern man, the Tea Party patriot, the late-life libertarian, the midterm election voter. Don't touch my junk, Obamacare—get out of my doctor's examining room, I'm wearing a paper-thin gown slit down the back. Don't touch my junk, Google—Street View is cool, but get off my street. Don't touch my junk, you airport security goon—my package belongs to no one but me, and do you really think I'm a Nigerian nut job preparing for my 72-virgin orgy by blowing my johnson to kingdom come?

In *Up in the Air*, that ironic take on the cramped freneticism of airport life, George Clooney explains why he always follows Asians in the security line:

"They pack light, travel efficiently and they got a thing for slip-on shoes, God love 'em."

"That's racist!"

"I'm like my mother. I stereotype. It's faster."

That riff is a crowd-pleaser because everyone knows that the entire apparatus of the security line is a national homage to political correctness. Nowhere do more people meekly acquiesce to more useless inconvenience and needless indignity for less purpose. Wizened seniors strain to untie their shoes. Beltless salesmen struggle comically to hold up their pants. Three-year-olds scream while being searched insanely for explosives—when everyone, everyone, knows that none of these people is a threat to anyone.

The ultimate idiocy is the full-body screening of the pilot. The pilot doesn't need a bomb or box cutter to bring down a plane. All he has to do is drive it into the water, like the EgyptAir pilot who crashed his plane off Nantucket while intoning "I rely on God," killing all on board.

But we must not bring that up. We pretend that we go through this nonsense as a small price paid to ensure the safety of air travel. Rubbish. This has nothing to do with safety—95% of these inspections, searches, shoe removals and pat-downs are ridiculously unnecessary. The only reason we continue to do this is that people are too cowed to even question the absurd taboo against profiling—when the profile of the airline attacker is narrow, concrete, uniquely definable and universally known. So instead of seeking out terrorists, we seek out tubes of gel in stroller pouches.

The junk man's revolt marks the point at which a docile public declares that it will tolerate only so much idiocy. Metal detector? Back-of-the-hand pat? Okay. We will swallow hard and pretend airline attackers are randomly distributed in the population.

But now you insist on a full-body scan, a fairly accurate representation of my naked image to be viewed by a total stranger? Or alternatively, the full-body pat-down, which, as the junk man correctly noted, would be sexual assault if performed by anyone else?

This time you have gone too far, Big Bro'. The sleeping giant awakes. Take my shoes, remove my belt, waste my time and try my patience. But don't touch my junk.

The Washington Post, November 19, 2010

ACCENTS AND AFFECTATIONS

When I was a kid, movie Indians said things like "me no like-um paleface." No one ever explained the origins of the peculiar "-um" declension, but no matter. Logic was not expected of Indians, and the same held for other native peoples in other movies, from *Tarzan* on up.

Things have changed. The dignity of language has been restored to movie Indians (well, PBS Indians—there are none left in the movies). They speak in their own tongue now, and the subtitles report them saying lyrical things like, "The cry of the night pierces the soul of my darkness."

This process of language decolonization follows the general political decolonization of the last 30 years. It also follows modern recognition of the dignity and complexity of native cultures. That is all to the good. It even makes more fictional sense for Indians to be speaking something other than a bizarre variant of Ellis Island English.

The trend, however, has not stopped there. It never does. Linguistic emancipation, it seems, is for everyone. Even, say, cavemen. Twenty years ago, the Hollywood Neanderthal communicated with a pound on the chest and a wield of the club. It is hard to see one today for whom some consultant anthropologist has not invented a language as elaborate as it is bogus. And honored, like the highest German, with subtitles. Thankfully, the movement to subtitle dolphins is stalled.

I find these good intentions strained but tolerable. Less tolerable is the direction of another wing of the language decolonization movement, the school of Militant Anti-Colonials—MACs for short. MACs insist that whenever, in conversation, you cross an international border, you must turn in your English and go native. A MAC is the guy (English-speaking) who, in the middle of a discourse (in

English) about Central America, tells you that you totally misunderstand the situation in Neeeee-kahh-RAAAHH-gwahhh.

Neeeee-kahh-RAAAHH-gwahhh? Pronouncing Nicaragua the Spanish way is perhaps a sign of sophistication, but it is also an advertisement of one's raised consciousness. More annoying still is the ringingly rococo "elll sahl-vahh-DOHRRRRR," all liquid *l*'s and rolling *r*'s, climaxed in the triumphantly accented last syllable. All this to signify hopes for a liberated El Salvador and, some day, a liberated listener.

MACs can easily be picked out of a crowd even before their conversation has wandered south. A MAC is anyone who carefully and aggressively says "North America" to mean "United States" (as in "North American aggression") to demonstrate that he has transcended the imperial (North) American tendency to appropriate for one country the name of two continents.

I can take this oblique swipe at the Monroe Doctrine. What I cannot take is the follow-up reference to, say, the drug problem in "Kohl-LOHHHHM-bia." My habit now is to respond with the observation that the problem is seen very differently in Paa-RRREEEE, is ignored totally in Mohs-KVA, though it has provoked street demonstrations in KUE-bin-hah-ven (DAN-mark).

Not that such an anti-MAC attack ever satisfies. But it does make the point that what drives English-speaking MACs is not a sense of linguistic authenticity but merely a bad colonial conscience. They would never think of assaulting you with "Mahhh-DRRREEED." We never sent a Marine there.

In my calmer moments I do admit the existence of a real dilemma here. It is a problem: How do you pronounce a foreign-language word when speaking English?

My answer: When in Rome, speak Roman; when in America (what some call the United States), speak English. Drop the umlauts, the aigues and graves, and give foreign words their most mundane English rendering.

About the use of fancy accents in mundane situations, I speak from experience. When I was five, my family moved to Montreal, in part because it was French-speaking (my mother being Belgian, my father French). But our French was not the kind spoken in Quebec. Ours was what Montrealers called "Parisian" French, the language of Quebec's upper class (i.e., snobs, such as Pierre Elliott Trudeau, who once dismissed Robert Bourassa, the current Quebec premier and of working-class origins, as "a hot dog eater"). This bit of local sociology was unknown to me the first time I got on a bus and asked, in my Parisian French, for directions. The bus driver did not take kindly to being linguistically patronized by a creature four feet tall and wearing short pants. I learned my lesson. From then on I used only English in public.

But one can't totally avoid foreign words, even when speaking English. I still did not know what to do with French words that pop up in everyday English. For years, I doggedly, and self-consciously, pronounced *déjà vu* precisely as my folks insisted at home, with sharps and flats and lips pursed ("vuh") as if to whistle.

Then came *Déjà Vu,* the album. It's been "vooo" ever since. One does not discuss Crosby, Stills, Nash and Young in an Inspector Clouseau accent. The gig was up. Time to learn to embrace English, jettison flatulent foreignness and say *ciao* to all that. So how about it, guys? Ni-cuh-rag-wa.

The Washington Post, July 11, 1986

THE APPEAL OF ORDEAL

William Butler Yeats tells of Icelandic peasants who found a skull in a cemetery and suspected it might be that of the poet Egill. "Its great thickness made them feel certain it was," he writes, but "to be doubly sure they put it on a wall and hit it hard blows with a hammer." When it did not break, "they were convinced that it was in truth the skull of the poet and worthy of every honor."

The human propensity to test the worthiness of a thing by seeing how well it stands up to abuse—the instinct to kick the tires on a used car—is an ancient and, if Yeats is to be trusted, occasionally charming habit. It can also be painful. Trial by ordeal, the venerable and once widespread practice by which fire or poison or some other divining element is used to determine a person's guilt or innocence, is the kick-to-test instinct applied to living subjects. It used to be a popular method for deciding whether or not someone was a witch, perhaps because what the practice lacked in fairness—the ancient Hindus tied a bag of cayenne pepper around the head of an accused witch, and suffocation was the only proof of innocence—it made up for in finality.

We have come a long way since those dark days. Or have we? We no longer pick our witches or our poets this way, but that is because moderns have little interest in either. When it comes to things they are interested in—doctors, lawyers, presidents—they have replaced skull-bashing and suffocation with more subtle ordeals. Aspiring doctors must first survive the pressure cooker of a sleepless year of internship, aspiring lawyers the cutthroat paper chase of first-year law school. And those who aspire to the most exalted title of all, president, are required to traverse a campaign trail of Homeric peril. Its length is ludicrous: three years for any serious candidate; its requirements absurd: giving up privacy, often family and almost always a job ("You have to be unemployed to run for president," says Senate

Majority Leader Howard Baker, who leaves the Senate in January
and is pondering a run for the presidency in 1988); and its purpose
obscure: posing with funny hats has, on the face of it, little to do with
the subject at hand, namely, governing.

The ritual seems strange. Things just aren't done that way anymore. Not even in Chad, where ten years ago President Ngarta Tom-
balbaye ordered all high government officials to undergo Yondo, a
sometimes fatal initiation ritual combining physical abuse (e.g., flog-
ging, mock burial) with ingeniously gruesome tests of stamina (e.g.,
crawling naked through a nest of termites). For his pains, Tombal-
baye was assassinated within a year, and his people danced in the
streets. Americans bear their burdens with better humor. They show
no inclination to deal nearly so decisively with, say, the Hubert Humphrey test of presidential toughness. Humphrey once questioned
whether Walter Mondale had the "fire in the belly" to run for president, a charge so serious that to meet it Mr. Mondale had to submit
to a three-year diet of rubber chicken and occasional crow. Mondale
may have other political liabilities, but the absence of a burning belly
is no longer one of them.

There is only one point to these trials: to humble. The imposed,
often improbable ordeal is a form of payment, dues demanded of people who are about to be rewarded with high position. It is a form of
democratic practice, laying low the mighty before we bestow upon
them prestige and power. It is, as an Icelandic peasant might see it,
poetic justice.

But what of the ordeal not mandated by others? How to understand the current passion for the self-imposed, the recreational
ordeal? A marathon, after all, is a voluntary thing, and for 99.9% of
the 95,000 Americans who run marathons every year, there is nothing awaiting them at the finish line except a blanket and bottled oxygen. Yet the marathon has become so commonplace that a new sport
had to be created: the triathlon, a monstrous composite of three consecutive marathons (swimming, biking and running a total of often
a hundred miles or more). And now the upper classes have taken

the fun indoors. A few years ago the rage was *Napoleon*, a silent film 4½ hours long. Then came the stage production of *Nicholas Nickleby*, 9½ hours, including snack-and-comfort breaks. Now we're up to 15½ hours with Fassbinder's *Berlin Alexanderplatz*, shown in either five, two or occasionally one grand sitting of "sheer exhilarating length" (Vincent Canby, *New York Times*)—and subtitles.

To be sure, the self-inflicted ordeal was not invented yesterday. The 1920s had marathon dancing, and the *Guinness Book of World Records* is full of champion oyster eaters and HulaHoopers. But such activities used to be recognized as exotic, the province of the down-and-out or the eccentric. The 24-hour underwater Parcheesi game was for slightly nutty college freshmen. Running 26 miles at a shot was for the most hardened athlete, preferably a barefoot Ethiopian. Nowadays, a 26-mile run is Sunday afternoon recreation, an alternative to a day at the beach or on the lawn mower. As for evening recreation, Fassbinder's epic is so popular that the *Wall Street Journal* dubbed it "the *Flashdance* of the intelligentsia."

What's new is not the odd individual who rows the Atlantic left-handed while eating only salted peanuts, nor the collegians perched atop flagpoles for reasons still unknown. It is the midday, mainstream, Main Street marathoner. The modern wonder is to be found on America's heartbreak hills, where it has become impossible to drive without running across (and nearly over) at least one bedraggled jogger drenched in sweat and close to collapse, the very picture of agony. Why do they do it?

The participants will tell you that they go to marathon movies for culture. They run for health. They spend 48 consecutive hours locked in a Holiday Inn ballroom in enforced communion with complete strangers and call it therapy. (Sartre had another word for it: He once wrote a play based on the convincing premise that hell was being locked in a room forever with other people.) But surely there are less trying ways to acquire culture, health or psychological succor.

There are, but the ordeal offers as a bonus two very chic commodities. One is survivorship, the highest achievement of the modern self-celebratory ethic, best exemplified by the I-SURVIVED-THE-BLIZZARD-OF-'77 T-shirt. Survivorship, however, is capriciously doled out. Not everyone can live in Buffalo or have a Malibu beach house obliterated by a mud slide. For the average Joe, there is no cachet in surviving the 5:22 to White Plains. How, then, to earn the badge of honor that is survivorship? Create an ordeal. Run the Western States 100 (miles, that is) over the Sierra Nevada (they say that horses have died racing the trail), and live to talk about it. Or attend the first modern showing of *Napoleon*, held in the Colorado Rockies, outdoors, from 10:30 p.m. to 3:30 a.m., and feel, in the words of the man who put the film together, "Like survivors of the retreat from Moscow."

The other modern good greatly in demand is the learning experience. Ordeal is a great teacher. A group of adventuresome souls staged an unbelievable race on New York's Randall's Island last year: a six-day run, the winner being the person who could traverse the most ground and survive. The race was run around an oval track, subjecting the runners not only to blisters, dehydration and shin splints, but to the overwhelming ennui of unchanging scenery. When reporters swarmed around the runners to ask why they did it, many replied that they had learned a lot about themselves. They never said exactly what it was they learned, but they seemed satisfied that it was important. "Because it is there" has become "Because I am here."

Like the ancients, moderns believe that one can learn about something by subjecting it to the ultimate test: beat the skull, and find the poet. Only today we insist on beating our own skulls, and not quite for the pleasure of stopping.

Why, then? The prestige of survivorship and the hunger for learning experiences are only partial explanations. The somewhat misanthropic economist Thorstein Veblen described the larger phenomenon. He hypothesized a new kind of good, demand for which, contrary to economic law and common sense, increases with price. In the end, the recreational ordeal is just the latest example of a Veblenesque status good, periodically invented for the amusement and prestige of the leisured classes. Now that everyone can afford status items like designer jeans, conspicuous consumption gives way to conspicuous exertion. Sheer exhilarating length becomes a value in itself. And the triathlon comes to represent, to quote a winner of the Hawaiian Ironman race (2.4-mile ocean swim, 112-mile bike ride, 26.2-mile marathon run), "the ultimate expression of the Southern California life-style."

Which is why, outside a cluster of easeful lands, the recreational ordeal is not wildly popular. In America, people run for fun. In Beirut, they run for their lives. People there listen not for the starter's gun, but for the sniper's. In some parts of the world, when a man runs 26 miles it's because he's come from Marathon and he's strictly on business.

Time, May 14, 1984

CHAPTER 3

PRIDE AND PREJUDICES

THE PARIAH CHESS CLUB

once met a physicist who as a child had been something of a chess prodigy. He loved the game and loved the role. He took particular delight in the mortification older players felt upon losing to a kid in short pants.

"Still play?" I asked.

"Nope."

"What happened?"

"Quit when I was 21."

"Why?"

"Lost to a kid in short pants."

The Pariah Chess Club, where I play every Monday night, admits no one in short pants. Even our youngest member, in his twenties, wears trousers. The rest of us are more grizzled veterans numbering about a dozen, mostly journalists and writers, with three lawyers, an academic and a diplomat for ballast. We've been meeting at my house for almost a decade for our weekly fix.

Oh, yes, the club's name. Of the four founding members, two were social scientists who, at the time we started playing, had just written books that had made their college lecture tours rather physically hazardous. I too sported a respectable enemies list (it was the heady Clinton years). And we figured that the fourth member, a music critic and perfectly well-liked, could be grandfathered in as a pariah because of his association with the three of us.

Pariah status has not been required of subsequent members, though it is encouraged. Being a chess player already makes you suspect enough in polite society, and not without reason. Any endeavor that has given the world Paul Morphy, the first American champion, who spent the last 17-odd years of his life wandering the streets of New Orleans, and Bobby Fischer, the last American champion, now descended John Nash-like into raving paranoia, cannot be expected to be a boon to one's social status.

Our friends think us odd. They can understand poker night or bridge night. They're not sure about chess. When I tell friends that three of us once drove from Washington to New York to see Garry Kasparov play a game, it elicits a look as uncomprehending as if we had driven 200 miles for an egg-eating contest.

True, we chess players can claim Benjamin Franklin as one of our own. He spent much of his time as ambassador to France playing chess at the Café de la Régence, where he fended off complaints that he was not being seen enough at the opera by explaining, "I call this my opera." But for every Franklin, there is an Alexander Alekhine, who in 1935 was stopped while trying to cross the Polish-German frontier without any papers. He offered this declaration instead: "I am Alekhine, chess champion of the world. This is my cat. Her name is Chess. I need no passport." He was arrested.

Or Aron Nimzovich, author of perhaps the greatest book on chess theory ever written, who, upon being defeated in a game, threw the pieces to the floor and jumped on the table screaming, "Why must I lose to this idiot?"

I know the feeling, but at our club, when you lose with a blunder that instantly illuminates the virtues of assisted suicide, we have a cure. Rack 'em up again. Like pool. A new game, right away. We play fast, very fast, so that memories can be erased and defeats immediately avenged.

I try to explain to friends that we do not sit in overstuffed chairs smoking pipes in five-hour games. We play like the vagrants in the park—at high speed with clocks ticking so that thinking more than 10 or 20 seconds can be a fatal extravagance. In speed ("blitz") chess, you've got 5 or 10 minutes to play your entire game. Some Mondays we get in a dozen games each. No time to recriminate, let alone ruminate.

And we have amenities. It's a wood-paneled library, chess books only. The bulletin board has the latest news from around the world, this month a London newspaper article with a picture of a doe-eyed brunette languishing over a board, under the headline "Kournikova of Chess Makes Her Move." The mini-jukebox plays k.d. lang and Mahler. (We like lush. We had Roy Orbison one night, till our lone Iowan begged for mercy.) *Monday Night Football* in the background, no sound. Barbecue chips. Sourdough pretzels. Sushi when we're feeling extravagant. And in a unique concession to good health, Nantucket Nectar. I'm partial to orange mango.

No alcohol, though. Not even a beer. It's not a prohibition. You can have a swig if you want, but no one ever does. The reason is not ascetic but aesthetic. Chess is a beautiful game, and though amateurs playing fast can occasionally make it sing, we know there are riffs—magical symphonic combinations—that we either entirely miss or muck up halfway through. Fruit juice keeps the ugliness to a minimum.

The Washington Post, December 27, 2002

OF DOGS AND MEN

The way I see it, dogs had this big meeting, oh, maybe 20,000 years ago. A huge meeting—an international convention with delegates from everywhere. And that's when they decided that humans were the up-and-coming species and dogs were going to throw their lot in with them. The decision was obviously not unanimous. The wolves and dingoes walked out in protest.

Cats had an even more negative reaction. When they heard the news, they called their own meeting—in Paris, of course—to denounce canine subservience to the human hyperpower. (Their manifesto—*La Condition Féline*—can still be found in provincial bookstores.)

Cats, it must be said, have not done badly. Using guile and seduction, they managed to get humans to feed them, thus preserving their superciliousness without going hungry. A neat trick. Dogs, being guileless, signed and delivered. It was the beginning of a beautiful friendship.

I must admit that I've been slow to warm to dogs. I grew up in a non-pet-friendly home. Dogs do not figure prominently in Jewish-immigrant households. My father was not very high on pets. He wasn't hostile. He just saw them as superfluous, an encumbrance. When the Cossacks are chasing you around Europe, you need to travel light. (This, by the way, is why Europe produced far more Jewish violinists than pianists. Try packing a piano.)

My parents did allow a hint of zoological indulgence. I had a pet turtle. My brother had a parakeet. Both came to unfortunate ends. My turtle fell behind a radiator and was not discovered until too late. And the parakeet, God bless him, flew out a window once, never to be seen again. After such displays of stewardship, we dared not ask for a dog.

My introduction to the wonder of dogs came from my wife, Robyn.

She's Australian. And Australia, as lovingly recounted in Bill Bryson's *In a Sunburned Country*, has the craziest, wildest, deadliest, meanest animals on the planet. In a place where every spider and squid can take you down faster than a sucker-punched boxer, you cherish niceness in the animal kingdom. And they don't come nicer than dogs.

Robyn started us off slowly. She got us a border collie, Hugo, when our son was about six. She knew that would appeal to me because the border collie is the smartest species on the planet. Hugo could (1) play outfield in our backyard baseball games, (2) do flawless front-door sentry duty and (3) play psychic weatherman, announcing with a wail every coming thunderstorm.

When our son Daniel turned 10, he wanted a dog of his own. I was against it, using arguments borrowed from seminars on nuclear nonproliferation. It was hopeless. One giant "Please, Dad," and I caved completely. Robyn went out to Winchester, Virginia, found a litter of black Labs and brought home Chester.

Chester is what psychiatrists mean when they talk about unconditional love. Unbridled is more like it. Come into our house, and he was so happy to see you, he would knock you over. (Deliverymen learned to leave things at the front door.)

In some respects—Ph.D. potential, for example—I don't make any great claims for Chester. When I would arrive home, I fully expected to find Hugo reading the newspaper. Not Chester. Chester would try to make his way through a narrow sliding door, find himself stuck halfway and then look at me with total and quite genuine puzzlement. I don't think he ever got to understand that the rear part of him was actually attached to the front.

But it was Chester, who dispensed affection as unreflectively as he breathed, who got me thinking about this long-ago pact between humans and dogs. Cat lovers and the pet averse will just roll their eyes at such dogophilia. I can't help it. Chester was always at your foot or your hand, waiting to be petted and stroked, played with and talked to. His beautiful blocky head, his wonderful overgrown puppy's body, his baritone bark filled every corner of house and heart.

Then last month, at the tender age of eight, he died quite suddenly. The long, slobbering, slothful decline we had been looking forward to was not to be. When told the news, a young friend who was a regular victim of Chester's lunging love-bombs said mournfully, "He was the sweetest creature I ever saw. He's the only dog I ever saw kiss a cat."

Some will protest that in a world with so much human suffering, it is something between eccentric and obscene to mourn a dog. I think not. After all, it is perfectly normal—indeed, deeply human—to be moved when nature presents us with a vision of great beauty. Should we not be moved when it produces a vision—a creature—of the purest sweetness?

Time, June 16, 2003

In Defense of the F-Word

I am sure there is a special place in heaven reserved for those who have never used the F-word. I will never get near that place. Nor, apparently, will Dick Cheney.

Washington is abuzz with the latest political contretemps. Cheney, taking offense at Sen. Pat Leahy's imputation of improper vice-presidential conduct regarding Halliburton contracts in Iraq, let the senator know as much during a picture-taking ceremony on the floor of the Senate. The F-word was used. Washington is scandalized.

The newspapers were full of it. Lamentations were heard about the decline of civility. The *Washington Post* gave special gravitas to the occasion, spelling out the full four letters (something that it had done only three times previously). Democrats, feeling darned outraged, demanded apologies. The vice president remained defiant, offering but the coyest concession—that he "probably" cursed—coupled with satisfaction: "I expressed myself rather forcefully, felt better after I had done it."

The Federal Communications Commission just last year decreed that the F-word could be used as an adjective, but not as a verb. Alas, this Solomonic verdict, fodder for a dozen Ph.D. dissertations, was recently overturned. It would not get Cheney off the hook anyway. By all accounts, he deployed the pungent verb form, in effect a suggestion as to how the good senator from Vermont might amuse himself.

Flood-the-zone coverage by investigative reporters has not, however, quite resolved the issue of which of the two preferred forms passed Cheney's lips: the priceless two-worder—"[verb] you"—or the more expansive three-worder, a directive that begins with "go."

Though I myself am partial to the longer version, I admit that each formulation has its virtues. The deuce is the preferred usage when time is short and concision is of the essence. Enjoying the benefits of economy, it is especially useful in emergencies. This is why it is a favorite of major league managers going nose to nose with umpires. They know that they have only a few seconds before getting tossed out of the game, and as a result television viewers have for years delighted in the moment the two-worder is hurled, right on camera. No need for sound. The deuce was made for lip reading.

Which makes it excellent for drive-by information conveyance. When some jerk tailgater rides my bumper in heavy traffic, honking his horn before passing and cutting me off, I do a turn-to-the-left, eyeball-to-eyeball, through-the-driver's-window two-worder—mouthed slowly and with exaggerated lip movements. No interlocutor has yet missed my meaning.

Nonetheless, while the two-worder has the directness of the dagger, the three-worder has the elegance of the wide-arced saber slice. It is more musical and, being more clearly spelled out, more comprehensible to the non-English speaker (a boon in major urban areas). It consists of a straightforward directive containing both a subject and an object—charmingly, the same person.

According to the *Post*, the local authority on such matters, Cheney went for a variant of the short form, employing the more formal "yourself." And given the location, the floor of the Senate, it seems a reasonable choice: Time was short, and he undoubtedly reserves the right to revise and extend his remarks.

Ah, but the earnest chin-pullers are not amused. Cheney's demonstration of earthy authenticity in a chamber in which authenticity of any kind is to be valued has occasioned anguished meditations on the loss of civility in American politics. Liberals in particular have expressed deep concern about this breach of decorum.

Odd. The day before first reports of Cheney's alleged indiscretion, his Democratic predecessor, Al Gore, delivered a public speech in which he spoke of the administration's establishing a "Bush gulag" around the world and using "digital brown shirts" to intimidate the media. The former vice president of the United States compared the current president to both Hitler and Stalin in the same speech—a first not just in hyperbole but in calumny—and nary a complaint is heard about a breach of civility.

If you suspect that this selective indignation may be partisan, you guessed right. But here's an even more important question. In the face of Gore's real breach of civil political discourse, which of the following is the right corrective: (a) offer a reasoned refutation of the charge that George Bush is both Stalinist and Hitlerian; (b) suggest an increase in Gore's medication; or (c) do a Cheney.

The correct answer is (c). And given the circumstances, go for the deuce.

The Washington Post, Friday, July 2, 2004

THE CENTRAL AXIOM OF PARTISAN POLITICS

To understand the workings of American politics, you have to understand this fundamental law: Conservatives think liberals are stupid. Liberals think conservatives are evil.

For the first side of this equation, I need no sources. As a conservative, I can confidently attest that whatever else my colleagues might disagree about—Bosnia, John McCain, precisely how many orphans we're prepared to throw into the snow so the rich can have their tax cuts—we all agree that liberals are stupid.

We mean this, of course, in the nicest way. Liberals tend to be nice, and they believe—here is where they go stupid—that most everybody else is nice too. Deep down, that is. Sure, you've got your multiple felon and your occasional war criminal, but they're undoubtedly depraved 'cause they're deprived. If only we could get social conditions right—eliminate poverty, teach anger management, restore the ozone, arrest John Ashcroft—everyone would be holding hands smiley-faced, rocking back and forth to "We Shall Overcome."

Liberals believe that human nature is fundamentally good. The fact that this is contradicted by, oh, 4,000 years of human history simply tells them how urgent is the need for their next seven-point program for the social reform of everything.

Liberals suffer incurably from naïveté, the stupidity of the good heart. Who else but that oracle of American liberalism, the *New York Times*, could run the puzzled headline: "Crime Keeps On Falling, but Prisons Keep On Filling." *But?* How about this wild theory: If you lock up the criminals, crime declines.

Accordingly, the conservative attitude toward liberals is one of compassionate condescension. Liberals are not quite as reciprocally charitable. It is natural. They think conservatives are mean. How can conservatives believe in the things they do—self-reliance, self-discipline, competition, military power—without being soulless?

How to understand the conservative desire to actually abolish welfare, if it is not to punish the poor? The argument that it would increase self-reliance and thus ultimately *reduce* poverty is dismissed as meanness rationalized—or as Rep. Major Owens (D-N.Y.) put it more colorfully in a recent House debate on welfare reform, "a cold-blooded grab for another pound of flesh from the demonized welfare mothers."

Liberals, who have no head (see above), believe that conservatives have no heart. When Republicans unexpectedly took control of the House of Representatives in 1994, conventional wisdom immediately attributed this disturbance in the balance of the cosmos to the vote of the "angry white male" (an invention unsupported by the three polls that actually asked about anger and found three-quarters of white males *not* angry).

The "angry white male" was thus a legend, but a necessary one. It was unimaginable that conservatives could be given power by any sentiment less base than anger, the selfish fury of the former top dog—the white male—forced to accommodate the aspirations of women, minorities and sundry upstarts.

The legend lives. Years ago it was Newt Gingrich as the Grinch who stole Christmas. Today, *New York Times* columnist Paul Krugman declares the Bush administration the moral equivalent of Jean-Marie Le Pen, France's far right, xenophobic, antisemitic heir to European fascism. Both apparently represent the "angry right." But in America, writes Krugman, it is worse: "Here the angry people are already running the country."

This article of liberal faith—that conservatism is not just wrong but angry, mean and, well, bad—produces one paradox after another. Thus the online magazine *Slate* devoted an article to attempting to explain the "two faces" of Paul Gigot, editorial page editor of the *Wall Street Journal*. The puzzle is how a conservative could have such a "winning cocktail-party personality and talk-show cordiality." Gigot, it turns out, is "Janus-faced": regular guy—"plays basketball with working reporters"—yet conservative! "By day he wrote acid editorials . . . by night he polished his civilized banter [on TV]."

A classic of the genre—liberal amazement when it finds conservatism coexisting with human decency in whatever form—is the *New
York Times* news story speaking with unintended candor about bio-
ethicist Leon Kass: "Critics of Dr. Kass' views call him a neoconservative thinker. . . . But critics and admirers alike describe him as
thoughtful and dignified."

But? Neoconservative *but* thoughtful and dignified. A sighting:
rare, oxymoronic, newsworthy.

The venerable David Halberstam, writing in praise of the recently
departed Ted Williams, offered yet another sighting: "He was
politically conservative but in his core the most democratic of men."
Amazing.

The most troubling paradox of all, of course, is George W. Bush.
Compassionate, yet conservative? Reporters were fooled during the
campaign. "Because Bush seemed personally pleasant," explained
Slate, "[they] assumed his politics lay near the political center."

What else could one assume? Pleasant and *conservative*? Ah, yes,
Grampa told of seeing one such in the Everglades. But that was 1926.

The Washington Post, July 26, 2002

KRAUTHAMMER'S FIRST LAW

Strange doings in Virginia. George Allen, former governor, one-term senator, son of a famous football coach and in the midst of a heated battle for reelection, has just been outed as a Jew. An odd turn of events, given that his having Jewish origins has nothing to do with anything in the campaign and that Allen himself was oblivious to the fact until his 83-year-old mother revealed to him last month the secret she had kept concealed for 60 years.

Apart from its political irrelevance, it seems improbable in the extreme that the cowboy-boots-wearing football scion of Southern manner and speech should turn out to be, at least by origins, a son of Israel. For Allen, as he quipped to me, it's the explanation for a life-long affinity for Hebrew National hot dogs. For me, it is the ultimate confirmation of something I have been regaling friends with for 20 years and now, for the advancement of social science, feel compelled to publish.

Krauthammer's Law: *Everyone is Jewish until proven otherwise.* I've had a fairly good run with this one. First, it turns out that John Kerry—windsurfing, French-speaking, Beacon Hill aristocrat—had two Jewish grandparents. Then Hillary Clinton—methodical Methodist—unearths a Jewish stepgrandfather in time for her run as New York senator.

A less jaunty case was that of Madeleine Albright, three of whose Czech grandparents had perished in the Holocaust and who most improbably contended that she had no idea they were Jewish. To which we can add the leading French presidential contender (Nicolas Sarkozy), a former supreme allied commander of NATO (Wesley Clark) and Russia's leading antisemite (Vladimir Zhirinovsky). One must have a sense of humor about these things. Even Fidel Castro claims he is from a family of Marranos.

For all its tongue-in-cheek irony, Krauthammer's Law works

because when I say "everyone," I don't mean everyone you know personally. Depending on the history and ethnicity of your neighborhood and social circles, there may be no one you know who is Jewish.
But if "everyone" means anyone that you've heard of in public life, the
law works for two reasons. Ever since the Jews were allowed out of
the ghetto and into European society at the dawning of the Enlightenment, they have peopled the arts and sciences, politics and history
in astonishing disproportion to their numbers.

There are 13 million Jews in the world, one-fifth of 1% of the
world's population. Yet 20% of Nobel Prize winners are Jewish, a
staggering hundredfold surplus of renown and genius. This is similarly true for a myriad of other "everyones"—the household names
in music, literature, mathematics, physics, finance, industry, design,
comedy, film and, as the doors opened, even politics.

But it is not just Jewish excellence at work here. There is a dark side
to these past centuries of Jewish emancipation and achievement—an
unrelenting history of persecution. The result is the other, more som-
ber and poignant reason for the Jewishness of public figures being
discovered late and with surprise: concealment.

Look at the Albright case. Her distinguished father was Jewish,
if tenuously so, until the Nazi invasion. He fled Czechoslovakia and,
shortly thereafter, converted. Over the centuries, suffering—most
especially the Holocaust—has proved too much for many Jews. Many
survivors simply resigned their commission.

For some, the break was defiant and theological: A God who could
permit the Holocaust—ineffable be His reasons—had so breached
the Covenant that it was now forfeit. They were bound no longer to
Him or His faith.

For others, the considerations were far more secular and practical.
Why subject one's children to the fear and suffering, the stigmatization and marginalization, the prospect of being hunted until death
that being Jewish had brought to an entire civilization in Europe?

In fact, that was precisely the reason Etty Lumbroso, Allen's
mother, concealed her identity. Brought up as a Jew in French Tuni-

sia during World War II, she saw her father, Felix, imprisoned in a concentration camp. Coming to America was her one great chance to leave that forever behind, for her and for her future children. She married George Allen Sr., apparently never telling her husband's family, her own children or anyone else of her Jewishness.

Such was Etty's choice. Multiply the story in its thousand variations and you have Kerry and Clinton, Albright and Allen, a world of people with a whispered past. Allen's mother tried desperately to bury it forever. In response to published rumors, she finally confessed the truth to him, adding heartbreakingly, "Now you don't love me anymore"—and then swore him to secrecy.

The Washington Post, September 25, 2006

CHAPTER 4

FOLLIES

SAVE THE BORDER COLLIE

Alas, not many British dukes are bred as closely as their poorest shepherd's dogs. Even fewer dukes are bred for accomplishment.
—Donald McCaig, *Eminent Dogs, Dangerous Men*

The dumbing of America has gone far enough. Yes, we have gotten used to falling SAT scores, coming in dead last in international math comparisons, high schoolers who cannot locate the Civil War to the nearest half-century. But we have got to draw the line somewhere. I say we draw it at dogs.

Last month, the American Kennel Club, the politburo of American dog breeding, decided to turn the world's smartest dog, the border collie, into a moron. Actually, it voted 11–1 to begin proceedings to turn it into a show dog, which will amount to the same thing. A dog bred for 200 years exclusively for smarts will now be bred for looks. Its tail, its coat, its ears, its bite, its size will have to be just so. That its brains will likely turn to mush is of no consequence.

What is the border collie? A breed developed in the border country between England and Scotland for one thing only: its ability to herd sheep, though, if necessary, it can work cattle or hogs or even turkeys. (Our border collie, deprived of such gainful employment, likes to swim out to the middle of a pond and herd ducks.)

It is a creature of uncanny intelligence and a jaw-dropping capacity to communicate with humans, able to herd 300 sheep at a time at a distance of a mile and a half from its shepherd. It is, testifies Baxter Black (NPR's "cowboy poet, philosopher and former large-animal veterinarian"), "one of the greatest genetic creations on the face of the earth."

Now it faces genetic ruin. When bred for looks, great swaths of the border collie population, which comes in all shapes and sizes, will be condemned to genetic oblivion.

It would be nice to breed for beauty and brains, but history and genetics teach that the confluence of the two is as rare in dogs as it is in humans. Inbreeding in the pursuit of man-made standards of beauty has reduced other breeds to ruin: In the 1950s, writes Mark Derr in the *Atlantic Monthly*, show people turned the German shepherd into a weak-hipped animal with a foul temper and bizarre downward-sloping hindquarters. The cocker spaniel lost its ability to hunt. The bulldog and the Boston terrier have been given such exaggerated heads that the females regularly need C-sections to give birth. As for the AKC's Irish setters, says veterinarian Michael W. Fox, "they're so dumb they get lost on the end of their leash."

The genetics behind such sad stories is straightforward. "In genetics, selection for one trait usually comes at the expense of another," explains Jasper Rine, professor of genetics and former director of the Human Genome Center at the Lawrence Berkeley Labs. "The notion that one could achieve a standard conformation for border collies and maintain their working qualities is simply foolish." Which is why the border collie people are prepared to sue to keep the AKC's snout from under their tent.

Why should anyone else care? Well, a society that grieves for the accidental demise of the snail darter and the spotted owl that not one in a million Americans has ever seen should not easily acquiesce to the deliberate destruction of a unique breed of animals whose fate is so intimately entwined with man's. "Border collies: Are they truly smarter than a chimpanzee?" asks Black. "Can they change course in mid-air, drag Nell from the tracks and locate missing microfiche? Yes. I believe they can. They are the best of the best."

And for those who find such fascination with dogs self-indulgent sentimentalism, who care as little for the border collie as they do for the snail darter, consider this: In a world of rising crime and falling standards, of broken cities and failing schools, the border collie is one of the few things that works. Must we ruin this too? Reduce it to imbecility in the name of prettiness?

In the brief interval of calm between our latest capitulation to North Korea and our invasion of Haiti, it is worth pondering this small but telling domestic folly. Face it: Our kids are not going to beat the South Koreans at math for decades. But we can still produce a thinking dog. For now.

The Washington Post, July 15, 1994

BUSH DERANGEMENT SYNDROME

> **Diane Rehm:** *"Why do you think he [Bush] is suppressing that [Sept. 11] report?"*
>
> **Howard Dean:** *"I don't know. There are many theories about it. The most interesting theory that I've heard so far—which is nothing more than a theory, it can't be proved—is that he was warned ahead of time by the Saudis. Now who knows what the real situation is?"*
>
> —*The Diane Rehm Show,* NPR, Dec. 1, 2003

It has been 25 years since I discovered a psychiatric syndrome (for the record: "Secondary Mania," *Archives of General Psychiatry,* November 1978), and in the interim I haven't been looking for new ones. But it's time to don the white coat again. A plague is abroad in the land.

Bush Derangement Syndrome: *the acute onset of paranoia in otherwise normal people in reaction to the policies, the presidency—nay—the very existence of George W. Bush.* Now, I cannot testify to Howard Dean's sanity before this campaign, but five terms as governor by a man with no visible tics and no history of involuntary confinement is pretty good evidence of a normal mental status. When he avers, however, that "the most interesting" theory as to why the president is "suppressing" the Sept. 11 report is that Bush knew about Sept. 11 in advance, it's time to check on Thorazine supplies. When Rep. Cynthia McKinney (D-Ga.) first broached this idea before the 2002 primary election, it was considered so nutty it helped make her *former* representative McKinney. Today the Democratic presidential front-runner professes agnosticism as to whether the president of the United States was tipped off about 9/11 by the Saudis, and it goes unnoticed. The virus is spreading.

It is, of course, epidemic in New York's Upper West Side and the

tonier parts of Los Angeles, where the very sight of the president—
say, smiling while holding a tray of Thanksgiving turkey in a Baghdad
mess hall—caused dozens of cases of apoplexy in otherwise healthy
adults. What is worrying epidemiologists about the Dean incident,
however, is that heretofore no case had been reported in Vermont or
any other dairy state.

Moreover, Dean is very smart. Until now, Bush Derangement
Syndrome (BDS) had generally struck people with previously compromised intellectual immune systems. Hence its prevalence in Hollywood. Barbra Streisand, for example, wrote her famous September
2002 memo to Dick Gephardt warning that the president was drag-
ging us toward war to satisfy, among the usual corporate malefactors
who "clearly have much to gain if we go to war against Iraq," the
logging industry—timber being a major industry in a country that is
two-thirds desert.

It is true that BDS has struck some pretty smart guys—Bill Moyers ranting about a "right-wing wrecking crew" engaged in "a deliberate, intentional destruction of the United States way of governing"
and *New York Times* columnist Paul Krugman, whose recent book
attacks the president so virulently that Krugman's British publisher
saw fit to adorn the cover with images of Vice President Cheney in a
Hitler-like mustache and Bush stitched up like Frankenstein. Nonetheless, some observers took that to be satire; others wrote off Moyers
and Krugman as simple aberrations, the victims of too many years of
neurologically hazardous punditry.

That's what has researchers so alarmed about Dean. He had none
of the usual risk factors: Dean has never opined for a living and has
no detectable sense of humor. Even worse is the fact that he is now
exhibiting symptoms of a related illness, Murdoch Derangement
Syndrome (MDS), in which otherwise normal people believe that
their minds are being controlled by a single, very clever Australian.

Chris Matthews: *"Would you break up Fox?"*
Howard Dean: *"On ideological grounds, absolutely yes, but . . . I
don't want to answer whether I would break up Fox or not. . . .*

What I'm going to do is appoint people to the FCC that believe democracy depends on getting information from all portions of the political spectrum, not just one."

Some clinicians consider this delusion—that Americans can get their news from only one part of the political spectrum—the gravest of all. They report that no matter how many times sufferers in padded cells are presented with flash cards with the symbols ABC, NBC, CBS, CNN, MSNBC, NPR, PBS, *Time, Newsweek, New York Times, Washington Post, L.A. Times*—they remain unresponsive, some in a terrifying near-catatonic torpor.

The sad news is that there is no cure. But there is hope. There are many fine researchers seeking that cure. Your donation to the BDS Foundation, no matter how small, can help. Mailing address: Republican National Committee, Washington, D.C., Attention: psychiatric department. Just make sure your amount does not exceed $2,000 ($4,000 for a married couple).

The Washington Post, December 5, 2003

LIFE BY MANUAL

My channel surfing was arrested by the news reporter at the Manhattan courthouse recounting the day's doings at the Woody Allen–Mia Farrow custody fight. "Testimony today," she said, "focused on Woody Allen's lack of parenting skills." By this she meant that on the witness stand Allen had admitted that he (1) could not name a single one of his children's friends, (2) had never taken the children to the barber or given them a bath, (3) did not know who their dentist was, (4) had never attended a parent-teacher conference for son Satchel. In fact, the three children whose custody he seeks had never spent a night at his apartment.

Lack of parenting skills? One might as well say that Jeffrey Dahmer lacked interpersonal skills or that Robespierre could have used some sensitivity training. The problem here is not some absence of technique. It is an absence of something far more basic: an instinct, a feeling, the normal bond that ties the average parent to his child.

Allen's problem is self-absorption taken, as with most everything in his life, to the point of parody. Here is the artiste so jealous of his autonomy, so disdainful of attachment, that his children may not spend the night at his apartment, though this should not prevent the court from awarding him custody.

Of course, given the alternative, the hysterical Ms. Farrow, whose narcissism expresses itself not in detachment but in a self-indulgence that acquires children like stray pets, Allen may turn out to be the better choice. The sight of these two vying for custody of that pathetic brood makes you wonder how a society that requires licenses for drivers manages without requiring them for parents.

The reason is that nature endows most people in all cultures with an instinctive parental feeling that translates into often clumsy, sometimes wrongheaded, but generally benign and benevolent care. The fact that the grotesque absence of these qualities in Allen could be interpreted as a lack of "parenting skills" shows how far we've gone in the belief in the mechanization of ordinary human feeling.

Sexual intimacy, for example. "A skill like any other," concludes Pulitzer Prize–winning journalist Richard Rhodes in his recent sexual autobiography. There are entire bookshelves of wildly successful manuals (*How to Satisfy a Woman Every Time*—55 weeks on the best-seller list) to show how far from alone Rhodes is in this belief.

Self-improvement through the acquisition of skill is, of course, hardly a new American theme. First mass-marketed by Dale Carnegie, it owes its popularity to the marriage of two powerful American beliefs: human perfectibility and the power of technology.

In the past, however, tradition and community acted as partial antidotes to this tendency. But with the modern decline of tradition and community as guides to experience, the mechanization of behavior is complete. Every human activity is now the subject of the how-to industry.

A visit to the local bookstore shows how far things have gone. Not just parenting and loving, but everything—eating and drinking, running and sunning, living itself—is a skill to be learned and mastered. There are books, videos, multibillion-dollar industries for teaching people such exotic skills as losing weight (try eating less!) and exercise (try running around). The business succeeds because Americans have come to believe that only an expert can teach them the correct way to, say, walk, or bend their knees or think well of themselves.

The idea that everything is a skill to be learned, like a golf swing, applies far beyond the field of family and sexual intimacy. We now have training for the proper love of strangers. Marge Schott, owner of the Cincinnati Reds and given to racist remarks, is sentenced by baseball owners to sensitivity training. This will make her nice. Five years ago, a religious student at the University of Michigan expressed the view that homosexuality is immoral. He was made to recant and ordered a dose of sensitivity training. This will make him broad-minded.

This project for the inculcation of proper human feelings through behavioral technique is either sinister or idiotic. It is sinister when it works, as in Communist China, where they have learned how to break one's character through extremes of coercion, deprivation and torture. These means are not yet available to American educators and family therapists. Which explains their low success rate. Some things, alas, cannot be taught.

Woody Allen, the movie character, once said: I've had 17 years of psychotherapy—one more and I'm going to Lourdes. Time's up, Woody. You've tried technique. Now get on that plane.

The Washington Post, April 2, 1993

FROM PEOPLE POWER TO POLENTA

When Katherine Ann Power—'60s radical, bank robber, fugitive—turned herself in last week after 23 years on the run, she added another entry to her already crowded résumé: unwitting historian. Her brief explanatory statement released upon her surrender to Boston police is a document historians of the future, puzzling over what happened to the '60s, will find useful.

They will ignore the usual mitigating phrases about actions she now characterizes as "naïve and unthinking." One does not ordinarily think of a bank robbery in which a policeman, father of nine, is shot in the back, as an act of naïveté. "My intention was never to damage any human life," she says. It apparently never occurred to her that when robbing a bank in the company of three ex-cons, a shotgun and a submachine gun, somebody might get hurt.

Nor is there anything unusual about her spirit-of-the-age defense, wherein she insists that her deeds should be seen in the context of a time when many others—she cites, for example, Daniel Ellsberg, leaker of the Pentagon papers—were breaking the law. There is a certain moral gap between unauthorized leaking and armed robbery that this defense does not bridge.

No matter. These run-of-the-mill self-justifications are window dressing. What everyone wants to know is not why Katherine Power robbed a bank in 1970—we know: She wanted to save the world—but why she finally gave it up in 1993. It is her account of the return that yields the one truly memorable line in this text, the one historians will ponder to their benefit: "I know that I must answer this accusation from the past, in order to live with full authenticity in the present."

So Katherine Power came in from the cold in search of "full authenticity." Not out of remorse or resignation. Not seeking forgiveness or repentance. "She did not return out of guilt," explained her husband. She just tired of telling lies, of living as Alice Metzinger, wife, cook, restaurateur, but with a shrouded past and troubled future. "She wanted her life back," said her husband. "She wanted her truth back. She wants to be whole."

That Officer Schroeder will not get his life back troubled her ("his death was shocking to me"), but that is not why she surrendered—or she would have done so 23 years ago. In fact, as elaborated in a front-page *New York Times* story about her psychotherapy for depression, her surrender—for the sake of "full authenticity"—was a form of therapy, indeed the final therapeutic step toward regaining her sense of self.

Allan Bloom once described a man who had just gotten out of prison, where he had undergone "therapy." "He said he had found his identity and learned to like himself," writes Bloom. "A generation earlier, he would have found God and learned to despise himself as a sinner."

In an age where the word *sin* has become quaint—reserved for such offenses against hygiene as smoking and drinking (which alone merit "sin taxes")—surrendering to the authorities for armed robbery and manslaughter is not an act of repentance but of personal growth. Explains Jane Alpert, another '60s radical who served time (for her part in a series of bombings that injured 21 people): "Ultimately, I spent many years in therapy, learning to understand, to tolerate and forgive both others and myself."

Learning to forgive oneself. Very important nowadays for revolutionaries with a criminal bent. What a pathetic trajectory from the '60s to the '90s: from revolutionary slogans to New Age psychobabble, from Frantz Fanon to Robert Fulghum, from the thrill of the underground to the banalities of the couch.

But the banality does not stop there. This revolution has not just gone into therapy. It is heavily into food. When Bobby Seale, cofounder and chairman of the Black Panthers, finally produced his oeuvre, it was *Barbeque'n with Bobby*. Karleton Lewis Armstrong, jailed for a 1970 University of Wisconsin bombing that injured four and killed one, now runs a fruit-juice business in Madison, Wisconsin. And Katherine Power, expert chef and cooking instructor, was renowned in her adopted Oregon for her recipes. Power's therapist, reports the *New York Times*, found it impossible "to believe that this bespectacled cook with the terrific polenta recipe . . . had spent 14 years as one of the Federal Bureau of Investigation's 10 Most Wanted fugitives."

It starts with people power. It ends in polenta. A fitting finish to the radical '60s.

But it is not quite right to close the book with this touch of cute domesticity. Let's remember who Katherine Power was and what she did. This was not a flower child caught up some wild afternoon in a robbery. She was found to have in her apartment three rifles, a carbine, a pistol, a shotgun and a huge store of ammunition. She is accused of having firebombed a National Guard armory. She took part in a bank robbery in which a hero cop, father of nine, was shot dead. This is someone very hard who has now softened—out of feelings of loss, principally for herself.

"After all these years," concludes *Newsweek*, "it's hard to know whom to feel the most sympathy for: the [Schroeder] children who lost a father . . . [or] the young woman who lost her way in the tumult of the '60s."

That's a hard one? Reflecting on the man who learned to like himself in prison, Bloom notes that in the mind of this ex-con, "the problem lay with his sense of self, not with any original sin or devils in him. We have here the peculiarly American way of digesting Continental despair. It is nihilism with a happy ending."

Except for the orphans.

Annals of "Art"

Culture wars, chapter 36. The Brooklyn Museum of Art readies an exhibition of high decadence called "Sensation." The mayor of New York threatens to close down the museum if the exhibit is not canceled. The mayor is pilloried by the usual suspects—a consortium of New York museums, the ACLU, the highbrow press—for philistinism and/or First Amendment abuse.

The exhibit itself is nothing very special, just the usual fin de siècle celebration of the blasphemous, the criminal and the decadent. The item that caught Rudy Giuliani's attention is a portrait of the Virgin Mary adorned with elephant dung and floating bits of female pornography. The one that caught my attention is the giant portrait of a child molester and murderer—made to look as if composed of tiny children's handprints.

The culture-guardians scream "censorship." The mayor makes the quite obvious point that these artists can do anything the hell they want, but they have no entitlement to have their work exhibited in a museum subsidized by the taxpayers of New York City to the tune of $7 million a year.

It is an old story. Art whose very purpose is *épater les bourgeois* is at the same time demanding the bourgeois' subsidy. Of course, if the avant-garde had any self-respect, it would shock the bourgeoisie on its own dime.

But how silly. Self-respect is a hopelessly bourgeois value. The avant-garde lives by a code of fearless audacity and uncompromising authenticity. And endless financial support. The art world has sustained this cultural blackmail by counting on the status anxiety of the middle class. They are afraid to ask the emperor's-new-clothes question—Why are we being forced to subsidize willful, offensive banality?—for fear of being considered terminally unsophisticated.

This cultural blackmail has gone on for decades, with the artist loudly blaspheming everything his patrons hold dear—while suckling at their teats. Every once in a while, however, someone refuses to play the game. This time it is Giuliani. And sure enough, he has been charged with philistinism, or as the *New York Times* editorial put it, with making "the city look ridiculous."

"The mayor's rationale," says the *Times* with unintended hilarity, "derives from the fact that the city owns the Brooklyn Museum of Art and provides nearly a third of its operating budget."

Rationale? It is self-evident: You own an institution—whether you are an individual, a corporation, or a city with duly elected authorities acting on its behalf—you regulate its activity. This is no "rationale." It is a slam-dunk, argument-ending, QED clincher.

Let's be plain. No one is preventing these art works from being made or displayed. The only question is whether artists have a claim on the taxpayer's dollar in displaying it.

The answer is open and shut: no. It is a question not of censorship but of sensibility. Can there ever be a limit to the tolerance and generosity of the paying public? Of course. Does this particular exhibit forfeit whatever claim art has to public support—and the legitimacy and honor conferred upon it by the stamp of the city-owned Brooklyn Museum?

The Virgin Mary painting alone would merit an answer of yes. Add the child molester painting, the 3-D acrylic women with erect penises for noses, *Spaceshit* and *A Thousand Years* ("Steel, glass, flies, maggots, MDF, insect-o-cutor, cow's head, sugar, water, 213 x 427 x 213 centimeters"), and you get a fuller picture: an artistic sensibility that is a peculiar combination of the creepy and the banal.

Of course everyone loves to play victim, the status of victim being, as Anthony Daniels put it in the *New Criterion*, "the personal equivalent of most favored nation." But the idea that art of this type is under assault or starved for funds is quite ridiculous. Art of this type is now the norm. It is everywhere. Galleries, museums, private collections are filled with it.

It is classical representational art that is starved for funds. Try finding a school in your town that teaches classical drawing or painting. As James Cooper noted some years ago in the *American Arts Quarterly*, "A modest grant to a small art academy was recently denied by the National Endowment for the Arts because, the terse NEA memo explained, 'teaching students to draw the human figure is revisionist and stifles creativity.'"

Add some dung, though, and you've got yourself a show.

The role of the artist has changed radically in the last century and a half. It was once the function of the artist to represent beauty and transcendence and possibly introduce it into the life of the beholder. With the advent of photography and film, the perfect media for both representation and narration, art has fought its dread of obsolescence by seeking some other role.

Today the function of the artist is to be an emissary to the aberrant: to live at the cultural and social extremes, to go over into the decadent and even criminal, to scout forbidden emotional and psychic territory—and bring back artifacts of that "edgy" experience to a bourgeoisie too cozy and cowardly to make the trip itself.

This has been going on for decades. It must be said, however, that at the beginning of the transformation there was an expectation that the artist would bring skill and a sense of craft to his work. Whether their conceit was dandyism, criminality or sexual adventurism (free love, homosexuality and the other once shocking taboos of yesterday), artists of the early modern period still felt a need to render their recreation of shock with style and technique.

Having reached a time, however, when technique itself is considered revisionist, anti-creative and, of course, bourgeois, all we are left with is the raw stinking shock. On display, right now, at the Brooklyn Museum of Art.

It is important to note that the artists and promoters who provoked the great Brooklyn contretemps are not feigning their surprise at Giuliani's counterattack. They genuinely feel entitled to their subsidy. They genuinely feel they perform a unique and priceless service, introducing vicarious extremism into the utterly compromised lives of their bourgeois patrons.

Ah, but every once in a while a burgher arises and says to the artist: No need to report back from the edge. You can stay where you are. We'll have our afternoon tea without acid, thank you.

And then the fun begins.

The Weekly Standard, October 11, 1999

"NATURAL" CHILDBIRTH

Nancy Miner wanted to give birth to her baby at home. The fact that she was 39, that this was her first child, that there was no electricity in her "rustic Middleburg cottage" did not daunt her. Assisting her were her husband, a friend and a lay midwife. During the delivery, the baby's umbilical cord became compressed. The baby died. The midwife has now been charged with manslaughter.

Lay midwifery is not certified and not legal in Virginia, but the midwife's lawyer says she should not be held liable because she was simply doing what the parents wanted. I'm with the lawyer. If there was real justice in this world, it is the parents who would be in the dock, charged with criminal self-indulgence.

"This case is all about the rights of parents to make decisions about the welfare of their children," says Erin Fulham, a Maryland nurse and member of Maryland Friends of Midwives. Welfare of the children? If Nancy Miner had had the slightest concern about the welfare of her child, this at-risk 39-year-old primigravida would have had her child in a hospital where, when the breech birth and compressed cord had been discovered, she could have had an emergency C-section and a good chance of saving her child.

"Should parents have the choice about the health care of their newborn?" asks Fulham rhetorically. Of course. But the Miners' choice, as the subsequent tragedy proved, was hardly about the newborn's health care. It was about the mother's karma. It was about the narcissistic pursuit of "experience," the Me Generation's insistence on turning every life event—even those fraught with danger for others—into a personalized Hallmark moment.

Miner protests in her own defense: "Everyone was born at home a generation ago. Now they act like it is outrageous." More like 80 years ago, but no matter. Yes, 80 years ago babies were born at home.

And they died in droves. Almost 1 in 10 newborns died then. Fewer than 1 in 100 does now.

Yes, childbirth used to be natural. But so were the accompanying death, disability, deformity and disease. A parent's duty is to avoid these "natural" phenomena by all possible means. Today we have those means. They are called modern medicine.

The whole natural childbirth phenomenon is an astonishing triumph of ideology over experience. Pain is normally—indeed, "naturally"—something humans try to avoid. And the pain of childbirth is among life's most searing. It is also, today, entirely unnecessary.

My older brother was born 50 years ago in Rio de Janeiro. Postwar Brazil not being a mecca of high-tech obstetrics, my mother delivered without anesthetics and suffered accordingly. Four years later in New York, she had the opportunity to give birth differently. She quite sensibly chose to deliver (me) in a state of blissful unconsciousness. To this day she has no doubt which was the more desirable experience. (As for me, I must have entered the world as zonked as Janis Joplin left it, but with no apparent side effects. I don't even like beer.)

In the '60s and '70s, natural childbirth made a comeback, fueled by a peculiar combination of New Age mysticism and macho feminism. Today, thankfully, some feminist writers argue that hospital childbirth is alright, that it is not a betrayal of sisterhood, that there is no earthly reason to willfully embrace pain for the mother and danger for the child as a protest against the alleged patriarchal structure and technological tyranny of modern medicine. They could usefully use as text the case of Nancy Miner.

I will no doubt be charged with lack of sympathy for a bereaved mother. I plead guilty. I reserve my sympathy instead for the lost child. Perhaps if we reserved for these wanton parents less sympathy and more scorn, less understanding and more opprobrium, we might deter some and save a few children.

The Miners have every right to be Luddites, free spirits, foes of modern technology. But the original 18th-century industrial saboteurs sought to destroy the satanic textile mills by throwing their wooden shoes (sabots) into the machines. They didn't throw their children.

The Washington Post, May 24, 1996

THE INNER MAN? WHO CARES

As Bob Woodward likes to say, he is the gift that keeps on giving. Richard Nixon, that is. And an endless source of amusement he is. We have all been having a great chuckle listening to Nixon again. More tapes, more titillation, most notably his ranting and raving about Jews. ("Generally speaking, you can't trust the bastards," etc.)

As a Jew, I have been asked several times about these revelations. I am entirely unmoved.

First, I wonder how anyone would fare who had an open microphone in his office for 3,700 hours running. Second, Nixon was suspicious and paranoid about everyone. So what else is new?

Third and most important: I don't really care what a public figure thinks. I care about what he does. Let God probe his inner heart. Tell me about his outer acts.

And what were Nixon's outer acts vis-à-vis Jews? Well, in 1973, he saved Israel from possible destruction with his massive weapons airlift during the Yom Kippur War. He even put the U.S. military on worldwide alert to keep the Russians from intervening on Egypt's behalf.

I feel about Nixon the way I feel reading about Truman's occasional ethnic lapses. "In private, Truman was a man who still . . . could use a word like 'kike,'" writes David McCullough, "or, in a letter to his wife, dismiss Miami as nothing but 'hotels, filling stations, Hebrews and cabins.'" So what? Truman remains a hero to Jews for having recognized the State of Israel at the crucial moment of its birth in 1948.

Herb Stein, who died last month, was chairman of Nixon's Council of Economic Advisers. Reflecting on Nixon's Jewish problem, he wrote that he never felt anything but the utmost respect and friendship from Nixon. Whatever Nixon's private thoughts, both in his personal relations and in his public actions as president, he was a friend of the Jews.

It is part of the trivialization of politics that we give endless attention to the inner life of the politician—his private thoughts, his inner demons—at the expense of his outer life. I cannot, for example, imagine Pat Buchanan ever saying even in private anything as nasty about Jews as did Nixon. But the public Pat Buchanan goes around fanning hatred for Jews with his sly and not so sly allusions to Jewish power, Jewish influence, Jewish disloyalty. So who is the antisemite?

Obsession with self is the motif of our time. It carries over into our thinking about public figures, to our preoccupation—long predating our fascination with Gary Hart's nocturnal trysts—with their inner life.

The reductio ad absurdum of this tendency is Edmund Morris' disastrous book on Reagan. The subject of the book is really not Reagan but Morris, and when Morris does get around to Reagan, it is the inner "Dutch" that interests him, not the politician, the leader, the president.

The results are comical. Seven pages spent on imagining Reagan's thoughts while making his first movie, four pages on the momentous years 1976–80, when Reagan remade American politics. Between Reagan's losing the nomination in '76 and winning the presidency in '80, the book is a near total blank. We hear about Morris' encounter with Jimmy Carter, Morris' publication of his Theodore Roosevelt biography, then get one page—out of 674—on the 1980 campaign.

One modern conceit is that the inner man is more important than the outer man. The second conceit is that somehow, thanks to Freud and modern psychobabble, we have real access to the inner man.

As a former psychiatrist, I know how difficult it is to try to understand the soul of even someone you have spent hundreds of hours alone with in therapy. To think that one can decipher the inner life of some distant public figure is folly.

Even the experts haven't a clue. Remember that group of psychiatrists, 1,189 strong, who in 1964 signed a statement asserting their professional judgment that Barry Goldwater was psychologically unfit to be president? The very attempt to make such a diagnosis at a distance is malpractice.

Even Nixon, his private thoughts spilled out on tape forever, is no open book. Sure, the seething cauldron of inchoate hatreds and fears helps explain Watergate. But how do you match that with the man who cut through the paranoia and fear and opened the door to China, fashioned détente and ushered in the era of arms control— something less psychically roiled presidents had not been able to do?

"Know thyself" is a highly overrated piece of wisdom. As for knowing the self of others, forget it. Know what they do and judge them by their works.

The Washington Post, October 15, 1999

THE MIRROR-IMAGE FALLACY

"As is evident just from the look on his face," observes *The New Yorker* in a recent reflection on the Lincoln Memorial, "[Lincoln] would have liked to live out a long life surrounded by old friends and good food." Good food? *New Yorker* readers have an interest in successful soufflés, but it is hard to recall the most melancholy and spiritual of presidents giving them much thought. *New Yorker* editors no doubt dream of living out their days grazing in gourmet pastures. But did Lincoln really long to retire to a table at Lutèce?

Solipsism is the belief that the whole world is me, and as mathematician Martin Gardner points out, its authentic version is not to be found outside mental institutions. What is to be found outside the asylum is its philosophic cousin, the belief that the whole world is *like* me. This species of solipsism—plural solipsism, if you like—is far more common because it is far less lonely. Indeed, it yields a very congenial world populated exclusively by creatures of one's own likeness, a world in which Lincoln pines for his dinner with André or, more consequentially, where KGB chiefs and Iranian ayatollahs are, well, folks just like us.

The mirror-image fantasy is not as crazy as it seems. Fundamentally, it is a radical denial of the otherness of others. Or to put it another way, a blinding belief in "common humanity," in the triumph of human commonality over human differences. It is a creed rarely fully embraced (it has a disquieting affinity with martyrdom), but in a culture tired of such ancient distinctions as that between children and adults (in contemporary movies the kids are, if anything, wiser than their parents) or men and women ("I was a better man as a woman with a woman than I've ever been as a man with a woman," says Tootsie), it can acquire considerable force.

Its central axiom is that if one burrows deep enough beneath the

Mao jacket, the *shapka* or the chador, one discovers that people everywhere are essentially the same. Eleven-year-old American anthropologist Samantha Smith was invited to Moscow by Yuri Andropov for
firsthand confirmation of just that proposition—a rare Soviet concession to the principle of on-site inspection. After a well-photographed
sojourn during which she took in a children's festival at a Young Pio-
neer camp (but was spared the paramilitary training), she got the
message: "They're just . . . almost . . . just like us," she announced
at her last Moscow press conference. Her mother, who is no longer
eleven but makes up for it in open-mindedness, supplied the corollary: "They're just like us . . . they prefer to work at their jobs than to
work at war."

That completes the syllogism. We all have "eyes, hands, organs,
dimensions, senses, affections, passions." We are all "fed with the
same food, hurt with the same weapons, subject to the same diseases,
healed by the same means, warmed and cooled by the same winter
and summer." It follows, does it not, that we must all want the same
things? According to Harvard cardiologist Bernard Lown, president
of International Physicians for the Prevention of Nuclear War, that's
not just Shakespeare, it's a scientific fact "that Russian and American
hearts are indistinguishable, that both ache for peace and survival."

Such breathtaking non sequiturs, cardiological or otherwise, are
characteristic of plural solipsism. For it is more than just another
happy vision. It is meant to have practical consequences. If people
everywhere, from Savannah to Sevastopol, share the same hopes and
dreams and fears and love of children (and good food), they should
get along. And if they don't, then there must be some misunderstand-
ing, some misperception, some problem of communication.

As one news report of the recent conference of Soviet and American peace activists in Minneapolis put it, "The issue of human rights
sparked a heated discussion . . . and provided participants with a firsthand view of the obstacles to communication which so often charac-
terize U.S.-Soviet relations."

It is the broken-telephone theory of international conflict, and it suggests a solution: repair service by the expert "facilitator," the Harvard negotiations professor. Hence the vogue for peace academies, the mania for mediators, the belief that the world's conundrums would yield to the right intermediary, the right presidential envoy, the right socialist international delegation. Yet Iraq's Saddam Hussein and Iran's Ayatollah Khomeini have perfectly adequate phone service. They need only an operator to make the connection. Their problem is that they have very little to say to each other.

There are other consequences. If the whole world is like me, then certain conflicts become incomprehensible; the very notion of intractability becomes paradoxical. When the U.S. embassy in Tehran is taken over, Americans are bewildered. What does the ayatollah want? The U.S. government sends envoys to find out what token or signal or symbolic gesture might satisfy Iran. It is impossible to believe that the ayatollah wants exactly what he says he wants: the head of the shah. Things are not done that way anymore in the West (even the Soviet bloc has now taken to pensioning off deposed leaders). It took a long time for Americans to get the message.

Other messages from exotic cultures are never received at all. The more virulent pronouncements of Third World countries are dismissed as mere rhetoric. The more alien the sentiment, the less seriously it is taken. Diplomatic fiascoes follow, like Secretary Shultz's recent humiliation in Damascus. He persisted in going there despite the fact that President Assad had made it utterly plain that he rejected efforts by the U.S. (the "permanent enemy") to obtain withdrawal of Syrian forces from Lebanon.

Or consider the chronic American frustration with Saudi Arabia. The Saudis consistently declare their refusal to accept the legitimacy of a Jewish state in the Middle East, a position so at variance with the Western view that it is simply discounted. Thus successive American governments continue to count on Saudi support for U.S. peace plans, only to be rudely let down. When the Saudis finally make it unmistakably clear that they will support neither Camp David nor the Reagan plan nor the Lebanon accord, the U.S. reacts with consternation.

It might have spared itself the surprise if it had not in the first place imagined that underneath those kaffiyehs are folks just like us, sharing our aims and views.

"The wise man shows his wisdom in separation, in gradation, and his scale of creatures and of merits is as wide as nature," writes Emerson. "The foolish have no range in their scale, but suppose every man is as every other man." Ultimately to say that people all share the same hopes and fears, are all born and love and suffer and die alike, is to say very little. For it is after commonalities are accounted for that politics becomes necessary. It is only when values, ideologies, cultures and interests clash that politics even begins. At only the most trivial level can it be said that people want the same things. Take peace. The North Vietnamese want it, but apparently they wanted to conquer all of Indochina first. The Salvadoran right and left both want it, but only after making a desert of the other. The Reagan administration wants it, but not if it has to pay for it with pieces of Central America.

And even if one admits universal ends, one still has said nothing about means, about what people will risk, will permit, will commit in order to banish their (common) fears and pursue their (common) hopes. One would think that after the experience of this century the belief that a harmony must prevail between peoples who share a love of children and small dogs would be considered evidence of a most grotesque historical amnesia.

From where does the idea of a world of likes come? In part from a belief in universal brotherhood, a belief that is parodied, however, when one pretends that the ideal already exists. In part from a trendy ecological pantheism with its misty notions of the oneness of those sharing this lonely planet. In part from the Enlightenment belief in a universal human nature, a slippery modern creation that for all its universality manages in every age to take on a decidedly middle-class look.

For the mirror-image fantasy derives above all from the coziness of middle-class life. The more settled and ordered one's life—and in particular one's communal life—the easier it becomes for one's imagination to fail. In Scarsdale, destitution and desperation, cruelty and zeal are the stuff of headlines, not life. Thus a single murder can create a sensation; in Beirut it is a statistic. When the comfortable encounter the unimaginable, the result is not only emotional but cognitive rejection. Brutality and fanaticism beyond one's ken must be made to remain there; thus, for example, when evidence mounts of biological warfare in faraway places, the most fanciful theories may be produced to banish the possibility.

To gloss over contradictory interests, incompatible ideologies and opposing cultures as sources of conflict is more than anti-political. It is dangerous. Those who have long held a mirror to the world and seen only themselves are apt to be shocked and panicked when the mirror is removed, as inevitably it must be. On the other hand, to accept the reality of otherness is not to be condemned to a war of all against all. We are not then compelled to see in others the focus of evil in the world. We are still enjoined to love our neighbors as ourselves. Only it no longer becomes an exercise in narcissism.

But empathy that is more than self-love does not come easily. Particularly not to a culture so fixed on its own image that it can look at Lincoln, gaunt and grave, and see a man ready to join the queue at the pâté counter at Zabar's.

Time, August 15, 1983

CHAPTER 5

PASSIONS AND PASTIMES

THE JOY OF LOSING

Among my various idiosyncrasies, the most baffling to my friends is my steadfast devotion to the Washington Nationals. When I wax lyrical about having discovered my own private paradise at Nationals Park, eyes begin to roll and it is patiently explained to me that my Nats have been not just bad, but prodigiously—epically—bad.

As if I don't know. They lost 102 games in 2008; 103 in 2009. That's no easy feat. Only three other teams in the last quarter-century have achieved back-to-back 100-loss seasons.

Now understand: This is not the charming, cuddly, amusing incompetence of, say, the '62 Mets, of whom their own manager, Casey Stengel, famously asked, "Can't anybody here play this game?"—and whose stone-gloved first baseman, Marv Throneberry, was nicknamed Marvelous Marv, the irony intended as a sign of affection.

Nor am I talking about heroic, stoic, character-building losing. The Chicago Cubs fan knows that he's destined for a life of Sisyphean suffering and perpetual angst. Mr. Cub, Ernie Banks, may have said, "Let's play two," but in 19 years he never got to play even one postseason game. These guys go 58 years without winning, then come within five outs of the National League pennant, only to have one of their own fans deflect a ball about to settle into a Cub outfielder's glove, killing the play and bringing on the unraveling.

The fan was driven into hiding and the fateful ball ritually exor-
cised, blown to smithereens on TV. Sorry, that's not my kind of losing. Been there. I'm a former Red Sox fan, now fully rehabilitated.
No, I don't go to games to steel my spine, perfect my character, journey into the dark night of the soul. I get that in my day job watching
the Obama administration in action.

I go for relief. For the fun, for the craft (beautifully elucidated in
George Will's just-reissued classic *Men at Work*) and for the sweet,
easy cheer at Nationals Park.

You get there and the twilight's gleaming, the popcorn's popping,
the kids're romping and everyone's happy. The joy of losing consists
in this: Where there are no expectations, there is no disappointment.
In Tuesday night's game, our starting pitcher couldn't get out of the
third inning. Gave up four straight hits, six earned runs, and as he
came off the mound, actually got a few scattered rounds of applause.

Applause! In New York, he'd have been booed mercilessly. In
Philly, he'd have found his car on blocks and missing a headlight.

No one's happy to lose, and the fans cheer lustily when the Nats
win. But as starters blow up and base runners get picked off, there is
none of the agitation, the angry, screaming, beer-spilling, red-faced
ranting you get at football or basketball games.

Baseball is a slow, boring, complex, cerebral game that doesn't
lend itself to histrionics. You "take in" a baseball game, something
odd to say about a football or basketball game, with the clock running and the bodies flying.

And for a losing baseball team, the calm is even more profound.
I've never been to a park where the people are more relaxed, tolerant
and appreciative of any small, even moral, victory. Sure, you root,
root, root for the home team, but if they don't win "it's a shame"—
not a calamity. Can you imagine arm-linked fans swaying to such
a sweetly corny song of early-20th-century innocence—as hard to
find today as a manual typewriter or a 20-game winner—at the two-
minute warning?

But now I fear for my bliss. Hope, of a sort, is on the way—in the form of Stephen Strasburg, the greatest pitching prospect in living memory. His fastball clocks 103 mph and his slider, says Tom Boswell, breaks so sharply it looks like it hit a bird in midair. In spring training, center fielder Nyjer Morgan nicknamed him Jesus. Because of the kid's presence, persona, charisma? Nope. Because "that's what everybody says the first time they see Strasburg throw," explained Morgan. "Jeeee-sus."

But now I'm worried. Even before Strasburg has arrived from the minor leagues, the Nats are actually doing well. They're playing .500 ball for the first time in five years. They are hovering somewhere between competent mediocrity and respectability. When Jesus arrives—my guess is late May—they might actually be good.

They might soon be, gasp, a contender. In the race deep into September. Good enough to give you hope. And break your heart.

Where does one then go for respite?

The Washington Post, April 23, 2010

BEAUTY, TRUTH AND HITCHCOCK

While the rest of the sporting world was distracted with sideshows—the World Series, the Douglas-Holyfield fight—the main event was being played out in utter silence at the Hudson Theater on Broadway, where the two best players in the world, Garry Kasparov and Anatoly Karpov, were fighting it out for the championship of chess. (After 12 games, the match is tied.)

Now, mention chess and most people's eyes glaze over. They think of two old geezers, one of whom has died but no one has noticed, in overstuffed armchairs at the Diogenes Club. Know how chess crowds do the wave? guffawed a CBS newsreader. With their eyebrows.

Ho, ho. What the benighted don't understand is that modern chess is played not just against an opponent but against a clock. It thus produces a heart-stopping equivalent of football's two-minute drill. At Move 32 of Game 8, for example, challenger Karpov, losing, was forced to make nine moves in less than three minutes. He executed them in a dazzling flurry that didn't just leave him winning; it left the crowd stunned and silent. Except, that is, for one patron who, unnerved by Karpov's preposterous escape, let out a loud, shocking laugh.

Moreover, the place to watch world-championship chess is not in the theater but five floors up, in the analysis room. There the action is frenzied. One TV monitor shows the players and the running time clocks. The other shows the latest board position. Scattered about are a score of the greatest players in the world, a couple of whom are standing at the front trying dozens of follow-on combinations on a large demonstration board. The result is a tumult of lightning analysis, inspired second-guessing, withering criticism, contemptuous asides, suggestions and refutations as the pros search for the best possible "lines" into the future.

During Game 8, I found myself in a room with the U.S. chess

champion (Lev Alburt), four grandmasters and one legend, former World Champion Mikhail Tal. It was like watching the World Series with five Hall of Famers parsing every pitch and Cy Young correcting them. On Karpov's 23rd move the parsing got slightly crazy: If Kasparov does A, then Karpov must do B. If Kasparov then tries C and Karpov answers with D, look out: E, F and G follow. But if Kasparov does Z, then . . .

Some of these lines were harmony, variations on the main theme of the game. Some were jazz riffs, freestyle and whimsical. Some were just fanciful trills, exotic and occasionally atonal. They all went up on the board fast and furious, as patzers—plodding amateurs—like me struggled to follow the logic.

Then Karpov did the unexpected: He advanced a pawn, unbalancing the position and not a few grandmasters. Instantly all the heretofore examined lines, entire symphonies of hypothetical variation, vanished into the ether. "Unheard melodies," murmured the yellow-tied patzer sitting near me. His tone was wry and regretful.

The move done, the grandmasters wiped the slate clean and began composing fresh music, speculating on what might follow next. This greatly disturbed the dapper young Yugoslav grandmaster Ljubomir Ljubojevic. Shaking his head in disapproval, Ljubo strode up to the board, took down all the moves now being assayed and brought the position back not to Move 23 but to Move 22. If Karpov had pushed the pawn in Move 22 instead of first delivering that ridiculous check, the now animated Ljubo insisted, it would have been a triumph. He then gave a long demonstration of the truth of his analysis.

Of course by then it was irrelevant. Karpov had played the check first. Enough of history, said the others, impatient to get on with analyzing the world as it now existed. Ljubo insisted on analyzing the world as it should exist. As the groans grew louder, Ljubo's retort was indignant: "Let's find some truth here."

The yellow-tied patzer had come for beauty, but Ljubo had come for truth. In chess, that means finding not just a good move or even a harmonious move but the perfect move. God's move.

Playing chess with divinity can be dangerous, however. The great Steinitz, who once claimed to have played against God and won (he neglected to leave a record of the game), went quite mad. The last great practitioner of truth, Bobby Fischer, after winning the world championship in 1972, disappeared into some apocalyptic sect in California and had the fillings in his teeth removed to stop the KGB transmissions.

Melodies you can get in any record store. But truth? Where else can you find truth? The next day I saw Ljubo again. It was 12 hours later and he was still shaking his head.

Down on the Hudson stage, however, the protagonists were engaged not so much in truth seeking as in attempted murder. Kasparov, who calls Karpov "a creature of darkness," had declared his intent not just to defeat Karpov but to destroy him. Accordingly, Kasparov played the opening games with the confident, reckless belligerence of a young Ali. Karpov, though, was fully Frazier's equal. The result was mayhem rarely seen at that level of play. It was like a title fight with 10 knockdowns by Round 3 or, for the more delicate, like a ballet performed not on a stage but on a trampoline.

Even the exalted were amazed by the innovations, the sacrifices, the speculative attacks, the kind of stuff a patzer like me tries out in Washington's Lafayette Square, not the kind world champions play with $1.7 million at stake. I asked the great and wizened Tal what he thought of the opening games of the match. "Hitchcock movies," he replied with a grin.

Beauty, truth and Hitchcock. Now that's entertainment.

Time, November 19, 1990

FERMAT SOLVED

Fermat's Last Theorem is solved, and a generation of tormented German graduate students can now go fishing.

Imagine you have some interest in biblical archaeology and see advertised a lecture on, say, "Calibrated Radiocarbon Chronology of Royal Judean Storage Jars," or some such. You go to the lecture at the end of which the speaker says, "And, oh, by the way, on Thursday I found the Holy Grail in the basement of a bed-and-breakfast in downtown Jericho. Here it is."

Well, something comparable happened in Cambridge, England, last week. A group of mathematicians attended a conference on—hold on—"P-adic Galois Representations, Iwasawa Theory and the Tamagawa Numbers of Motives." They went, as audiences do, expecting entertainment and instruction. What they got was astonishment.

They went to hear Prof. Andrew Wiles deliver three lectures on "Modular Forms, Elliptic Curves and Galois Representations." At the end of the third lecture, Wiles noted that his presentation had just proved Fermat's Last Theorem, the most famous and elusive mathematical puzzle of the last 300 years.

If Wiles' claim holds up—and its 200 pages of reasoning are so difficult that only a handful of mathematicians are in a position to judge—he will be hailed for his mathematical genius. He should be equally hailed for his modesty. Dropping his bombshell at the end of a lecture, without a hint of the now usual "cold fusion"–type advance publicity, is in itself an achievement in this age of hype.

In science, modesty and genius do not coexist well together. (In Washington, modesty and cleverness don't.) Einstein is perhaps the most famous exception to the rule. Yet even Watson and Crick, discoverers of the genetic code and not known for their modesty, proved themselves capable of one admirable, indeed immortal, act of understatement. Toward the end of their epic two-page paper revealing the structure of DNA, they noted drily: "It has not escaped our notice that the specific pairing [i.e., zipper-like structure of DNA] we have postulated immediately suggests a possible copying mechanism for the replication of the genetic material."

For hundreds of years humans had known that hereditary traits are transmitted from parent to child. But they hadn't a clue as to how. Watson and Crick had just provided the clue.

Wiles, however, is due homage not just for his genius and his modesty, but for his courage. Courage is not a quality one normally associates with mathematicians. Yet it should apply to people who work in their attics in secret for seven years without cease on a problem that has eluded the greatest mathematical minds since first proposed in 1637.

I once had a friend at Oxford who drifted into the study of Hegel, that famously impenetrable German philosopher, and was never seen again. There are intellectual black holes, vortexes of endless regression, that mortals ought to stay clear of. Many mathematicians have felt that way about Fermat's Last Theorem.

Its allure lies not just in its longevity but in its simplicity. It can be written on one line: "$X^n + Y^n = Z^n$ is impossible when $n > 2$," meaning that while a square can broken into two smaller squares—25 (the square of 5) can be broken into 16 (the square of 4) plus 9 (the square of 3)—one cannot divide a cube into two smaller cubes, and for that matter, one cannot divide any higher power into two smaller numbers of the same power.

It is a proposition so vexing and mathematically profound that the French Academy of Sciences offered a gold medal and 300 francs for its solution. That was in 1815, the year Napoleon was just settling into his new digs on St. Helena.

It is a proposition so famous that perhaps the one person on Earth most grateful for the Wiles solution, after the professor's wife and daughters ("Daddy's back!"), is Dr. Martin Kneser of the Göttingen Academy of Sciences. He administers another Fermat prize, the Wolfskehl prize (first offered in 1908, now 7,500 marks). Which means that poor Dr. Kneser must fight his way through the "three meters of correspondence" from every crank on the planet who is sure he has bested Fermat.

How does he handle the mountain of mail? "In recent decades," wrote Kneser's predecessor, "it was handled in the following way: the Secretary of the Akademie divides the arriving manuscripts into (1) complete nonsense, which is sent back immediately, and into (2) material which looks like mathematics." The second category is given to young research assistants forced by poverty and induced by payment to search for the inevitable mistakes.

One would-be Fermat slayer sent half a solution and demanded 1,000 Marks before he would produce the other half. Another also demanded money up front, promising 10% of the radio and TV take that would follow his fame and threatening, if denied, to send his solution to Russia.

Consider, then, what Wiles has wrought. A generation of tormented German graduate students can now go fishing. Kneser is free at last. Fermat is vindicated. And the rest of us are treated to a rare, irrefutable demonstration that the hairless ape with the opposable thumb is indeed, now and then, capable of something that deserves the name progress.

The Washington Post, July 2, 1993

BE AFRAID

As was to be expected, the end of civilization as we know it was announced on the back pages. On Feb. 10, 1996, in Philadelphia, while America was distracted by the rise of Pat Buchanan, the fall of Phil Gramm and other trifles, something large happened. German philosophers call such large events world-historical. This was larger. It was species-defining. The *New York Times* carried it on page A32.

On Feb. 10, Garry Kasparov, the best chess player in the world and quite possibly the best chess player who ever lived, sat down across a chessboard from a machine, an IBM computer called Deep Blue, and lost.

True, it was only one game. What kind of achievement is that? Well—as Henny Youngman used to say when asked, "How's your wife?"—compared to what? Compared to human challengers for the world championship? Just five months ago, the same Kasparov played a championship match against the next best player of the human species. The No. 2 human played Kasparov 18 games and won 1. Deep Blue played Kasparov and won its very first game. And it was no fluke. Over the first four games, the machine played Kasparov dead even—one win, one loss, two draws—before the champ rallied and came away with the final two games.

Kasparov won the match. That was expected. Game 1, however, was not supposed to happen. True, Kasparov had lost to machines in speed games and other lesser tests. And lesser grandmasters have lost regulation games to machines. But never before in a real game played under championship conditions had a machine beaten the best living human.

Indeed Kasparov, who a few weeks ago single-handedly took on the entire national chess team of Brazil, was so confident of winning that he rejected the offer that the $500,000 purse be split 60–40 between winner and loser. Kasparov insisted on winner-take-all. They settled on 80–20. (What, by the way, does Deep Blue do with its 100-grand purse? New chips?)

Asked when he thought a computer would beat the best human, Kasparov had said 2010 or maybe never. A mutual friend tells me Garry would have gladly offered 1–10, perhaps even 1–100 odds on himself. That was all before Game 1. After Game 1, Kasparov was not offering any odds at all. "He was devastated," said his computer coach, Frederick Friedel. "It was a shattering experience. We didn't know what the game meant. There was the theoretical possibility that the computer would be invincible, and that he would lose all six games."

True, we have already created machines that can run faster, lift better, see farther than we can. But cars, cranes and telescopes shame only our limbs and our senses, not our essence. Thinking is our specialty, or so we think. How could a device capable of nothing more than calculation (of the possible moves) and scoring (of the relative strengths of the resulting positions) possibly beat a human with a lifetime of experience, instant pattern recognition, unfathomable intuition and a killer instinct?

How? With sheer brute force: calculation and evaluation at cosmic speeds. At the height of the game, Deep Blue was seeing about 200 million positions every second. You and I can see one; Kasparov, two. Maybe three. But 200 million? It was style vs. power, and power won. It was like watching Muhammad Ali, floating and stinging, try to box a steamroller in a very small ring. The results aren't pretty.

What is Deep Blue's secret? Grandmaster Yasser Seirawan put it most succinctly: "The machine has no fear." He did not just mean the obvious, that silicon cannot quake. He meant something deeper: Because of its fantastic capacity to see all possible combinations some distance into the future, the machine, once it determines that its own position is safe, can take the kind of attacking chances no human would. The omniscient have no fear.

In Game 1, Blue took what grandmaster Robert Byrne called

"crazy chances." On-site expert commentators labeled one move "insane." It wasn't. It was exactly right.

Here's what happened. Late in the game, Blue's king was under savage attack by Kasparov. Any human player under such assault by a world champion would be staring at his own king trying to figure out how to get away. Instead, Blue ignored the threat and quite nonchalantly went hunting for lowly pawns at the other end of the board. In fact, at the point of maximum peril, Blue expended two moves—many have died giving Kasparov even one—to snap one pawn. It was as if at Gettysburg, General Meade had sent his soldiers out for a bit of apple picking moments before Pickett's charge because he had calculated that they could get back to their positions with a half-second to spare.

In humans, that is called *sangfroid*. And if you don't have any *sang*, you can be very *froid*. But then again if Meade had known absolutely—by calculating the precise trajectories of all the bullets and all the bayonets and all the cannons in Pickett's division—the time of arrival of the enemy, he could indeed, without fear, have ordered his men to pick apples.

Which is exactly what Deep Blue did. It had calculated every possible combination of Kasparov's available moves and determined with absolute certainty that it could return from its pawn-picking expedition and destroy Kasparov exactly one move before Kasparov could destroy it. Which it did.

It takes more than nerves of steel to do that. It takes a silicon brain. No human can achieve absolute certainty because no human can be sure to have seen everything. Deep Blue can.

Now, it cannot see everything forever—just everything within its horizon, which for Deep Blue means everything that can happen within the next 10 or 15 moves or so. The very best human player could still beat it (as Kasparov did subsequently) because he can intuit—God knows how—what the general shape of things will be 20 moves from now.

But it is only a matter of time before, having acquired yet more sheer computing power, Blue will see farther than Garry can feel. And then it's curtains. Then he gets shut out, 6–0. Then we don't even bother to play the brutes again. The world championship will consist of one box playing another. Men stopped foot racing against automobiles long ago.

Blue's omniscience will make it omnipotent. It can play—fight—with the abandon of an immortal. Kasparov himself said that with Deep Blue, quantity had become quality. When you can calculate so fast and so far, you rise to another level. At some point that happened in biology. There are neurons firing in lemmings and squid, but put them together in gigantic enough numbers and fantastic enough array, as in humans—and, behold, a thought, popping up like a cartoon bubble from the brain.

We call that consciousness. Deep Blue is not there yet, though one day we will be tempted to ask him. In the meantime he's done alchemy, turning quantity into quality. That in itself is scary.

At least to me. However, my son, age 10, who lives as comfortably with his computer as he does with his dog, was rooting for Deep Blue all along. "What are you worried about, Dad?" he says. "After all, we made the machine, didn't we? So we're just beating ourselves."

The next generation has gone over to Them. No need to wait for the rematch. It's over.

Time, February 26, 1996

The Best Show in Town

In that fleeting interval between natural disaster (earthquake, hurricane) and the president's 57th (or so) major national address next Thursday, I can finally devote a summer column to the finest efflorescence of that season this city has to offer: the Washington Nationals.

They are a baseball team. Not yet very good, mind you, but it matters not. When you live in a town with a great team, you go to see them win. When you live in a town with a team that is passing rapidly through mediocrity on its way to contention—the Nats have an amazing crop of upcoming young players—you go for the moments.

I go to see Ryan Zimmerman charge a slowly hit grounder down the third-base line. This happens roughly once a game. Zim comes flying in, picks up the ball barehanded and throws it across his body to first base, *perpendicular* to the direction he's running.

Except that this cannot be done. You could never get enough (velocity) on the throw to get the out at first. So Zimmerman dives forward, leaving his feet and hovering there for an instant, his body parallel to the ground in order to get more arm extension and thus more on the throw, which by now is nearly underhanded, his fingers almost scraping the ground. Batter out.

Try this yourself. Aim for a barn door. You will miss. And also dislocate your shoulder.

Another attraction is rookie second baseman Danny Espinosa. He has what in baseball parlance is known as range. A hard shot is hit to the hole between first and second, and Espy ranges to his left to snag it. Three weeks ago, one shot was hit so hard and so deep that he had to dive onto the outfield grass to reach it, sliding on his side in the general direction of the right-field foul pole.

Nice grab, but unless you can get the ball to first, it's just for show. Espy starts to get up. But there is no time for standing. So, from his knees, while still sliding on the grass out toward the stands, he forces himself into a counterclockwise 180-degree spin to throw back toward first base—except that he actually begins his throw mid-turn, *while facing the outfield*, thereby gaining velocity from the centrifugal force (and probably the rotation of the Earth, although this remains unverified). It's like throwing on your knees from a spinning merry-go-round that is itself moving laterally in a landslide. Try *that*.

Batter out.

The pièce de résistance, however, is what center fielder Rick Ankiel pulled off last Sunday. It's the bottom of the ninth, one out. The Reds have just tied the game with a solo homer. They need one more run to win. Batter crushes the ball to right-center field. If it clears the wall, game over.

But it doesn't. It bounces off the wall, eluding our right fielder. Ankiel, who had dashed over from center, charges after the ball, picks it up barehanded and, in full running stride, fires it to third, to which the batter is headed and from which he is very likely to later score and win the game (there being only one out).

Now, when mortals throw a ball, they give it arc to gain distance. That's how artillery works. Ankiel is better than artillery. He releases the ball at the top of his throwing motion, the ball rocketing out as if tracing a clothesline. It bounces five feet from third base, perfectly on line, arriving a millisecond before the batter and maybe 20 inches above the bag.

Quick tag. Batter out. Game saved. (Blown five innings later. But remember, it's the Nats.) Said Nats broadcaster and former major leaguer F. P. Santangelo: "That might be the best throw I've ever seen." Me too, except that I didn't see it personally, as it were. Only saw it on TV. They were playing in Cincinnati. I may be a fan, but I'm not a lunatic. I don't travel with the team.

Yet.

Yes, I know that the world is going to pieces and that the prowess of three gifted players doesn't amount to a hill of beans in this crazy world. But I remind you that FDR wanted baseball to continue during World War II. I make no claim that elegance and grace on any field will ward off the apocalypse. But if it comes in summer, I'll be waiting for it at Nats Park, Section 128, hard by the Dippin' Dots.

The Washington Post, September 1, 2011

CHAPTER 6

HEAVEN AND EARTH

YOUR ONLY HALLEY'S

A Lutheran minister once called comets the "thick smoke of human sins," a hypothesis that finds little support nowadays among scientists. They prefer to see comets as big dirty snowballs trailing tails of gas and enthralled by gravitation. And coming not from God but from the equally ineffable Oort cloud, a gigantic shell far beyond the solar system where aspiring comets spend eons of quiet desperation until disturbed by some celestial accident and called to race toward the sun and make men weep.

Except that men don't weep anymore. Halley's Comet may have brought victory to the Normans in 1066, heralded the descent of Turkish armies on Belgrade in 1456 and, in 1910, killed Mark Twain and then Edward VII. This time around all is forgiven. After all, it knows not what it does. And we know what it is: a forlorn mass of rock and ice, a few miles across, caught in endless revolution around our sun. Now an object, not an omen, it is the source not of panic but of curiosity. Five earthly spacecraft have been sent to greet it and snap its picture.

Science has thoroughly desacrilized the universe. It is in the language. When in the last election Walter Mondale warned against militarizing "the heavens," the usage seemed quaint. After Neil Armstrong and George Lucas, what's up there now is simply "space." The heavens were a place for angels, gods and portentous messengers. Space is home to extraterrestrials, the Force and now snowballs cruising through emptiness.

Don't get me wrong. I am not pining for the days of the witch doctor. Things are much better now. There are costs to demystifying the universe and turning it over to science—the ubiquity of Carl Sagan is among the heavier ones—but the gain is great.

Halley's, like the rest of space, is friendly now, tamed. This will probably be the first time in history that Halley's will bring wonder unalloyed with fear. Halley's has turned into a celebration, a scientific romance.

The romance is in the return. Halley's comes back, always exactly on time. After its current pass, it will travel 3 billion miles away from Earth and then turn to revisit your children. It is the grandest reminder that an individual can behold of the constancy of nature. This, because of its cycle: It returns about every 75 years, once in a lifetime.

The sun rises regularly, too, but so often that we can't help being dulled to the wonder of its rhythm. And what rhythms, beyond that of the familiar year, really touch us? Sunspots come every 11 years, and what layman cares? Economists are forever coming up with "long waves" (50 years) and other putative business cycles. Even Freud's theory of neurosis was built on the notion of a distant return, the return of the child to the mind of the man. Such cycles can most charitably be called speculative.

Others are merely too long. The ice age will be back too. Fit that in your calendar. Halley's alone is made to human scale. Its span is precisely a lifetime. Birth and death are perhaps the only events that match Halley's periodicity. And neither is nearly as reliable. Birth and death come with regular irregularity (to borrow a term from cardiology). Halley's you can count on.

We know, for example, absolutely nothing about what the world will be like in 2061. Except one thing. In that unimaginable year, a year whose very number has an otherworldly look, Halley's will light up the sky.

One price of demystifying the universe is that science, unlike religion, asks only how, not why. As to the purpose of things, science is silent. But if science cannot talk about meaning, it can talk about harmony. And Halley's is at once a symbol and a proof of a deep harmony of the spheres.

The great author of that harmony was Newton. And one of the earliest empirical demonstrations of his gravitational theories was provided by his friend, Edmond Halley. Twenty-three years after the great comet of 1682, Halley deciphered its logic. He predicted its return in 1758. Halley died 17 years before he could be proved right. The return of the comet was a sensation. It made Halley immortal. True to its nature, science wed the comet forever to the man who did not discover it but was the first to understand it.

This time around, there will be no sensation. Halley's will give one of the worst shows ever. This may be its dimmest apparition in more than 2,000 years. What we will celebrate, then, is not the spectacle but the idea.

Halley's is a monument to science, a spokesman for its new celestial harmonies—and an intimation of mortality. It is at once recurring and, for us individually, singular. This will be my only Halley's and, if you're old enough to read this without moving your lips, your last one too, I'm afraid.

Halley's speaks to me especially acutely. As it turns around the sun, the midpoint on its journey, I will be marking the midpoint in mine, or so say the Metropolitan Life tables. Our perihelions match. Mark Twain was rather pleased with the fact that he came in with Halley's and would go out with it. Ashes to ashes, Oort to Oort. Hail Halley's.

The Washington Post, December 13, 1985

HUMBLED BY THE HAYDEN

Bantam Books will soon reissue its updated—illustrated—edition of Stephen Hawking's wildly popular *A Brief History of Time*. Beware. As part-time scientific food-taster for my readers, I can report that, having devoured Hawking's original book not once but twice, it leaves no trace. That is because it is entirely incomprehensible. Illustrating the book seems to me akin to tarting up hieroglyphics with Etruscan annotation.

Want an invigorating scientific experience? I have a better idea: the new Hayden Planetarium in New York.

The building itself is worth the trip. It is an immense 10-story cube of glass inside of which seems to float a huge sphere (which houses the sky-show viewing room) surrounded by a curving walkway (tracing the origins of the universe) seemingly suspended in the void.

The intelligence of this design is as striking as its beauty. It is a brilliant metaphor for the attempt of the human imagination to wrap itself around the natural world.

Why? Because (apart from crystals) there are few straight lines in nature. Nature is more sinews: curves, waves, ellipses and, when we are blessed, perfect spheres.

Look up at the sky. It is a festival of spheres. It is we, the bipeds with the fat heads and opposable thumbs, who impose straight lines on nature. We connect the dots between the stars to make dippers, large and small. We take the human form—as in Vitruvian Man, the famous geometrical drawing by Leonardo and Cesariano and others—and fit it with axes, right angles and diagonals.

That is what we do to grasp the incomprehensible. And on a magnificent scale that is what the new Hayden building does. It wraps an enormous cube around interior curves and spheres, just as science creates the lines that give order and solidity to the bending ephemera of nature.

That is your impression from the outside. Inside is even more thrilling. The vastness of the empty space of the cube allows for demonstrations of scale by analogy. You stand on the walkway, look down at a display housing a small ball and a plaque informing you that if the ball represents Earth, the gigantic sphere hovering above you—the sky show auditorium—represents the sun.

Lessons in scale are everywhere. One corridor, for example, features wall-size composite photos taken by astronauts on the moon. You can see a hundred pictures of the moon, but until you've seen one the size of a storefront window showing an astronaut in his little dune buggy in one tiny corner of the immensity of a desolate moonscape, you have not quite experienced the vastness of the void and the insignificance of man.

And yet, oddly, that very insignificance adds to the glory of the creature that dares challenge such cosmic disparities. You feel it most acutely walking down the great floating ramp, where every inch represents 3.6 million years of the evolution of the universe; each stride, 75 million. You trace the story from the Big Bang through dozens of Hubble telescope pictures displayed along the way. Then you come to Now.

You've been walking for about 20 minutes; you've traversed more than 100 yards. And you come upon a glass case containing nothing but a human hair—and a little notification that, on the scale of the events you have just traversed, the width of that hair represents all of human history.

The Hayden Planetarium thus acts as a counterpart to the great Air and Space Museum in Washington. At Air and Space everything is on a human scale: The Lindbergh plane, the jets, even the rockets are approachable. You can wrap, if not your arms, then your mind around them.

It is the universe as seen and conquered by man; the Hayden is the unconquerable universe as seen by God. Air and Space is a shrine to human defiance; the Hayden is a palace of wonder. You come out of Air and Space exhilarated; you come out of the Hayden humbled.

Humbled in more ways than one. Some visitors are overwhelmed by the sophistication of the exhibits. The curators have chosen to talk down to no one. Be prepared to have Hubble's Constant (a mathematical formula that represents the rate at which the universe is expanding) thrown out at you without a puppet show illustration. Indeed, just a month after Hayden reopened, the *New York Times* ran a piece summarizing visitors' complaints that the museum was often too difficult to grasp.

In a culture where everything from textbooks to television to SATs has been renormed and dumbed down, one should be grateful for an intellectual challenge. A building devoted to explaining the cosmos that does not leave you scratching your head and humbled—has failed. The Hayden succeeds splendidly.

The Washington Post, September 1, 2000

Lit Up for Liftoff?

Someone's gotta do it. No one's gonna do it. So I'll do it. Your honor, I rise in defense of drunken astronauts.

You've all heard the reports, delivered in scandalized tones on the evening news or as guaranteed punch lines for the late-night comics, that at least two astronauts had alcohol in their systems before flights. A stern and sober NASA has assured an anxious nation that this matter, uncovered by a NASA-commissioned study, will be thoroughly looked into and appropriately dealt with.

To which I say: Come off it. I know NASA has to get grim and do the responsible thing, but as counsel for the defense—the *only* counsel for the defense, as far as I can tell—I place before the jury the following considerations:

Have you ever been to the shuttle launchpad? Have you ever seen that beautiful and preposterous thing the astronauts ride? Imagine it's you sitting on top of a 12-story winged tube bolted to a gigantic canister filled with 2 million liters of liquid oxygen and liquid hydrogen. Then picture your own buddies—the "closeout crew"—who met you at the pad, fastened your emergency chute, strapped you into your launch seat, sealed the hatch and waved smiling to you through the window. Having left you lashed to what is the largest bomb on planet Earth, they then proceed 200 feet down the elevator and drive not one, not two, but three miles away to watch as the button is pressed that lights the candle that ignites the fuel that blows you into space.

Three miles! That's how far they calculate they must go to be beyond the radius of incineration should anything go awry on the launchpad on which, I remind you, these insanely brave people are sitting. Would you not want to be a bit soused? Would you be all aflutter if you discovered that a couple of astronauts—out of dozens—were mildly so? I dare say that if the standards of today's fussy flight surgeons had been applied to pilots showing up for morning duty in the Battle of Britain, the signs in Piccadilly would today be in German.

Cut these cowboys some slack. These are not wobbly Northwest Airlines pilots trying to get off the runway and steer through clouds and densely occupied airspace. An ascending space shuttle, I assure you, encounters very little traffic. And for much of liftoff, the astronaut is little more than spam in a can—not pilot but guinea pig. With opposable thumbs, to be sure, yet with only one specific task: to come out alive.

And by the time the astronauts get to the part of the journey that requires delicate and skillful maneuvering—docking with the international space station, outdoor plumbing repairs in zero-G—they will long ago have peed the demon rum into their recycling units.

Okay?

The most dismaying part of this brouhaha is not the tipsy Captain Kirk or two but the fact that space makes the news today only as mini-scandal or farce. It all started out as a great romance in the 1960s, yet by the 1970s—indeed, the morning after the 1969 moon landing—romance had turned to boredom.

When the *Apollo 13* astronauts gave their live broadcast from space, not a single network carried it. No interest. Until, that is, the explosion that nearly killed them, at which point the world tuned in with rapt and morbid attention.

Well, we are now in stage three of our space odyssey: mockery and amusement. The last big space story was the crazed lady astronaut on her diapered drive to a fatal-attraction rendezvous.

It's hard to entirely blame this state of affairs on a fickle public. Blame also belongs to the idiot politicians who decided 30 years ago to abandon the moon and send us on a pointless and endless journey into low-Earth orbit. President Bush has sensibly called an end to this nonsense and committed us to going back to the moon and, ultimately, to Mars. If his successors don't screw it up, within 10 years NASA will have us back to where we belong—on other worlds.

At which point, we'll remember why we did this in the first place.

And when we once again thrill at seeing humans on the moon—this time, making it their home—we won't much care whether the extra bounce in their gait is the effect of the one-sixth gravity or a touch of moonshine.

The Washington Post, August 3, 2007

Farewell, the New Frontier

As the space shuttle *Discovery* flew three times around Washington, a final salute before landing at Dulles airport for retirement in a museum, thousands on the ground gazed upward with marvel and pride. Yet what they were witnessing, for all its elegance, was a funeral march.

The shuttle was being carried—its pallbearer, a 747—because it cannot fly, nor will it ever again. It was being sent for interment. Above ground, to be sure. But just as surely embalmed as Lenin in Red Square.

Is there a better symbol of willed American decline? The pity is not *Discovery*'s retirement—beautiful as it was, the shuttle proved too expensive and risky to operate—but that it died without a successor. The planned follow-on—the Constellation rocket-capsule program to take humans back into orbit and from there to the moon—was suddenly canceled in 2010. And with that, control of manned spaceflight was gratuitously ceded to Russia and China.

Russia went for the cash, doubling its price for carrying an astronaut into orbit to $55.8 million. (Return included. Thank you, Boris.)

China goes for the glory. Having already mastered launch and rendezvous, the Chinese plan to land on the moon by 2025. They understand well the value of symbols. And nothing could better symbolize China overtaking America than its taking our place on the moon, walking over footprints first laid down, then casually abandoned, by us.

Who cares, you say? What is national greatness, scientific prestige or inspiring the young—legacies of NASA—when we are in economic distress? Okay. But if we're talking jobs and growth, science and technology, R&D and innovation—what President Obama insists are the keys to "an economy built to last"—why on earth cancel an incomparably sophisticated, uniquely American technological enterprise?

We lament the decline of American manufacturing, yet we stop production of the most complex machine ever made by man—and cancel the successor meant to return us to orbit. The result? Abolition of thousands of the most highly advanced aerospace jobs anywhere—its workforce abruptly unemployed and drifting away from space flight, never to be reconstituted.

Well, you say, we can't afford all that in a time of massive deficits.

There are always excuses for putting off strenuous national endeavors: deficits, joblessness, poverty, whatever. But they shall always be with us. We've had exactly five balanced budgets since Alan Shepard rode *Freedom 7* in 1961. If we had put off space exploration until these earthbound social and economic conundrums were solved, our rocketry would be about where North Korea's is today.

Moreover, today's deficits are not inevitable, nor even structural. They are partly the result of the 2008 financial panic and recession. Those are over now. The rest is the result of a massive three-year expansion of federal spending.

But there is no reason the federal government has to keep spending 24% of GDP. The historical post-war average is just over 20%—and those budgets sustained a robust manned space program.

NASA will tell you that it's got a new program to go way beyond low-Earth orbit and, as per Obama's instructions, land on an asteroid by the mid-2020s. Considering that Constellation did not last even five years between birth and cancellation, don't hold your breath for the asteroid landing.

Nor for the private sector to get us back into orbit, as Obama assumes it will. True, hauling MREs up and trash back down could be done by private vehicles. But manned flight is infinitely more complex and risky, requiring massive redundancy and inevitably larger expenditures. Can private entities really handle that? And within the next lost decade or two?

Neil Armstrong, James Lovell and Gene Cernan are deeply skeptical. "Commercial transport to orbit," they wrote in a 2010 open letter, "is likely to take substantially longer and be more expensive than we would hope." They called Obama's cancellation of Constellation a "devastating" decision that "destines our nation to become one of second or even third rate stature."

"Without the skill and experience that actual spacecraft operation provides," they warned, "the USA is far too likely to be on a long downhill slide to mediocrity." This, from "the leading space faring nation for nearly half a century."

Which is why museum visits to the embalmed *Discovery* will be sad indeed. America rarely retreats from a new frontier. Yet today we can't even do what John Glenn did in 1962, let alone fly a circa-1980 shuttle.

At least *Discovery* won't suffer the fate of the *Temeraire*, the British warship tenderly rendered in Turner's famous *The Fighting Temeraire Tugged to Her Last Berth to Be Broken Up, 1838*. Too beautiful for the scrapheap, *Discovery* will lie intact, a magnificent and melancholy rebuke to constricted horizons.

The Washington Post, April 19, 2012

Are We Alone in the Universe?

Huge excitement last week. Two Earth-size planets found orbiting a sun-like star less than a thousand light-years away. This comes two weeks after the stunning announcement of another planet orbiting another star at precisely the right distance—within the "habitable zone" that is not too hot and not too cold—to allow for liquid water and therefore possible life.

Unfortunately, the planets of the right size are too close to their sun, and thus too scorching hot, to permit Earth-like life. And the Goldilocks planet in the habitable zone is too large. At 2.4 times the size of Earth, it is probably gaseous, like Jupiter. No earthlings there. But it's only a matter of time—perhaps a year or two, estimates one astronomer—before we find the right one of the right size in the right place.

And at just the right time. As the romance of manned space exploration has waned, the drive today is to find our living, thinking counterparts in the universe. For all the excitement, however, the search betrays a profound melancholy—a lonely species in a merciless universe anxiously awaits an answering voice amid utter silence.

That silence is maddening. Not just because it compounds our feeling of cosmic isolation but because it makes no sense. As we inevitably find more and more exo-planets where intelligent life *can* exist, why have we found no evidence—no signals, no radio waves—that intelligent life *does* exist?

It's called the Fermi Paradox, after the great physicist who once asked, "Where *is* everybody?" Or as was once elaborated: "All our logic, all our anti-isocentrism, assures us that we are not unique—that they *must* be there. And yet we do not see them."

How many of them should there be? The Drake Equation (1961) tries to quantify the number of advanced civilizations in just our own galaxy. To simplify slightly, it's the number of stars in the galaxy . . .

- multiplied by the fraction that form planets . . .
- multiplied by the average number of planets in the habitable zone . . .
- multiplied by the fraction of these that give birth to life . . .
- multiplied by the fraction of these that develop intelligence . . .
- multiplied by the fraction of these that produce interstellar communications . . .
- multiplied by the fraction of the planet's lifetime during which such civilizations survive.

Modern satellite data, applied to the Drake Equation, suggest that the number should be very high. So why the silence? Carl Sagan (among others) thought that the answer is to be found, tragically, in the final variable: the high probability that advanced civilizations destroy themselves.

In other words, this silent universe is conveying not a flattering lesson about our uniqueness but a tragic story about our destiny. It is telling us that intelligence may be the most cursed faculty in the entire universe—an endowment not just ultimately fatal but, on the scale of cosmic time, nearly instantly so.

This is not mere theory. Look around. On the very day that astronomers rejoiced at the discovery of the two Earth-size planets, the National Science Advisory Board for Biosecurity urged two leading scientific journals not to publish details of lab experiments that had created a lethal and highly transmittable form of bird flu virus, lest that fateful knowledge fall into the wrong hands.

Wrong hands, human hands. This is not just the age of holy terror but also the threshold of an age of hyperproliferation. Nuclear weapons in the hands of half-mad tyrants (North Korea) and radical apocalypticists (Iran) are only the beginning. Lethal biologic agents may soon find their way into the hands of those for whom genocidal pandemics loosed upon infidels are the royal road to redemption.

And forget the psychopaths: Why, a mere 17 years after *Homo sapiens*—born 200,000 years ago—discovered atomic power, those most stable and sober states, America and the Soviet Union, came within inches of mutual annihilation.

Rather than despair, however, let's put the most hopeful face on the cosmic silence and on humanity's own short, already baleful history with its new Promethean powers: Intelligence is a capacity so godlike, so protean that it must be contained and disciplined. This is the work of politics—understood as the ordering of society and the regulation of power to permit human flourishing while simultaneously restraining the most Hobbesian human instincts.

There could be no greater irony: For all the sublimity of art, physics, music, mathematics and other manifestations of human genius, everything depends on the mundane, frustrating, often debased vocation known as politics (and its most exacting subspecialty—statecraft). Because if we don't get politics right, everything else risks extinction.

We grow justly weary of our politics. But we must remember this: Politics—in all its grubby, grasping, corrupt, contemptible manifestations—is sovereign in human affairs. Everything ultimately rests upon it.

Fairly or not, politics is the driver of history. It will determine whether we will live long enough to be heard one day. Out there. By them, the few—the only—who got it right.

The Washington Post, December 29, 2011

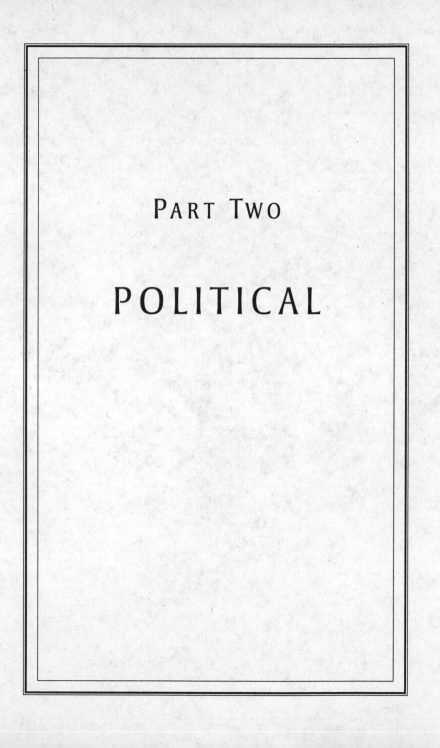

PART TWO

POLITICAL

CHAPTER 7

CITIZEN AND STATE

REFLECTIONS ON THE
REVOLUTION IN FRANCE

Two hundred years ago today a mob stormed the Bastille and freed its seven prisoners: four forgers, two lunatics and an aristocrat imprisoned at his family's request for "libertinism." It might have been eight had not the Marquis de Sade—whose cell contained a desk, a wardrobe, a dressing table, tapestries, mattresses, velvet cushions, a collection of hats, three kinds of fragrances, night lamps and 133 books—left a week earlier.

When the battle was lost, the governor of the Bastille, a minor functionary named Bernard-René de Launay, could have detonated a mountain of gunpowder, destroying himself, the mob and much of the surrounding faubourg Saint-Antoine. He chose instead to surrender. His reward was to be paraded through the street and cut down with knives and pistol shots. A pastry cook named Desnot, declining a sword, sawed off his head with a pocket knife.

For the French Revolution, it was downhill from there on. Now, after 200 years, the French themselves seem finally to be coming to terms with that reality. There is a tentativeness to this week's bicentennial celebration that suggests that French enthusiasm for the revolution has tempered. This circumspection stems from two decades of revisionist scholarship that stresses the reformist impulses of the ancien régime and the murderous impulses of the revolutionary regime that followed. Simon Schama's *Citizens* is but the culmination of this trend.

But the receptivity to such revisionism stems from something deeper: the death of doctrinaire socialism, which in France had long claimed direct descent from the revolution. Disillusion at the savage failure of the revolutions in our time—Russian, Chinese, Cuban, Vietnamese—has allowed reconsideration of the event that was father to them all.

One might say that romance with revolution died with Solzhenitsyn. The line from the Bastille to the gulag is not straight, but the connection is unmistakable. Modern totalitarianism has its roots in 1789. "The spirit of the French Revolution has always been present in the social life of our country," said Gorbachev during his visit to France last week. Few attempts at ingratiation have been more true or more damning.

Indeed, the French Revolution was such a model for future revolutions that it redefined the word. That is why 1776 has long been treated as a kind of pseudo-revolution, as Irving Kristol pointed out in a prescient essay written during America's confused and embarrassed bicentennial celebration of 1976. The American Revolution was utterly lacking in the messianic, bloody-minded idealism of the French. It rearranged the constitutional furniture. Its revolutionary leaders died in their own beds. What kind of revolution was that?

Thirteen years later, Kristol's answer has become conventional wisdom: a successful revolution, perhaps the only successful revolution of our time.

The French Revolution failed, argues Schama, because it tried to create the impossible: a regime both of liberty and of "patriotic" state power. The history of the revolution is proof that these goals are incompatible.

The American Revolution succeeded because it chose one, liberty. The Russian Revolution became deranged when it chose the other, state power. The French Revolution, to its credit and sorrow, wanted both. Its great virtue was to have loosed the idea of liberty upon Europe. Its great vice was to have created the model, the monster, of the mobilized militarized state—revolutionary France invented universal conscription, that scourge of the 20th century only now beginning to wither away.

The French cannot be blamed for everything, alas, but their revolution, with its glamour and influence, did not only popularize, it deified revolution. There are large parts of the world where even today the worst brutality and arbitrariness are justified by the mere invocation of the word *revolution*—without reference to any other human value.

For the Chinese authorities to shoot a dissident in the back of the head, they have only to show that he is a "counterrevolutionary." In Cuba, Gen. Arnaldo Ochoa Sanchez, erstwhile hero of the revolution, is condemned to death in a show trial and upon receiving his sentence confesses his sins and declares that at his execution his "last thought would be of Fidel and of the great revolution."

The fate, then, of all messianic revolution—revolution, that is, on the French model—is that in the end it can justify itself and its crimes only by reference to itself. In Saint-Just's famous formulation: "The Republic consists in the extermination of everything that opposes it." This brutal circularity of logic is properly called not revolution but nihilism.

The Washington Post, July 14, 1989

DID THE STATE MAKE YOU GREAT?

If you've got a business—you didn't build that. Somebody else made that happen.
—Barack Obama, Roanoke, Va., July 13, 2012

And who might that somebody else be? Government, says Obama. It built the roads you drive on. It provided the teacher who inspired you. It "created the Internet." It represents the embodiment of "we're in this together" social solidarity that, in Obama's view, is the essential origin of individual and national achievement.

To say that all individuals are embedded in and the product of society is banal. Obama rises above banality by means of fallacy: equating society with government, the collectivity with the state. Of course we are shaped by our milieu. But the most formative, most important influence on the individual is not government. It is civil society, those elements of the collectivity that lie outside government: family, neighborhood, church, Rotary club, PTA, the voluntary associations that Tocqueville understood to be the genius of America and source of its energy and freedom.

Moreover, the greatest threat to a robust, autonomous civil society is the ever-growing Leviathan state and those like Obama who see it as the ultimate expression of the collective.

Obama compounds the fallacy by declaring the state to be the font of entrepreneurial success. How so? It created the infrastructure—roads, bridges, schools, Internet—off which we all thrive.

Absurd. We don't credit the Swiss postal service with the Special Theory of Relativity because it transmitted Einstein's manuscript to the *Annalen der Physik*. Everyone drives the roads, goes to school, uses the mails. So did Steve Jobs. Yet only he created the Mac and the iPad.

Obama's infrastructure argument is easily refuted by what is essentially a controlled social experiment. Roads and schools are the constant. What's variable is the energy, enterprise, risk-taking, hard work and genius of the individual. It is therefore precisely those individual characteristics, not the communal utilities, that account for the different outcomes.

The ultimate Obama fallacy, however, is the conceit that belief in the value of infrastructure—and willingness to invest in its creation and maintenance—is what divides liberals from conservatives.

More nonsense. Infrastructure is not a liberal idea, nor is it particularly new. The Via Appia was built 2,300 years ago. The Romans built aqueducts, too. And sewers. Since forever, infrastructure has been consensually understood to be a core function of government.

The argument between left and right is about what you do *beyond* infrastructure. It's about transfer payments and redistributionist taxation, about geometrically expanding entitlements, about tax breaks and subsidies to induce actions pleasing to central planners. It's about free contraceptives for privileged students and welfare without work—the latest Obama entitlement-by-decree that would fatally undermine the great bipartisan welfare reform of 1996. It's about endless government handouts that, ironically, are crowding out necessary spending on, yes, infrastructure.

What divides liberals and conservatives is not roads and bridges but Julia's world, an Obama campaign creation that may be the most self-revealing parody of liberalism ever conceived. It's a series of cartoon illustrations in which a fictional Julia is swaddled and subsidized throughout her life by an all-giving government of bottomless pockets and "Queen for a Day" magnanimity. At every stage, the state is there to provide—preschool classes and cut-rate college loans, birth control and maternity care, business loans and retirement. The only time she's on her own is at her grave site.

Julia's world is totally atomized. It contains no friends, no community and, of course, no spouse. Who needs one? She's married to the provider state.

Or to put it slightly differently, the "Life of Julia" represents the paradigmatic Obama political philosophy: citizen as orphan child. For the conservative, providing for every need is the duty that government owes to actual orphan children. Not to supposedly autonomous adults.

Beyond infrastructure, the conservative sees the proper role of government as providing not European-style universal entitlements but a firm safety net, meaning Julia-like treatment for those who really cannot make it on their own—those too young or too old, too mentally or physically impaired, to provide for themselves.

Limited government so conceived has two indispensable advantages. It avoids inexorable European-style national insolvency. And it avoids breeding debilitating individual dependency. It encourages and celebrates character, independence, energy, hard work as the foundations of a free society and a thriving economy—precisely the virtues Obama discounts and devalues in his accounting of the wealth of nations.

The Washington Post, July 19, 2012

CONSTITUTIONALISM

For decades, Democrats and Republicans fought over who owns the American flag. Now they're fighting over who owns the Constitution.

The flag debates began during the Vietnam era when leftist radicals made the fatal error of burning it. For decades since, non-suicidal liberals have tried to undo the damage. Demeaningly, and somewhat unfairly, they are forever having to prove their fealty to the flag.

Amazingly, though, some still couldn't get it quite right. During the last presidential campaign, candidate Barack Obama, asked why he was not wearing a flag pin, answered that it represented "a substitute" for "true patriotism." Bad move. Months later, Obama quietly beat a retreat and began wearing the flag on his lapel. He does so still.

Today, the issue is the Constitution. It's a healthier debate because flags are pure symbolism and therefore more likely to evoke pure emotion and ad hominem argument. The Constitution, on the other hand, is a document that speaks. It defines concretely the nature of our social contract. Nothing in our public life is more substantive.

Americans are in the midst of a great national debate over the power, scope and reach of the government established by that document. The debate was sparked by the current administration's bold push for government expansion—a massive fiscal stimulus, Obamacare, financial regulation and various attempts at controlling the energy economy. This engendered a popular reaction, identified with the Tea Party but in reality far more widespread, calling for a more restrictive vision of government more consistent with the Founders' intent.

Call it constitutionalism. In essence, constitutionalism is the intellectual counterpart and spiritual progeny of the "originalism" movement in jurisprudence. Judicial "originalists" (led by Antonin Scalia and other notable conservative jurists) insist that legal interpretation

be bound by the text of the Constitution as understood by those who
wrote it and their contemporaries. Originalism has grown to become
the major challenger to the liberal "living Constitution" school, under
which high courts are channelers of the spirit of the age, free to create
new constitutional principles accordingly.

What originalism is to jurisprudence, constitutionalism is to governance: a call for restraint rooted in constitutional text. Constitutionalism as a *political* philosophy represents a reformed, self-regulating
conservatism that bases its call for minimalist government—for rein-
ing in the willfulness of presidents and legislatures—in the words
and meaning of the Constitution.

Hence that highly symbolic moment on Thursday, when the 112th
House of Representatives opened with a reading of the Constitution.
Remarkably, this had never been done before—perhaps because it had
never been so needed. The reading reflected the feeling, expressed
powerfully in the last election, that we had moved far, especially the
past two years, from a government constitutionally limited by its enu-
merated powers to a government constrained only by its perception of
social need.

The most galvanizing example of this expansive shift was, of
course, the Democrats' health-care reform, which will revolutionize
one-sixth of the economy and impose an individual mandate that lev-
ies a fine on anyone who does *not* enter into a private contract with
a health insurance company. Whatever its merits as policy, there is
no doubting its seriousness as constitutional precedent: If Congress
can impose such a mandate, is there anything that Congress may not
impose upon the individual?

The new Republican House will henceforth require, in writing, constitutional grounding for every bill submitted. A fine idea,
although I suspect 90% of them will simply make a ritual appeal
to the "general welfare" clause. Nonetheless, anything that reminds
members of Congress that they are not untethered free agents is
salutary.

But still mostly symbolic. The real test of the Republicans' newfound constitutionalism will come in legislating. Will they really cut government spending? Will they really roll back regulations? Earmarks are nothing. Do the Republicans have the courage to go after entitlements as well?

In the interim, the cynics had best tread carefully. Some liberals are already disdaining the new constitutionalism, denigrating the document's relevance and sneering at its public recitation. They sneer at their political peril. In choosing to focus on a majestic document that bears both study and recitation, the reformed conservatism of the Obama era has found itself not just a symbol but an anchor.

Constitutionalism as a guiding political tendency will require careful and thoughtful development, as did jurisprudential originalism. But its wide appeal and philosophical depth make it a promising first step to a conservative future.

The Washington Post, January 7, 2011

MYTH OF THE ANGRY WHITE MALE

The Angry White Male, suitably capitalized to indicate that the menace has become a media-certified trend, stalks the land, or at least the land of the media. In the 10 years before the Nov. 1994 election, there were 59 (Nexis) references to angry white men. There have been 1,400 since. A post-election front-page headline in *USA Today* was typical: "Angry White Men: Their votes turned the tide for the GOP."

By sheer numbing repetition, the legend grows. "The Republicans scraped together a majority," explains the genial Garrison Keillor, "by appealing to the sorehead vote, your brother-in-law and mine." By early April, the term receives its official presidential seal of approval when Bill Clinton confirms that "this is psychologically a difficult time for a lot of white males, the so-called angry white males."

Then comes Oklahoma City, and the legend has its poster boy: khaki-clad, hopping-mad, armed and dangerous. "Have angry white men gone too far?" asks the *Wall Street Journal* in a front-page headline right after the bombing. Apparently, yes. "Heart-breaking [Oklahoma] news reports," explains the *Journal*, "show the lengths to which the anger of the much-commented-upon angry white males can extend."

The Oklahoma bomber is now honorary class president of those conservative-leaning, Republican-voting agitated white males the media have been warning us about since November. First he gives Newt Gingrich the House. Then he blows up the federal building in Oklahoma City.

Where did this legend come from? Yes, white men shifted significantly toward Republicans in the November election. But where did the ubiquitous pejorative "angry" come from? Where is the evidence for the rage of this white male cohort? Anyone take their blood pressure in the voting booth?

USA Today's front-page "Angry White Men" story is again typical. It offered reams of polls, not one supporting the supposed "anger" of white men. Indeed, of the dozens of polls taken around Election Day, I could find only three that even raised the issue. Frank Luntz asked voters if they considered themselves "angry voters." Seven out of 10 white men did not.

The Voter News Service National Exit Poll asked respondents if they were angry "about the way the federal government works." Three out of four white males were not.

The *Washington Post*–ABC pre-election poll asked the same question. Four out of five white males were not. Moreover, the 21% who were exactly matches the average percentage of Americans overall who have identified themselves as angry in the last 10 such polls stretching back to early 1992. Where is the hormonally challenged, mad-as-hell, sexist, racist mob that ran the Democrats out of Congress in 1994?

The absence of facts must not be allowed to stand in the way of a good line or an ad hominem charge. And the charge of male anger has a history that predates the 1994 election. It began its recent career as the ultimate put-down of those critical of the first ladyhood of Hillary Clinton. As she herself explained in an interview in the *Wall Street Journal* on Sept. 30, "People are not really often reacting to me so much as they are reacting to their own lives. . . . If somebody has a female boss for the first time, and they've never experienced that— well, maybe they can't take out their hostility against her so they turn it on me."

Keillor puts it, again, more genially when he dubs the Republicans the "Party of Large White Men Who Feel Uneasy Around Gals." Clinton pollster Stanley Greenberg echoes the theme when he writes about Republicans becoming a home "for every angry group," among them "those who resent . . . strong women."

Really? Let's look at Maryland. State Delegate Ellen Sauerbrey, who last year lost the closest gubernatorial race in the country, is a Republican. She is a tough independent politician, so tough, in fact, that for nine weeks she doggedly tried to overturn what she charged was a tainted election before deigning to concede to her male opponent.

So here's a test of the Clinton-Keillor-Greenberg proposition. How did white males—so fearful and resentful of strong women— vote in Maryland? For Mrs. Sauerbrey, by a 2–1 landslide.

The *New York Times* post-election coverage cited speculation that apathy among women voters might have contributed to the huge Democratic losses of 1994. It noted a "lack of interest this year among women" compared with 1992—the so-called Year of the Woman— when "the fracas between Clarence Thomas and Prof. Anita F. Hill energized women voters."

Women, you see, are "energized." Men are enraged. When women show electoral clout, it is the Year of the Woman. When men do, it is the Year of the Angry White Male.

In fact, the Angry White Male is a myth, an invention of political partisans who wish to rationalize and ultimately de-legitimize the election of 1994. After all, neither anger, nor whiteness, nor maleness is a coveted attribute these days. The invention of the Angry White Male pointedly ascribes the current Republican ascendancy to a toxic constituency, akin to the petty bourgeoisie that brought fascists to power in the Europe of the 1930s.

A rabble of dispossessed white men—threatened by women, resentful of minorities, enthralled by talk radio—has been stirred, and that's why the Republicans won. The myth is not just useful but comforting too. Defeat becomes tolerable, indeed virtuous, when you've convinced yourself that you lost to a lynch mob.

GOING NEGATIVE

Delta Airlines, you might have noticed, does not run negative TV ads about USAir. It does not show pictures of the crash of USAir Flight 427, with a voice-over saying: "USAir, airline of death. Going to Pittsburgh? Fly Delta instead."

And McDonald's, you might also have noticed, does not run ads reminding viewers that Jack in the Box hamburgers once killed two customers. Why? Because Delta and McDonald's know that if the airline and fast-food industries put on that kind of advertising, America would soon be riding trains and eating box-lunch tuna sandwiches.

Yet every two years the American politics industry fills the airwaves with the most virulent, scurrilous, wall-to-wall character assassination of nearly every political practitioner in the country—and then declares itself puzzled that America has lost trust in its politicians.

Voters declare a burning desire to throw the bums out. Polls show an aversion to politicians that can only be called malignant. And the sages pull on their beards, stumped.

The economy? It is in better shape than it has been in years.

Gridlock? People so thoroughly disgusted with their politicians want gridlock. They approve of a system that promises to stop them before they legislate again. It is not the system they dislike. It is the players they cannot abide.

Why? No need for exotic theories. The simplest explanation is always the best. Politics is the only American industry whose participants devote their advertising budgets to the regular, public, savage undermining of one another. It is the only American industry whose participants devote prodigious sums to destroying whatever shred of allegiance any of them might once have won with their customers.

Compare. About the only other business that indulges in negative advertising is the long-distance phone business. MCI tells you that AT&T overcharges. Not so, says AT&T. This piddling stuff is about as nasty as it gets.

Moreover, picking a long-distance operator hardly demands a relationship of trust. Whereas picking an airline that suspends you in a sealed aluminum tube at 30,000 feet is a matter of trust. So is picking a fast-food restaurant that presents you with heavily camouflaged meat confected by a 16-year-old with acne. So is picking a politician, who rifles your paycheck and regulates your life. Yet only the politicians work systematically to kill that trust.

Turn on the tube and watch what one candidate—any candidate—has to say about the other. Then remember that no matter who wins, one of these miserable, execrable human beings will end up representing you in Congress.

Sen. John Danforth of Missouri recalls that in his first Senate race in 1970, he ran against the popular Stuart Symington and lost. Yet both ran such positive and honorable campaigns that Danforth ended up one of best-liked politicians in Missouri. Six years later he ran again and won.

That was a long time ago in a galaxy far, far away. (Danforth is retiring now from a political environment turned toxic.) The politicians have since "gone negative." The reason is simple. Negative works. It gets individuals elected. Add up all the individual acts of political homicide, however, and you have a political class that is collectively committing suicide.

The basic theme of the 1994 campaign is that everyone running is a liar, a cheat, a crook or a fraud. Take the, oh, 3rd District of Tennessee, Button vs. Wamp. Wamp portrays Button as a fraud. Button calls Wamp a liar, and compliments Wamp for "kicking [his] chemical dependency." A nice touch.

In the most publicized case of mutual assured political destruction, the Virginia Senate race, Oliver North's TV ad starts with "Why can't Chuck Robb tell the truth?" which Robb's answers with "After lying about President Reagan and even lying to schoolchildren, now

Oliver North is lying about Chuck Robb." To schoolchildren, mind you.

The immutable fact is this: As of Nov. 9, one of these two highly advertised liars will be the next senator from Virginia. Every state in the union will be sending to Congress some brutally excoriated campaign survivor. The 104th Congress is guaranteed to be an assembly of the most vilified persons in every American community. And you thought the baseball owners were self-destructive.

Do we really need seminars on why voters loathe politicians?

The Washington Post, October 28, 1994

The Tirana Index

N ow that the campaign is over and the returns are in, analysis of the latest Albanian election begins. The facts are clear: Communist Party chief Enver Hoxha's slate of candidates for Parliament won by the comfortable margin of 1,627,959 to 1. The message seems to be: Stay the course.

The party ran well in all regions and among all classes—worker, peasant and apparatchik. It swept the atheist vote. The much ballyhooed gender gap never developed. On the other hand, it failed to make any inroads on opposition support. (In the last Albanian election there was also one vote against.) Some observers had been predicting that opposition support might double, but that prospect dimmed last December when a potential leader of the movement, Prime Minister Mehmet Shehu, committed suicide.

At the time Hoxha claimed that Shehu did so "in a moment of nervous crisis." Now party chairman Hoxha ("himself a successful candidate in the 210th district of Tirana," writes the *New York Times*) says that Mr. Shehu, whom he described variously as an American agent, a Soviet agent and a Yugoslav agent, had been ordered by Yugoslavia to kill Mr. Hoxha and other Albanian leaders, but finally met his demise when he "broke his head against the unity of the party and the people." (Mr. Hoxha's equivocation recalls the answer that the police captain in *Casablanca* gave to a question about the condition of a prisoner. "We are trying to decide whether he committed suicide or died trying to escape.") Since Albanian election law does not permit absentee ballots, analysts conclude that the one vote against Hoxha could not have been cast by Mr. Shehu. His voice will be missed.

Hoxha's victory margin, though impressive, is not unprecedented. President Assad of Syria won reelection in 1978 with 99.6% of the vote. The Soviet embassy informs us that candidates "always" win more than 99% of the vote, usually "around 99.5%." Indeed, it seems, anything less than 99% is considered a vote of no confidence.

Western observers are generally skeptical about these results. Because of their obsession with the authenticity of such elections, they tend to overlook their enormous value as scientific tools. For generations political science has been seeking a way to quantify freedom. Some, like Freedom House, annually classify countries according to their level of political and civil liberty. Others, like Morton Kondracke, propose the creation of a computerized despot-a-meter to take the guesswork out of such perennially taxing questions as: Who's worse, Idi Amin or Roberto d'Aubuisson?

The trouble with these pioneering schemes is that they are too complicated. I propose a simpler system, crude, but like all crude instruments, quick, easy to use and blunt. It is the Tirana Index: The higher the vote any government wins in an election, the more tyrannous it is.

The Tirana Index lends itself to easy rules of thumb. Very bad tyranny (known to some as totalitarian states) usually gets more than 95% of the vote, and the more efficient of these, more than 99%. Traditional autocracies and military governments (known to some as authoritarian states), such as Turkey and Mexico, can be counted on to clock in somewhere between 80% and 95%. (Turkey's last referendum passed by 92.) Well-functioning democracies produce winners who get between 50% and 80% of the vote.

Countries like Italy, Israel and others where driving is a life-threatening activity regularly produce winning margins of less than 50%. They can safely be classified as anarchies.

The New Republic, December 13, 1982

CHAPTER 8

CONUNDRUMS

WITHOUT THE NOOSE, WITHOUT THE GAG

At dawn on Tuesday, Robert Alton Harris, a double murderer, died in a California gas chamber, California's first execution in 25 years. There is no doubt that Harris deserved to die. In my view, however, California should not have killed him.

Not because there is anything unconstitutional about the death penalty. The Fifth Amendment takes it as a given. Moreover, capital punishment may be cruel, but it is not unusual. A measure that is approved by 36 states can hardly be deemed one against which Americans have turned their face, which is what "unusual" means in constitutional terms.

Nor is there any high principle that the state may not put people to death. There are reasons of state—war, for example—for which the state will put tens of thousands of people to death (and risk the lives of thousands of its own innocents as well).

Nor is capital punishment unjust. Indeed, justice is the most powerful argument in favor of capital punishment. When a man wantonly kills two boys, as did Harris, it is hard to think of any penalty short of death that would restore the moral order that has been so brutally violated.

Nonetheless, I oppose capital punishment on the following grounds: It is a mark of civilization to maintain order at the lowest possible level of official violence. One is not supposed to talk these days about higher and lower levels of civilization, but even political correctness would admit that the less a society has recourse to official violence the more civilized it is. We do not cut off the hands of thieves. We do not keelhaul miscreant sailors. We no longer have public floggings. Each abolition represents an advance of civilization. Abolition of the death penalty represents a further advance.

I do not oppose capital punishment in principle. If capital punishment could be demonstrated to deter murder, I might be persuaded to tolerate a few exemplary hangings to save many innocents. But there is no convincing evidence that the death penalty deters. Murder rates in states with the death penalty are just as high as in neighboring states without it. In states where the death penalty has been introduced, murder rates do not, on average, go down. And in states where the death penalty has been abolished, murder rates do not go up.

When something as barbaric as cold-blooded execution by the state makes no appreciable contribution to public safety, it deserves abolition. True, justice militates for capital punishment. But on balance, it seems to me worth forgoing the satisfactions of perfect justice—as all of Western Europe has done—to live in a society civilized enough to maintain order without judicial killing.

Now, this kind of argument against the death penalty may have useful application to issues other than capital punishment. The idea of choosing a course that makes for a more refined, more advanced, more civilized society can be of help in thinking our way through political conundrums that are otherwise reduced to a clash of irreconcilable principles. Take free speech, for example. We have a serious debate in this country, particularly in the universities, over the establishment of legal codes outlawing racist, sexist or otherwise hostile speech.

Several democracies—Canada and Germany, for example—have laws banning the advocacy of racist ideas. I would oppose such laws for the United States, again not on grounds of principle but on grounds that, today and in this country, such laws are an unnecessary infringement on liberty and thus unworthy of an advanced democracy.

Nazism, communism and other intolerant extremisms are laughably marginal in American politics. David Duke's 15-minute rise and fall have made the point once again. Nonetheless, if some day some totalitarians posed a real challenge to our system of liberty (as did the Nazis to Weimar), I could see no reasonable argument against their suppression, forcible if necessary.

In a time of clear and present danger, liberty is not obliged to commit suicide. Lincoln certainly did not think so when he suspended habeas corpus during the Civil War. But we do not live in such a time of extreme danger. Far from it. Totalitarians are a fringe of the fringe. So long as they remain so, why diminish the first of all rights—speech—to deal with a threat that is not a threat?

Which brings us to the speech codes now being imposed in the universities. In principle, there might be a situation in which one would countenance such limits on speech. In the midst of an epidemic of racial and ethnic hostility that made normal life and scholarly discourse impossible, one might be willing to suspend the traditional rules and outlaw certain kinds of speech. But we are nowhere near such a situation. Where the situation does not apply, neither should curtailments of speech.

Thus, those who oppose capital punishment or who oppose speech codes need not do so in the name of some holy principle that the state may not take away life or liberty—it may—but on the grounds that an advanced, civilized society should strive to preserve public order and social peace with an absolute minimum of official violence to life and liberty.

Some day, some emergency might warrant the state aggressively hanging criminals and gagging dissidents. But until that day, it would be a credit to our society to try to get by without the noose and the gag.

The Washington Post, April 24, 1992

MOTHERHOOD MISSED

The screaming headline was tabloid size: "I WAS DESPERATE FOR A BABY AND I HAVE THE MEDICAL BILLS TO PROVE IT." Some love-struck movie star? A lesbian celebrity? No. Germaine Greer, icon of 20th-century feminism. "I still have pregnancy dreams," she confessed movingly in the premier issue of the British magazine *Aura*, "waiting with vast joy and confidence for something that will never happen."

The longing for children is hardly novel. What, then, makes this story so sensational, earning a 45-point type, "exclusive" treatment? What gives the story its man-bites-dog quality is that Greer is the great exemplar of the fiercely independent, aggressively sexual new woman. Iconoclastic to the point of fierceness, she reveled in her lovers and in telling about them.

The one adjective rarely attached to Greer was domestic. And now she reveals the hollowness that haunts her, the terrible sorrow she feels at what she lost: her chance for motherhood.

Many years ago, she now writes, she cared for the infant girl of a friend. "Ruby lit up my life in a way that nobody, certainly no lover, has ever done. I was not prepared for the incandescent sensuousness of this small child, the generosity of her innocent love."

Not prepared? Why? Because to the uncompromising feminism of those early days, she writes, childbearing was constricting, suffocating, an enemy of a liberated woman's larger hopes. "Getting pregnant meant the end of all good times . . . the mother-generation warned us darkly not to rush into childbearing, to have a 'good time' while we could."

And now, like Hannah, she weeps.

Greer is not the only such victim of ideology—and, it must be added, biology: When she finally decided to try to say yes to having a child, her body said no. At the 1998 Barnard commencement, Joyce

Purnick of the *New York Times* spoke of her deep regret at not having had a child. She felt that she had to choose between family and career. Her choice: the long days, the undivided attention, the single-minded ambition to succeed. "I am absolutely convinced I would not be the metro editor of the *Times* if I had had a family."

The poignancy of her dilemma lies in the lingering question: If she had it to do over again, would she still rather have the metro desk, or the soft comforts and inexpressible joys of motherhood?

In modern times we suffer not for our sins—sin having been abolished—but for ideology. The traditional victim of ideology is the communist betrayed by the "God that failed." As socialism recedes into history, there will be fewer such confessions. Feminism, a far nobler creed, commands the day. But like all gods, this one too exacts its tribute.

The early days of feminism did present stark choices. It was held, as Purnick put it, that "you cannot have it all." Unfair it was. Unfair it remains.

"Should men and women who have taken the detour of the Mommy/Daddy track be as far along as those who haven't?" asked Purnick. "I reluctantly have to say that it would not be fair." And is it fair that men and women with children lose out to "others who have been working the 12-hour days?" She believes it is.

Oh, my. This brought a storm of protest from younger feminists, women who, under the new dispensation, get the four-day weeks and the extended family leave—and expect nonetheless to remain on the same professional footing as their childless colleagues.

This is eminently fair, eminently nondiscriminatory. Indeed, earlier this month, President Clinton issued a federal ban on the "glass ceiling for parents." But imagine how it feels to those like Purnick. They are asked to stretch themselves and cover for a younger colleague so that she can go home and give her child a bath—a joy they will never know. A joy they deliberately gave up, under the terms of the original feminist contract, in the name of autonomy and advancement.

That contract has now been largely rewritten. But for them, alas, too late.

The good that feminism has wrought is quite incalculable. It gave half of humanity the chance to develop—something that had been denied it in practically every culture in every era. But like all great revolutions, feminism has its price and its victims.

The Washington Post, May 12, 2000

AMBIGUITY AND AFFIRMATIVE ACTION

The Supreme Court decision upholding affirmative action is incoherent, disingenuous, intellectually muddled and morally confused. Yet it is welcome.

Let me explain. Affirmative action began as an attempt to compensate for the effects of past discrimination against African Americans. Forty years after the passage of the Civil Rights Act, however, that justification is increasingly difficult to maintain. Proponents have accordingly reinvented the rationale. Affirmative action has metastasized into "diversity," in whose name an arbitrary selection of favored minorities (at Michigan, blacks, Hispanics and Native Americans) is entitled to favors denied other Americans purely because of their ethnicity and race.

In the Michigan law school case, the court justified allowing official racial discrimination—the majority opinion itself uses the term "racial preferences"—in order to achieve diversity. Why? Because a "critical mass" of minorities improves the educational environment. For this, the justices relied on some social science. In fact, there is contrary social science. But the real question is: Should we be violating the fundamental principle of equality before the law in order to attain a speculative, minor improvement in the study environment of a university?

And even if we grant the existence of this marginal gain, it is grossly outweighed by the huge social, moral and human costs of racial discrimination:

(1) The stigmatization of all minority achievement, as it gratuitously opens the question of whether any minority person in high position got there by merit or by skin color.

(2) The racial antagonism automatically engendered when race is used to prefer or penalize innocent citizens.

(3) The ruin of a legion of minority students who are artificially

promoted to institutions where they cannot compete academi-
cally and where they therefore fail—when they could have
been brilliant successes at institutions more suited to their
academic abilities. Before affirmative action was banned at
the University of California at Berkeley, the non-graduation
rate for whites was 16%; for blacks it was 42%. Guilty white
liberals could thus point proudly to high minority admissions
numbers, caring nothing about the fact that they had turned
almost half that cohort—bright young people who might have
succeeded elsewhere—into failures.

Why, then, am I glad the court, for all of its sophistry, upheld
affirmative action? For those who believe that affirmative action, for
all of its noble purposes, is extraordinarily destructive to both its beneficiaries and its victims, and to both race relations and constitutional
principles, it is tempting to wish it all swept away by the Supreme
Court.

It is a temptation to be resisted. Issues of this magnitude should
never be decided by nine robes. Affirmative action needs to be dealt
with by the people in the legislatures and in referendums. I believe
that the current dispensation is a travesty. But a very substantial
portion of the population reads the Constitution—and the nation's
needs—quite differently. Under these circumstances, the issue should
not be settled by judicial fiat.

We learned from the abortion issue the doleful consequences
of such judicial imperialism. In 1973 changes in public opinion and
action in state legislatures were altering the landscape on abortion. At
which point the court stepped in and took the issue out of the political arena. As Ruth Bader Ginsburg argued before she ascended to the
Supreme Court, "*Roe v. Wade* . . . halted a political process that was
moving in a reform direction and thereby, I believe, prolonged divisiveness and deferred stable settlement of the issue." The result has
been 30 years of strife and agitation, as a disenfranchised minority
continues to carry the fight against policy for which it has no political
recourse.

It would be a pity to reenact the experience with affirmative action. Popular referendums have already abolished racial preferences in California and Washington State. Such acts of abolition enjoy the kind of political legitimacy that—as conservatives, of all people, should acknowledge—is lacking when handed down by unelected judges.

Let's remember: The court did not mandate affirmative action. It only permitted affirmative action. The people and the politicians are entirely empowered to do away with it. True, the abolition movement has slowed since its successes in California and Washington, and most of the political class—both Democratic and Republican—lacks the courage to take up the fight.

But that should tell us something. It tells us that most Americans prefer to abide the current state of unprincipled, muddied racial incoherence so brilliantly reflected in the Supreme Court's Michigan law school decision.

It tells us, too, where the problem lies. We should not be blaming the Supreme Court for refusing to do for us what we the people, in Congress (and state legislatures) assembled, refuse to do for ourselves.

The Washington Post, June 27, 2003

MASSACRE AT NEWTOWN

Every mass shooting has three elements: the killer, the weapon and the cultural climate. As soon as the shooting stops, partisans immediately pick their preferred root cause with corresponding pet panacea. Names are hurled, scapegoats paraded, prejudices vented. The argument goes nowhere.

Let's be serious:

(1) THE WEAPON

Within hours of last week's Newtown, Connecticut, massacre, the focus was the weapon and the demand was for new gun laws. Several prominent pro-gun Democrats remorsefully professed new openness to gun control. Sen. Dianne Feinstein (D-Calif.) is introducing a new assault weapons ban. And the president emphasized guns and ammo above all else in announcing the creation of a new task force.

I have no problem in principle with gun control. Congress enacted (and I supported) an assault weapons ban in 1994. The problem was: It didn't work. (So concluded a University of Pennsylvania study commissioned by the Justice Department.) The reason is simple. Unless you are prepared to confiscate all existing firearms, disarm the citizenry and repeal the Second Amendment, it's almost impossible to craft a law that will be effective.

Feinstein's law, for example, would exempt 900 weapons. And that's the least of the loopholes. Even the guns that are banned can be made legal with simple, minor modifications.

Most fatal, however, is the grandfathering of existing weapons and magazines. That's one of the reasons the '94 law failed. At the time, there were 1.5 million assault weapons in circulation and 25 million large-capacity (i.e., more than 10 bullets) magazines. A reservoir that immense can take 100 years to draw down.

(2) THE KILLER

Monsters shall always be with us, but in earlier days they did not roam free. As a psychiatrist in Massachusetts in the 1970s, I committed people—often right out of the emergency room—as a danger to themselves or to others. I never did so lightly, but I labored under none of the crushing bureaucratic and legal constraints that make involuntary commitment infinitely more difficult today.

Why do you think we have so many homeless? Destitution? Poverty has *declined* since the 1950s. The majority of those sleeping on grates are mentally ill. In the name of civil liberties, we let them die with their rights on.

A tiny percentage of the mentally ill become mass killers. Just about everyone around Tucson shooter Jared Loughner sensed he was mentally ill and dangerous. But in effect, he had to kill before he could be put away—and (forcibly) treated.

Random mass killings were three times more common in the 2000s than in the 1980s, when gun laws were actually weaker. Yet a 2011 University of California at Berkeley study found that states with strong civil commitment laws have about a one-third lower homicide rate.

(3) THE CULTURE

We live in an entertainment culture soaked in graphic, often sadistic, violence. Older folks find themselves stunned by what a desensitized youth finds routine, often amusing. It's not just movies. Young men sit for hours pulling video-game triggers, mowing down human beings en masse without pain or consequence. And we profess shock when a small cadre of unstable, deeply deranged, dangerously isolated young men go out and enact the overlearned narrative.

If we're serious about curtailing future Columbines and Newtowns, everything—guns, commitment, culture—must be on the table. It's not hard for President Obama to call out the NRA. But will he call out the ACLU? And will he call out his Hollywood friends?

The irony is that over the last 30 years, the U.S. homicide rate has declined by 50%. Gun murders as well. We're living not through an epidemic of gun violence but through a historic decline.

Except for these unfathomable mass murders. But these are infinitely more difficult to prevent. While law deters the rational, it has far less effect on the psychotic. The best we can do is to try to detain them, disarm them and discourage "entertainment" that can intensify already murderous impulses.

But there's a cost. Gun control impinges upon the Second Amendment; involuntary commitment impinges upon the liberty clause of the Fifth Amendment; curbing "entertainment" violence impinges upon First Amendment free speech.

That's a lot of impingement, a lot of amendments. But there's no free lunch. Increasing public safety almost always means restricting liberties.

We made that trade after 9/11. We make it every time the Transportation Security Administration invades your body at an airport. How much are we prepared to trade away after Newtown?

The Washington Post, December 20, 2012

PANDORA AND POLYGAMY

And now, polygamy.

With the sweetly titled HBO series *Big Love*, polygamy comes out of the closet. Under the headline "Polygamists, Unite!" *Newsweek* informs us of "polygamy activists emerging in the wake of the gay-marriage movement." Says one evangelical Christian big lover: "Polygamy rights is the next civil-rights battle."

Polygamy used to be stereotyped as the province of secretive Mormons, primitive Africans and profligate Arabs. With *Big Love* it moves to suburbia as a mere alternative lifestyle.

As *Newsweek* notes, these stirrings for the mainstreaming of polygamy (or, more accurately, polyamory) have their roots in the increasing legitimization of gay marriage. In an essay 10 years ago, I pointed out that it is utterly logical for polygamy rights to follow gay rights. After all, if traditional marriage is defined as the union of (1) two people of (2) opposite gender, and if, as advocates of gay marriage insist, the gender requirement is nothing but prejudice, exclusion and an arbitrary denial of one's autonomous choices in love, then the first requirement—the number restriction (two and only two)—is a similarly arbitrary, discriminatory and indefensible denial of individual choice.

This line of argument makes gay activists furious. I can understand why they do not want to be in the same room as polygamists. But I'm not the one who put them there. Their argument does. Blogger and author Andrew Sullivan, who had the courage to advocate gay marriage at a time when it was considered pretty crazy, has called this the "polygamy diversion," arguing that homosexuality and polygamy are categorically different because polygamy is a mere "activity" while homosexuality is an intrinsic state that "occupies a deeper level of human consciousness."

But this distinction between higher and lower orders of love is precisely what gay rights activists so vigorously protest when the general culture "privileges" (as they say in the English departments) heterosexual unions over homosexual ones. Was *Jules et Jim* (and Jeanne Moreau), the classic Truffaut film involving two dear friends in love with the same woman, about an "activity" or about the most intrinsic of human emotions?

To simplify the logic, take out the complicating factor of gender mixing. Posit a union of, say, three gay women all deeply devoted to each other. On what grounds would gay activists dismiss their union as mere activity rather than authentic love and self-expression? On what grounds do they insist upon the traditional, arbitrary and exclusionary number of two?

What is historically odd is that as gay marriage is gaining acceptance, the resistance to polygamy is much more powerful. Yet until this generation, gay marriage had been sanctioned by no society that we know of, anywhere at any time in history. On the other hand, polygamy was sanctioned, indeed common, in large parts of the world through large swaths of history, most notably the biblical Middle East and through much of the Islamic world.

I'm not one of those who see gay marriage or polygamy as a threat to, or assault on, traditional marriage. The assault came from within. Marriage has needed no help in managing its own long, slow suicide, thank you. Astronomical rates of divorce and of single parenthood (the deliberate creation of fatherless families) existed before there was a single gay marriage or any talk of sanctioning polygamy. The minting of these new forms of marriage is a *symptom* of our culture's contemporary radical individualism—as is the decline of traditional marriage—and not its cause.

As for gay marriage, I've come to a studied ambivalence. I think it is a mistake for society to make this ultimate declaration of indifference between gay and straight life, if only for reasons of pedagogy. On the other hand, I have gay friends and feel the pain of their inability to have the same level of social approbation and confirmation of their relationship with a loved one that I'm not about to go to anyone's barricade to deny them that. It is critical, however, that any such fundamental change in the very definition of marriage be enacted democratically and not (as in the disastrous case of abortion) by judicial fiat.

Call me agnostic. But don't tell me that we can make one radical change in the one-man, one-woman rule and not be open to the claim of others that their reformation be given equal respect.

The Washington Post, March 17, 2006

EMPATHY OR RIGHT?

There are two ways to defend gay marriage. Argument A is empathy: One is influenced by gay friends in committed relationships yearning for the fulfillment and acceptance that marriage conveys upon heterosexuals. That's essentially the case President Obama made when he first announced his change of views.

No talk about rights, just human fellow feeling. Such an argument is attractive because it can be compelling without being compulsory. Many people, feeling the weight of this longing among their gay friends, are willing to redefine marriage for the sake of simple human sympathy.

At the same time, however, one can sympathize with others who feel great trepidation at the radical transformation of the most fundamental of social institutions, one that, until yesterday, was heterosexual in all societies in all places at all times.

The empathy argument both encourages mutual respect in the debate and lends itself to a political program of gradualism. State by state, let community norms and moral sensibilities prevail. Indeed, that is Obama's stated position.

Such pluralism allows for the kind of "stable settlement of the issue" that Ruth Bader Ginsburg once lamented had been "halted" by *Roe v. Wade* regarding abortion, an issue as morally charged and politically unbridgeable as gay marriage.

Argument B is more uncompromising: You have the right to marry anyone, regardless of gender. The right to "marriage equality" is today's civil rights, voting rights and women's rights—and just as inviolable.

Argument B has extremely powerful implications. First, if same-sex marriage is a right, then there is no possible justification for letting states decide for themselves. How can you countenance even one state outlawing a fundamental right? Indeed, half a century ago, states' rights was the cry of those committed to continued segregation and discrimination.

Second, if marriage equality is a civil right, then denying it on the basis of (innately felt) sexual orientation is, like discrimination on the basis of skin color, simple bigotry. California's Proposition 8 was overturned by a Ninth Circuit panel on the grounds that the referendum, reaffirming marriage as between a man and woman, was nothing but an expression of bias—"serves no purpose . . . other than to lessen the status and human dignity of gays and lesbians."

Pretty strong stuff. Which is why it was so surprising that Obama, after first advancing Argument A, went on five days later to adopt Argument B, calling gay marriage a great example of "expand[ing] rights" and today's successor to civil rights, voting rights, women's rights and workers' rights.

Problem is: It's a howling contradiction to leave up to the states an issue Obama now says is a right. And beyond being intellectually untenable, Obama's embrace of the more hard-line "rights" argument compels him logically to see believers in traditional marriage as purveyors of bigotry. Not a good place for a president to be in an evenly divided national debate that requires both sides to offer each other a modicum of respect.

No wonder that Obama has been trying to get away from the issue as quickly as possible. It's not just the *New York Times* poll showing his new position to be a net loser. It's that he is too intelligent not to realize he's embraced a logical contradiction.

Moreover, there is the problem of the obvious cynicism of his conversion. Two-thirds of Americans see his "evolution" as a matter not of principle but of politics. In fact, the change is not at all an evolution—a teleological term cleverly chosen to suggest movement toward a higher state of being—given that Obama came out for gay marriage 16 years ago. And then flip-flopped.

He was pro when running for the Illinois Legislature from ultraliberal Hyde Park. He became anti when running eight years later for the U.S. Senate and had to appeal to a decidedly more conservative statewide constituency. And now he's pro again.

When a Republican engages in such finger-to-the-wind political calculation (on abortion, for example), he's condemned as a flip-flopper. When a liberal goes through a similar gyration, he's said to have "evolved" into some more highly realized creature, deserving of a halo on the cover of a national newsmagazine.

Notwithstanding a comically fawning press, Obama knows he has boxed himself in. His "rights" argument compels him to nationalize same-sex marriage and sharpen hostility toward proponents of traditional marriage—a place he is loath to go.

True, he was rushed into it by his loquacious vice president. But surely he could have thought this through.

The Washington Post, May 17, 2012

FIRST A WALL—THEN AMNESTY

Every sensible immigration policy has two objectives: (1) to regain control of our borders so that it is we who decide who enters, and (2) to find a way to normalize and legalize the situation of the 11 million illegals among us.

Start with the second. No one of goodwill wants to see these 11 million suffer. But the obvious problem is that legalization creates an enormous incentive for new illegals to come.

We say, of course, that this will be the very last, very final, never-again, we're-not-kidding-this-time amnesty. The problem is that we say exactly the same thing with every new reform. And everyone knows it's phony.

What do you think was said when in 1986 we passed the Simpson-Mazzoli immigration reform? It turned into the largest legalization program in American history—nearly 3 million got permanent residency. And we are now back at it again with 11 million new illegals in our midst.

How can it be otherwise? We already have a river of people coming every day knowing they're going to be illegal and perhaps even exploited. They come nonetheless. The newest amnesty—the "earned legalization" now being dangled in front of them by proposed Senate legislation—can only increase the flow.

Those who think employer sanctions will control immigration are dreaming. Employer sanctions were the heart of Simpson-Mazzoli. They are not only useless, they are pernicious. They turn employers into enforcers of border control. That is the job of government, not landscapers.

The irony of this whole debate, which is bitterly splitting the country along partisan, geographic and ethnic lines, is that there is a silver bullet that would not just solve the problem but also create a national consensus behind it.

My proposition is the following: A vast number of Americans who oppose legalization and fear new waves of immigration would change their minds if we could radically reduce new—i.e., future—illegal immigration.

Forget employer sanctions. Build a barrier. It is simply ridiculous to say it cannot be done. If one fence won't do it, then build a second 100 yards behind it. And then build a road for patrols in between. Put cameras. Put sensors. Put out lots of patrols.

Can't be done? Israel's border fence has been extraordinarily successful in keeping out potential infiltrators who are far more determined than mere immigrants. Nor have very many North Koreans crossed into South Korea in the last 50 years.

Of course it will be ugly. So are the concrete barriers to keep truck bombs from driving into the White House. But sometimes necessity trumps aesthetics. And don't tell me that this is our Berlin Wall. When you build a wall to keep people in, that's a prison. When you build a wall to keep people out, that's an expression of sovereignty. The fence around your house is a perfectly legitimate expression of your desire to control who comes into your house to eat, sleep and use the facilities. It imprisons no one.

Of course, no barrier will be foolproof. But it doesn't have to be. It simply has to reduce the river of illegals to a manageable trickle. Once we can do that, everything becomes possible—most especially, humanizing the situation of our 11 million existing illegals.

If the government can demonstrate that it can control future immigration, there will be infinitely less resistance to dealing generously with the residual population of past immigration. And, as Mickey Kaus and others have suggested, that may require that the two provisions be sequenced. First, radical border control by physical means. Then shortly thereafter, radical legalization of those already here. To achieve national consensus on legalization, we will need a short lag time between the two provisions, perhaps a year or two, to demonstrate to the skeptics that the current wave of illegals is indeed the last.

This is no time for mushy compromise. A solution requires two acts of national will: the ugly act of putting up a fence and the supremely generous act of absorbing as ultimately full citizens those who broke our laws to come to America.

This is not a compromise meant to appease both sides without achieving anything. It is not some piece of hybrid legislation that arbitrarily divides illegals into those with five-year-old "roots" in America and those without, or some such mischief-making nonsense.

This is full amnesty (earned with back taxes and learning English and the like) with full border control. If we do it right, not only will we solve the problem, we will get it done as one nation.

The Washington Post, April 7, 2006

IN PLAIN ENGLISH—LET'S MAKE IT OFFICIAL

Growing up (as I did) in the province of Quebec, you learn not just the joys but also the perils of bilingualism. A separate national identity, revolving entirely around "Francophonie," became a raging issue that led to social unrest, terrorism, threats of separation and a referendum that came within a hair's breadth of breaking up Canada.

Canada, of course, had no choice about bilingualism. It is a country created of two nations at its birth and has ever since been trying to cope with that inherently divisive fact. The United States, by contrast blessed with a single common language for two centuries, seems blithely and gratuitously to be ready to import bilingualism with all its attendant divisiveness and antagonisms.

One of the major reasons for America's great success as the world's first "universal nation," for its astonishing and unmatched capacity for assimilating immigrants, has been that an automatic part of acculturation was the acquisition of English. And yet during the great immigration debate now raging in Congress, the people's representatives cannot make up their minds whether the current dominance of English should be declared a national asset, worthy of enshrinement in law.

The Senate could not bring itself to declare English the country's "official language." The best it could do was pass an amendment to the immigration bill tepidly declaring English the "national language." Yet even that was too much for Senate Democratic leader Harry Reid, who called that resolution "racist."

Less hyperbolic opponents point out that granting special official status to English is simply unnecessary: America has been accepting foreign-language-speaking immigrants forever—Brooklyn is so polyglot it is a veritable Babel—and yet we've done just fine. What's the great worry about Spanish?

The worry is this. Polyglot is fine. When immigrants, like those in Brooklyn, are members of a myriad of linguistic communities, each tiny and discrete, there is no threat to the common culture. No immigrant presumes to make the demand that the state grant special status to his language. He may speak it in the street and proudly teach it to his children, but he knows that his future and certainly theirs lie inevitably in learning English as the gateway to American life.

But all of that changes when you have an enormous, linguistically monoclonal immigration as we do today from Latin America. Then you get not Brooklyn's successful Babel but Canada's restive Quebec. Monoclonal immigration is new for the United States, and it changes things radically. If at the turn of the 20th century Ellis Island had greeted teeming masses speaking not 50 languages but just, say, German, America might not have enjoyed the same success at assimilation and national unity that it has.

Today's monoclonal linguistic culture is far from hypothetical. Growing rapidly through immigration, it creates large communities—in some places already majorities—so overwhelmingly Spanish speaking that, in time, they may quite naturally demand the rights and official recognition for Spanish that French has in French-speaking Quebec.

That would not be the end of the world—Canada is a decent place—but the beginning of a new one for the United States, a world far more complicated and fraught with division. History has blessed us with all the freedom and advantages of multiculturalism. But it has also blessed us, because of the accident of our origins, with a linguistic unity that brings a critically needed cohesion to a nation as diverse, multiracial and multiethnic as America. Why gratuitously throw away that priceless asset? How mindless to call the desire to retain it "racist."

I speak three languages. My late father spoke nine. When he became a naturalized American in midcentury, it never occurred to him to demand of his new and beneficent land that whenever its government had business with him—tax forms, court proceedings, ballot boxes—that it should be required to communicate in French, his best language, rather than English, his last and relatively weakest.

English is America's national and common language. But that may change over time unless we change our assimilation norms. Making English the official language is the first step toward establishing those norms. "Official" means the language of the government and its institutions. "Official" makes clear our expectations of acculturation. "Official" means that every citizen, upon entering America's most sacred political space, the voting booth, should minimally be able to identify the words *President* and *Vice President* and *county commissioner* and *judge*. The immigrant, of course, has the right to speak whatever he wants. But he must understand that when he comes to the United States, swears allegiance and accepts its bounty, he undertakes to join its civic culture. In English.

Time, June 5, 2006

OF COURSE IT'S A PONZI SCHEME

The Great Social Security Debate, Proposition 1: *Of course it's a Ponzi scheme.*

In a Ponzi scheme, the people who invest early get their money out with dividends. But these dividends don't come from any profitable or productive activity—they consist entirely of money paid in by later participants.

This cannot go on forever because at some point there just aren't enough new investors to support the earlier entrants. Word gets around that there are no profits, just money transferred from new to old. The merry-go-round stops, the scheme collapses and the remaining investors lose everything.

Now, Social Security is a pay-as-you-go program. A current beneficiary isn't receiving the money she paid in years ago. That money is gone. It went to her parents' Social Security check. The money in *her* check is coming from her son's FICA tax today—i.e., her "investment" was paid out years ago to earlier entrants in the system and her current benefits are coming from the "investment" of the new entrants into the system. Pay-as-you-go is the definition of a Ponzi scheme.

So what's the difference? Ponzi schemes are illegal, suggested one of my colleagues on *Inside Washington*.

But this is perfectly irrelevant. Imagine that Charles Ponzi had lived not in Boston but in the lesser parts of Papua New Guinea where the securities and fraud laws were, shall we say, less developed. He runs his same scheme among the locals—give me ("invest") one goat today, I'll give ("return") you two after six full moons—but escapes any legal sanction. Is his legal enterprise any less a Ponzi scheme? Of course not.

So what is the difference?

Proposition 2: *The crucial distinction between a Ponzi scheme and Social Security is that Social Security is mandatory.*

That's why Ponzi schemes always collapse and Social Security has not. When it's mandatory, you've ensured an endless supply of new participants. Indeed, if Charles Ponzi had had the benefit of the law forcing people into his scheme, he'd still be going strong—and a perfect candidate for commissioner of the Social Security Administration.

But there's a catch. Compulsion allows sustainability; it does not guarantee it. Hence . . .

Proposition 3: *Even a mandatory Ponzi scheme such as Social Security can fail if it cannot rustle up enough new entrants.*

You can force young people into Social Security, but if there just aren't enough young people *in existence* to support current beneficiaries, the system will collapse anyway.

When Social Security began making monthly distributions in 1940, there were 160 workers for every senior receiving benefits. In 1950, there were 16.5; today, 3; in 20 years, there will be but 2.

Now, the average senior receives in Social Security about a third of what the average worker makes. Applying that ratio retroactively, this means that in 1940, the average worker had to pay only 0.2% of his salary to sustain the older folks of his time; in 1950, 2%; today, 11%; in 20 years, 17%. This is a staggering sum, considering that it is in addition to all the other taxes he pays to sustain other functions of government, such as Medicare, whose costs are exploding.

The Treasury already steps in and borrows the money required to cover the gap between what workers pay into Social Security and what seniors take out. When young people were plentiful, Social Security produced a surplus. Starting now and for decades to come, it will add to the deficit, increasingly so as the population ages.

Demography is destiny. Which leads directly to Proposition 4: *This is one Ponzi scheme that can be saved by adapting to the new demographics.*

Three easy steps: Change the cost-of-living measure, means-test for richer recipients and, most important, raise the retirement age. The current retirement age is an absurd anachronism. Bismarck arbitrarily chose 70 when he created social insurance in 1889. Clever guy: Life expectancy at the time was under 50.

When Franklin Roosevelt created Social Security, choosing 65 as the eligibility age, life expectancy was 62. Today it is almost 80. FDR wanted to prevent the aged few from suffering destitution in their last remaining years. Social Security was not meant to provide two decades of greens fees for baby boomers.

Of course it's a Ponzi scheme. So what? It's also the most vital, humane and fixable of all social programs. The question for the candidates is: Forget Ponzi—are you going to fix Social Security?

The Washington Post, September 15, 2011

THE CHURCH OF GLOBAL WARMING

I'm not a global warming believer. I'm not a global warming denier. I'm a global warming agnostic who believes instinctively that it can't be very good to pump lots of CO_2 into the atmosphere but is equally convinced that those who presume to know exactly where that leads are talking through their hats.

Predictions of catastrophe depend on models. Models depend on assumptions about complex planetary systems—from ocean currents to cloud formation—that no one fully understands. Which is why the models are inherently flawed and forever changing. The doomsday scenarios posit a cascade of events, each with a certain probability. The multiple improbability of their simultaneous occurrence renders all such predictions entirely speculative.

Yet on the basis of this speculation, environmental activists, attended by compliant scientists and opportunistic politicians, are advocating radical economic and social regulation. "The largest threat to freedom, democracy, the market economy and prosperity," warns Czech president Vaclav Klaus, "is no longer socialism. It is, instead, the ambitious, arrogant, unscrupulous ideology of environmentalism."

If you doubt the arrogance, you haven't seen that *Newsweek* cover story that declared the global warming debate over. Consider: If Newton's laws of motion could, after 200 years of unfailing experimental and experiential confirmation, be overthrown, it requires religious fervor to believe that global warming—infinitely more untested, complex and speculative—is a closed issue.

But declaring it closed has its rewards. It not only dismisses skeptics as the running dogs of reaction, i.e., of Exxon, Cheney and now Klaus. By fiat, it also hugely re-empowers the intellectual left.

For a century, an ambitious, arrogant, unscrupulous knowledge class—social planners, scientists, intellectuals, experts and their left-wing political allies—arrogated to themselves the right to rule either in the name of the oppressed working class (communism) or, in its more benign form, by virtue of their superior expertise in achieving the highest social progress by means of state planning (socialism).

Two decades ago, however, socialism and communism died rudely, then were buried forever by the empirical demonstration of the superiority of market capitalism everywhere from Thatcher's England to Deng's China, where just the partial abolition of socialism lifted more people out of poverty more rapidly than ever in human history.

Just as the ash heap of history beckoned, the intellectual left was handed the ultimate salvation: environmentalism. Now the experts will regulate your life not in the name of the proletariat or Fabian socialism but—even better—in the name of Earth itself.

Environmentalists are Gaia's priests, instructing us in her proper service and casting out those who refuse to genuflect. (See *Newsweek* above.) And having proclaimed the ultimate commandment—carbon chastity—they are preparing the supporting canonical legislation that will tell you how much you can travel, what kind of light you will read by and at what temperature you may set your bedroom thermostat.

Only Monday, a British parliamentary committee proposed that every citizen be required to carry a carbon card that must be presented, under penalty of law, when buying gasoline, taking an airplane or using electricity. The card contains your yearly carbon ration to be drawn down with every purchase, every trip, every swipe.

There's no greater social power than the power to ration. And, other than rationing food, there is no greater instrument of social control than rationing energy, the currency of just about everything one does and uses in an advanced society.

So what does the global warming agnostic propose as an alternative? First, more research—untainted and reliable—to determine (a) whether the carbon footprint of man is or is not lost among the massive natural forces (from sunspot activity to ocean currents) that affect climate and (b) if the human effect is indeed significant, whether the planetary climate system has the homeostatic mechanisms (like the feedback loops in the human body, for example) with which to compensate.

Second, reduce our carbon footprint in the interim by doing the doable, rather than the economically ruinous and socially destructive. The most obvious step is a major move to nuclear power, which to the atmosphere is the cleanest of the clean.

But your would-be masters have foreseen this contingency. The Church of the Environment promulgates secondary dogmas as well. One of these is a strict nuclear taboo.

Rather convenient, is it not? Take this major coal-substituting fix off the table and we will be rationing all the more. Guess who does the rationing.

The Washington Post, May 30, 2008

CHAPTER 9

BODY AND SOUL

THE DUTCH EXAMPLE

In 1991 in the Dutch city of Assen, a perfectly healthy 50-year-old woman asked her doctor to help her die. Her two sons had died, one by suicide, one by cancer. She wanted to join them. After many hours of consultation, Dr. Boudewijn Chabot consented. He was at her side when she swallowed the lethal pills he prescribed for her death.

In Holland, physician-assisted suicide is for all practical purposes legal, but Dr. Chabot was tried anyway because this woman wasn't terminally ill. She wasn't even ill. In fact, she wasn't even psychiatrically ill, a point that at trial Dr. Chabot made in his own defense. She was as lucid as she was inconsolable.

The three-judge court in Assen acquitted Dr. Chabot. So did an appeals court. So did the Dutch Supreme Court. Thus, notes Dr. Herbert Hendin (in his indispensable study of euthanasia in Holland, *Seduced by Death: Doctors, Patients, and the Dutch Cure*), has Holland "legally established mental suffering as a basis for euthanasia."

Why is this important for Americans? Because on Wednesday the U.S. Supreme Court was asked to decide whether physician-assisted suicide should be legal in America, as in Holland. The two cases before the court both involved the terminally ill. But the deployment of these heartrending cases of terminal illness is part of the cunning of the euthanasia advocates. They are pulling heartstrings to get us to open the door. And once the door opens, it opens to everyone, terminally ill or not.

How do we know? At oral arguments on Wednesday, Justice David Souter asked that question in one form or another at least four times: Once you start by allowing euthanasia for the terminally ill, what evidence is there that abuses will follow?

The answer, in a word, is Holland. I'm not even talking here about the thousand cases a year—in the United States that would translate into 20,000 cases a year—of Dutch patients put to death by their doctors without their consent. (Most, by the way, are killed not for reasons of pain but, as the doctors put it, for "low quality of life" or because "all treatment was withdrawn but the patient did not die.") I'm talking here about Dutch doctors helping the suicide of people not terminally ill, not chronically ill, not ill at all but, like our lady of Assen, merely bereft.

Eugene Sutorius, the prominent Dutch attorney who defended Dr. Chabot, said after winning his case: "Euthanasia, which started with terminal illness, has moved to a different plane." And so it must. Why? Because in moving "to a different plane," the Dutch were not being perverse. They were being logical.

By what logical principle should the relief of death be granted only the terminally ill? Such a restriction is itself perverse. After all, the terminally ill face only a brief period of suffering. The chronically ill, or the healthy but bereft—they face a lifetime of agony. Why deny them the relief of a humane exit?

The litigants before the Supreme Court, however, claimed the right to assisted suicide on the grounds not of mercy but of liberty— the autonomy of individuals to determine when and how they will die.

But on what logical grounds can this autonomy be reserved only for the terminally ill? Why not for every mentally competent adult? Wednesday at the Supreme Court, the lawyers for the euthanasia side, Kathryn Tucker and Laurence Tribe, turned somersaults trying to answer the question. Tribe offered a riff on the stages of life—

"life, though it feels continuous to many of us, has certain critical thresholds: birth, marriage, child-bearing. I think death is one of those thresholds." It nearly got him laughed out of court when Justice Scalia cut him off with, "This is lovely philosophy. Where is it in the Constitution?"

Tribe had no answer because there is no answer. If assisted suicide is a right for the terminally ill, there is no argument that can be made to deny it on grounds of mercy or autonomy or nondiscrimination to anyone else who might request it.

That is why the Supreme Court decision in these two cases will be so fateful. That is why euthanasia advocates are so passionate about them. They know this is the beginning of something much larger: nothing less than historic legitimation—through the active, legal, societally blessed participation of the medical profession—of suicide.

In modern society, suicide is no longer punished (denial of burial on church grounds, denial of inheritance to the family). But it is still discouraged. When you see someone on a high ledge ready to jump, you are enjoined by every norm in our society to tackle him and pull him back from the abyss. We are now being asked to become a society where, when the tormented soul on the ledge asks for our help in granting him relief, we oblige him with a push.

They do it in Assen.

The Washington Post, January 10, 1997

Stem Cells and Fairy Tales

After the second presidential debate, in which John Kerry used the word *plan* 24 times, I said on television that Kerry has a plan for everything except curing psoriasis. I should have known there is no parodying Kerry's pandering. It turned out days later that the Kerry campaign has a plan—nay, a promise—to cure *paralysis*. What is the plan? Vote for Kerry.

This is John Edwards on Monday at a rally in Newton, Iowa: "If we do the work that we can do in this country, the work that we will do when John Kerry is president, people like Christopher Reeve are going to walk, get up out of that wheelchair and walk again."

In my 25 years in Washington, I have never seen a more loathsome display of demagoguery. Hope is good. False hope is bad. Deliberately, for personal gain, raising false hope in the catastrophically afflicted is despicable.

Where does one begin to deconstruct this outrage?

First, the inability of the human spinal cord to regenerate is one of the great mysteries of biology. The answer is not remotely around the corner. It could take a generation to unravel. To imply, as Edwards did, that it is imminent if only you elect the right politicians is scandalous.

Second, if the cure for spinal cord injury comes, we have no idea where it will come from. There are many lines of inquiry. Stem cell research is just one of many possibilities, and a very speculative one at that. For 30 years I have heard promises of miracle cures for paralysis (including my own, suffered as a medical student). The last fad, fetal tissue transplants, was thought to be a sure thing. Nothing came of it.

As a doctor by training, I've known better than to believe the hype—and have tried in my own counseling of people with new spinal cord injuries to place the possibility of cure in abeyance. I advise instead to concentrate on making a life (and a very good life it can be) with the hand one is dealt. The greatest enemies of this advice have been the snake-oil salesmen promising a miracle around the corner. I never expected a candidate for vice president to be one of them.

Third, the implication that Christopher Reeve was prevented from getting out of his wheelchair by the Bush stem cell policies is a travesty.

George Bush is the first president to approve federal funding for stem cell research. There are 22 lines of stem cells now available, up from one just two years ago. As Leon Kass, head of the President's Council on Bioethics, has written, there are 3,500 shipments of stem cells waiting for anybody who wants them.

Edwards and Kerry constantly talk of a Bush "ban" on stem cell research. This is false. There is no ban. You want to study stem cells? You get them from the companies that have the cells and apply to the National Institutes of Health for the federal funding.

In his Aug. 7 radio address to the nation, Kerry referred not once but four times to the "ban" on stem cell research instituted by Bush. At the time, Reeve was alive, so not available for posthumous exploitation. But Ronald Reagan was available, having recently died of Alzheimer's.

So what does Kerry do? He begins his radio address with the disgraceful claim that the stem cell "ban" is standing in the way of an Alzheimer's cure.

This is an outright lie. The President's Council on Bioethics, on which I sit, had one of the world's foremost experts on Alzheimer's, Dennis Selkoe from Harvard, give us a lecture on the newest and most promising approaches to solving the Alzheimer's mystery. Selkoe reported remarkable progress in using biochemicals to clear the "plaque" deposits in the brain that lead to Alzheimer's. He ended his presentation without the phrase "stem cells" having passed his lips.

So much for the miracle cure. Ronald D. G. McKay, a stem cell researcher at NIH, has admitted publicly that stem cells as an Alzheimer's cure are a fiction, but that "people need a fairy tale." Kerry and Edwards certainly do. They are shamelessly exploiting this fairy tale, having no doubt been told by their pollsters that stem cells play well politically for them.

Politicians have long promised a chicken in every pot. It is part of the game. It is one thing to promise ethanol subsidies here, dairy price controls there. But to exploit the desperate hopes of desperate people with the promise of Christ-like cures is beyond the pale.

There is no apologizing for Edwards' remark. It is too revealing. There is absolutely nothing the man will not say to get elected.

The Washington Post, October 15, 2004

THE TRUTH ABOUT
END-OF-LIFE COUNSELING

Let's see if we can have a reasoned discussion about end-of-life counseling.

We might start by asking Sarah Palin to leave the room. I've got nothing against her. She's a remarkable political talent. But there are no "death panels" in the Democratic health-care bills, and to say that there are is to debase the debate.

We also have to tell the defenders of the notorious Section 1233 of H.R. 3200 that it is not quite as benign as they pretend. To offer government reimbursement to any doctor who gives end-of-life counseling—whether or not the patient asked for it—is to create an incentive for such a chat.

What do you think such a chat would be like? Do you think the doctor will go on and on about the fantastic new million-dollar high-tech gizmo that can prolong the patient's otherwise hopeless condition for another six months? Or do you think he's going to talk about—as the bill specifically spells out—hospice care and palliative care and other ways of letting go of life?

No, say the defenders. It's just that we want the doctors to talk to you about putting in place a living will and other such instruments. Really? Then consider the actual efficacy of a living will. When you are old, infirm and lying in the ICU with pseudomonas pneumonia and deciding whether to (a) go through the long antibiotic treatment or (b) allow what used to be called "the old man's friend" to take you away, the doctor will ask you *at that time* what you want for yourself—no matter what piece of paper you signed five years earlier.

You are told constantly how very important it is to write your living will years in advance. But the relevant question is what you desire at the end—when facing death—not what you felt sometime in the past when you were hale and hearty and sitting in your lawyer's office barely able to contemplate a life of pain and diminishment.

Well, as pain and diminishment enter your life as you age, your calculations change and your tolerance for suffering increases. In the ICU, you might have a new way of looking at things.

My own living will, which I have always considered more a literary than a legal document, basically says: "I've had some good innings, thank you. If I have anything so much as a hangnail, pull the plug." I've never taken it terribly seriously because unless I'm comatose or demented, they're going to ask me *at the time* whether or not I want to be resuscitated if I go into cardiac arrest. The paper I signed years ago will mean nothing.

And if I'm totally out of it, my family will decide, with little or no reference to my living will. Why? I'll give you an example. When my father was dying, my mother and brother and I had to decide how much treatment to pursue. What was a better way to ascertain my father's wishes: what he checked off on a form one fine summer's day years before being stricken; or what we, who had known him intimately for decades, thought he would want? The answer is obvious.

Except for the demented orphan, the living will is quite beside the point. The one time it really is essential is if you think your fractious family will be only too happy to hasten your demise to get your money. That's what the law is good at—protecting you from murder and theft. But that is a far cry from assuring a peaceful and willed death, which is what most people imagine living wills are about.

So why get Medicare to pay the doctor to do the counseling? Because we know that if this white-coated authority whose chosen vocation is curing and healing is the one opening your mind to hospice and palliative care, we've nudged you ever so slightly toward letting go.

It's not an outrage. It's surely not a death panel. But it is subtle pressure applied by society through your doctor. And when you include it in a health-care reform whose major objective is to bend the cost curve downward, you have to be a fool or a knave to deny that it's intended to gently point the patient in a certain direction, toward the corner of the sickroom where stands a ghostly figure, scythe in hand, offering release.

The Washington Post, August 21, 2009

Mass Murder, Medicalized

What a surprise—that someone who shouts *"Allahu Akbar"* (the "God is great" jihadist battle cry) as he is shooting up a room of American soldiers might have Islamist motives. It certainly was a surprise to the mainstream media, which spent the weekend after the Fort Hood massacre playing down Nidal Hasan's religious beliefs.

"I cringe that he's a Muslim. . . . I think he's probably just a nut case," said *Newsweek*'s Evan Thomas. Some were more adamant. *Time*'s Joe Klein decried "odious attempts by Jewish extremists . . . to argue that the massacre perpetrated by Nidal Hasan was somehow a direct consequence of his Islamic beliefs." While none could match Klein's peculiar *cherchez-le-juif* motif, the popular story line was of an army psychiatrist driven over the edge by terrible stories he had heard from soldiers returning from Iraq and Afghanistan.

They suffered. He listened. He snapped.

Really? What about the doctors and nurses, the counselors and physical therapists at Walter Reed Army Medical Center who every day hear and live with the pain and the suffering of returning soldiers? How many of them then picked up a gun and shot 51 innocents?

And what about civilian psychiatrists—not the Upper West Side therapist treating Woody Allen neurotics, but the thousands of doctors working with hospitalized psychotics—who every day hear not just tales but cries of the most excruciating anguish, of the most unimaginable torment? How many of those doctors commit mass murder?

It's been decades since I practiced psychiatry. Perhaps I missed the epidemic.

But, of course, if the shooter is named Nidal Hasan, who National Public Radio reported had been trying to proselytize doctors and patients, then something must be found. Presto! Secondary post-traumatic stress disorder, a handy invention to allow one to ignore the obvious.

And the perfect moral finesse. Medicalizing mass murder not only exonerates. It turns the murderer into a victim, indeed a sympathetic one. After all, secondary PTSD, for those who believe in it (you won't find it in *DSM-IV-TR*, psychiatry's *Diagnostic and Statistical Manual*), is known as "compassion fatigue." The poor man—pushed over the edge by an excess of sensitivity.

Have we totally lost our moral bearings? Nidal Hasan cold-bloodedly killed 13 innocent people. His business card had his name, his profession, his medical degrees and his occupational identity. U.S. Army? No. "SoA"—Soldier of Allah. In such cases, political correctness is not just an abomination. It's a danger, clear and present.

Consider the army's treatment of Hasan's previous behavior. NPR's Daniel Zwerdling interviewed a Hasan colleague at Walter Reed about a hair-raising grand rounds that Hasan had apparently given. Grand rounds are the most serious academic event at a teaching hospital—attending physicians, residents and students gather for a lecture on an instructive case history or therapeutic finding.

I've been to dozens of these. In fact, I gave one myself on post-traumatic retrograde amnesia—as you can see, these lectures are fairly technical. Not Hasan's. His was an hour-long disquisition on what he called the Koranic view of military service, jihad and war. It included an allegedly authoritative elaboration of the punishments visited upon nonbelievers—consignment to hell, decapitation, having hot oil poured down your throat. This "really freaked a lot of doctors out," reported NPR.

Nor was this the only incident. "The psychiatrist," reported Zwerdling, "said that he was the kind of guy who the staff actually stood around in the hallway saying: Do you think he's a terrorist, or is he just weird?"

Was anything done about this potential danger? Of course not. Who wants to be accused of Islamophobia and prejudice against a colleague's religion?

One must not speak of such things. Not even now. Not even after we know that Hasan was in communication with a notorious Yemen-based jihad propagandist. As late as Tuesday, the *New York Times* was running a story on how returning soldiers at Fort Hood had a high level of violence.

What does such violence have to do with Hasan? He was not a returning soldier. And the soldiers who returned home and shot their wives or fellow soldiers didn't cry *"Allahu Akbar"* as they squeezed the trigger.

The delicacy about the religion in question—condescending, politically correct and deadly—is nothing new. A week after the first (1993) World Trade Center attack, the same *New York Times* ran the following front-page headline about the arrest of one Mohammed Salameh: "Jersey City Man Is Charged in Bombing of Trade Center."

Ah yes, those Jersey men—so resentful of New York, so prone to violence.

The Washington Post, November 13, 2009

THE DOUBLE TRAGEDY OF A STOLEN DEATH

"Dying is easy. Parking is hard." Art Buchwald's little witticism nicely captured his chosen path to a good death: mocking it to the very end. There is great courage and dignity in that, which is why Buchwald's extended good-bye (he died on Jan. 17) earned him such appreciation and admiration. But dying well is also a matter of luck. By unexpectedly living almost a full year after refusing dialysis for kidney failure, Buchwald won himself time to taunt the scythe.

Timing is everything. When former congressman—and distinguished priest and liberal luminary—Robert Drinan died earlier this year, the *Washington Post* published a special appreciation. It ran together with a tribute to another notable who died just one day later: Barbaro. The horse got top billing.

And does anyone remember when Mother Teresa died? The greatest saint of our time died on the frenzied eve of the funeral of the greatest diva of our time, Princess Di. In the popular mind, celebrity trumps virtue every time.

Consider Russian composer Sergei Prokofiev, tormented in life by Stalin, his patron and jailer. Prokofiev had the extraordinary bad luck of dying on the same day as the great man, "ensconcing him forever in the tyrant's shadow," wrote critic Sarah Kaufman of the *Washington Post*, "where he remains branded as a compromised artist."

We should all hope to die well. By that, I don't mean in the classic Greek sense of dying heroically, as in battle. I'm suggesting a much lower standard: just not dying badly. At a minimum, not dying comically—death by banana peel or pratfall or (my favorite, I confess) onstage, like the actor Harold Norman, killed in 1947 during an especially energetic sword fight in the last scene of *Macbeth*.

There is also the particularly unwelcome death that not just ends a life but also undoes it, indeed steals it. The way Kitty Genovese's was stolen. On March 13, 1964, she was repeatedly stabbed for 35 minutes in the street and in the foyer of her apartment building in Queens, New York. Many neighbors heard her scream. Not one helped. When the police eventually arrived, it was much too late. Her death became a sensation, her name a metaphor for urban alienation, her last hour an indictment of the pitiless American city.

I've always been struck by the double injustice of her murder. Not only did the killer cut short her life amid immense terror and suffering, but he defined it. He—a stranger, an intruder—gave her a perverse immortality of a kind she never sought, never expected, never consented to. She surely thought that in her 28 years she had been building a life of joys and loves, struggle and achievement, friendship and fellowship. That and everything else she built her life into were simply swallowed up by the notoriety of her death, a notoriety unchosen and unbidden.

That kind of double death can also result from an act of God. Disease, for example, can not just end your life; if it is exotic and dramatic enough, it can steal your identity as well. Without being consulted, you become an eponym. At least baseball great Lou Gehrig had the time and talent to be remembered for things other than what was generally known as ALS (amyotrophic lateral sclerosis). Ryan White, a teenager when he died in the early years of the AIDS epidemic, did not. He was hastily conscripted as poster boy for the Ryan White Comprehensive AIDS Resource Emergency (CARE) Act—defined by his dying, much like poor Megan Kanka, the little girl murdered by a sex offender in New Jersey, who lives today as Megan's Law.

No one grasps more greedily—and cruelly—the need for agency in death as does the greatest moral monster of our time: the suicide bomber. By choosing not only the time and place but the blood-soaked story that will accompany his death, he seeks to transcend and redeem an otherwise meaningless life. One day you are the alienated and insignificant Mohamed Atta; the next day, September 11, 2001, you join the annals of infamy with all the glory that brings in the darker precincts of humanity. It is the ultimate perversion of the "good death," done for the worst of motives—self-creation through the annihilation of others. People often denounce such suicide attacks as "senseless." On the contrary, they make all too much malevolent sense. There is great power in owning your own death—and even greater power in forever dispossessing your infidel victims of theirs.

Time, March 1, 2007

ESSAY: ON THE ETHICS OF
EMBRYONIC RESEARCH

THE PROBLEM

You were once a single cell. Every one of the 100 trillion cells in your body today is a direct descendant of that zygote, the primordial cell formed by the union of mother's egg and father's sperm. Each one is genetically identical (allowing for copying errors and environmental damage along the way) to that cell. Therefore, if we scraped a cell from, say, the inner lining of your cheek, its DNA would be the same DNA that, years ago in the original zygote, contained the entire plan for creating you and every part of you.

Here is the mystery: Why can the zygote, as it multiplies, produce every different kind of cell in the body—kidney, liver, brain, skin— while the skin cell is destined, however many times it multiplies, to remain skin forever? As the embryo matures, cells become specialized and lose their flexibility and plasticity. Once an adult cell has specialized—differentiated, in scientific lingo—it is stuck forever in that specialty. Skin is skin; kidney is kidney.

Understanding that mystery holds the keys to the kingdom. The Holy Grail of modern biology is regenerative medicine. If we can figure out how to make a specialized adult cell dedifferentiate— unspecialize, i.e., revert way back to the embryonic stage, perhaps even to the original zygotic stage—and then grow it like an embryo under controlled circumstances, we could reproduce for you every kind of tissue or organ you might need. We could create a storehouse of repair parts for your body. And, if we let that dedifferentiated cell develop completely in a woman's uterus, we will have created a copy of you—your clone.

That is the promise and the menace of cloning. It has already been done in sheep, mice, goats, pigs, cows, and now cats and rabbits (though cloning rabbits seems an exercise in biological redundancy). There is no reason in principle why it cannot be done in humans. The question is: Should it be done?

Notice that the cloning question is really two questions: (1) May we grow that dedifferentiated cell all the way into a cloned baby, a copy of you? That is called reproductive cloning. And (2) may we grow that dedifferentiated cell just into the embryonic stage and then mine it for parts, such as stem cells? That is called research cloning.

Reproductive cloning is universally abhorred. In July 2001 the House of Representatives, a fairly good representative of the American people, took up the issue and not a single member defended reproductive cloning. Research cloning, however, is the hard one. Some members were prepared to permit the cloning of the human embryo in order to study and use its component parts, with the proviso that the embryo be destroyed before it grows into a fetus or child. They were a minority, however. Their amendment banning baby-making but permitting research cloning was defeated by 76 votes. On July 31, 2001, a bill outlawing all cloning passed the House decisively.

Within weeks, perhaps days, the Senate will vote on essentially the same alternatives. On this vote will hinge the course of the genetic revolution at whose threshold we now stand.

THE PROMISE

This is how research cloning works. You take a donor egg from a woman, remove its nucleus, and inject the nucleus of, say, a skin cell from another person. It has been shown in animals that by the right manipulation you can trick the egg and the injected nucleus into dedifferentiating—that means giving up all the specialization of the skin cell and returning to its original state as a primordial cell that could become anything in the body.

In other words, this cell becomes totipotent. It becomes the equivalent of the fertilized egg in normal procreation, except that instead of having chromosomes from two people, it has chromosomes from one. This cell then behaves precisely like an embryo. It divides. It develops. At four to seven days, it forms a "blastocyst" consisting of about 100 to 200 cells.

The main objective of research cloning would be to disassemble this blastocyst: pull the stem cells out, grow them in the laboratory, and then try to tease them into becoming specific kinds of cells, say, kidney or heart or brain and so on.

There would be two purposes for doing this: study or cure. You could take a cell from a person with a baffling disease, like Lou Gehrig's, clone it into a blastocyst, pull the stem cells out, and then study them in order to try to understand the biology of the illness. Or you could begin with a cell from a person with Parkinson's or a spinal cord injury, clone it, and tease out the stem cells to develop tissue that you would reinject into the original donor to, in theory, cure the Parkinson's or spinal cord injury. The advantage of using a cloned cell rather than an ordinary stem cell is that, presumably, there would be no tissue rejection. It's your own DNA. The body would recognize it. You'd have a perfect match.

(Research cloning is sometimes called therapeutic cloning, but that is a misleading term. First, because therapy by reinjection is only one of the many uses to which this cloning can be put. Moreover, it is not therapeutic for the clone—indeed, the clone is invariably destroyed in the process—though it may be therapeutic for others. If you donate a kidney to your brother, it would be odd to call *your* operation a therapeutic nephrectomy. It is not. It's a sacrificial nephrectomy.)

The conquest of rejection is one of the principal rationales for research cloning. But there is reason to doubt this claim on scientific grounds. There is some empirical evidence in mice that cloned tissue may be rejected anyway (possibly because a clone contains a small amount of foreign—mitochondrial—DNA derived from the egg into which it was originally injected). Moreover, enormous advances are being made elsewhere in combating tissue rejection. The science of immune rejection is much more mature than the science of cloning. By the time we figure out how to do safe and reliable research cloning, the rejection problem may well be solved. And finally, there are less problematic alternatives—such as adult stem cells—that offer a promising alternative to cloning because they present no problem of tissue rejection and raise none of cloning's moral conundrums.

These scientific considerations raise serious questions about the efficacy of, and thus the need for, research cloning. But there is a stronger case to be made. Even if the scientific objections are swept aside, even if research cloning is as doable and promising as its advocates contend, there are other reasons to pause.

The most obvious is this: Research cloning is an open door to reproductive cloning. Banning the production of cloned babies while permitting the production of cloned embryos makes no sense. If you have factories all around the country producing embryos for research and commerce, it is inevitable that someone will implant one in a woman (or perhaps in some artificial medium in the farther future) and produce a human clone. What then? A law banning reproductive cloning but permitting research cloning would then make it a crime *not* to destroy that fetus—an obvious moral absurdity.

This is an irrefutable point and the reason that many in Congress will vote for the total ban on cloning. Philosophically, however, it is a showstopper. It lets us off too early and too easy. It keeps us from facing the deeper question: Is there anything about research cloning that *in and of itself* makes it morally problematic?

OBJECTION I:
INTRINSIC WORTH

For some people, life begins at conception. And not just life—if life is understood to mean a biologically functioning organism, even a single cell is obviously alive—but personhood. If the first zygotic cell is owed all the legal and moral respect due a person, then there is nothing to talk about. Ensoulment starts with Day One and Cell One, and the idea of taking that cell or its successor cells apart to serve someone else's needs is abhorrent.

This is an argument of great moral force but little intellectual interest. Not because it may not be right but because it is unprovable. It rests on metaphysics. Either you believe it or you don't. The discussion ends there.

I happen not to share this view. I do not believe personhood begins at conception. I do not believe a single cell has the moral or legal standing of a child. This is not to say that I do not stand in awe of the developing embryo, a creation of majestic beauty and mystery. But I stand in equal awe of the Grand Canyon, the spider's web and quantum mechanics. Awe commands wonder, humility, appreciation. It does not command inviolability. I am quite prepared to shatter an atom, take down a spider's web or dam a canyon for electricity. (Though we'd have to be very short on electricity before I'd dam the Grand.)

I do not believe the embryo is entitled to inviolability. But is it entitled to nothing? There is a great distance between inviolability, on the one hand, and mere "thingness," on the other. Many advocates of research cloning see nothing but thingness. That view justifies the most ruthless exploitation of the embryo. That view is dangerous.

Why? Three possible reasons. First, the Brave New World Factor: Research cloning gives man too much power for evil. Second, the Slippery Slope: The habit of embryonic violation is in and of itself dangerous. Violate the blastocyst today and every day, and the practice will inure you to violating the fetus or even the infant tomorrow. Third, Manufacture: The very act of creating embryos for the sole purpose of exploiting and then destroying them will ultimately predispose us to a ruthless utilitarianism about human life itself.

OBJECTION II:
THE BRAVE NEW WORLD FACTOR

The physicists at Los Alamos were not deterred from penetrating, manipulating and splitting uranium atoms on the grounds that uranium atoms possess intrinsic worth that entitled them to inviolability. Yet after the war, many fought to curtail atomic power. They feared the consequences of delivering such unfathomable power—and potential evil—into the hands of fallible human beings. Analogously, one could believe that the cloned blastocyst has little more intrinsic worth than the uranium atom and still be deeply troubled by the manipulation of the blastocyst because of the fearsome power it confers upon humankind.

The issue is leverage. Our knowledge of how to manipulate human genetics (or atomic nuclei) is still primitive. We could never construct ex nihilo a human embryo. It is an unfolding organism of unimaginable complexity that took nature 3 billion years to produce. It might take us less time to build it from scratch, but not much less. By that time, we as a species might have acquired enough wisdom to use it wisely. Instead, the human race in its infancy has stumbled upon a genie infinitely too complicated to create or even fully understand, but understandable enough to command and perhaps even control. And given our demonstrated unwisdom with our other great discovery—atomic power: As we speak, the very worst of humanity is on the threshold of acquiring the most powerful weapons in history—this is a fear and a consideration to be taken very seriously.

For example, female human eggs seriously limit the mass production of cloned embryos. Extracting eggs from women is difficult, expensive and potentially dangerous. The search is on, therefore, for a good alternative. Scientists have begun injecting human nuclei into the egg cells of animals. In 1996, Massachusetts scientists injected a human nucleus with a cow egg. Chinese scientists have fused a human fibroblast with a rabbit egg and have grown the resulting embryo to the blastocyst stage. We have no idea what grotesque results might come from such interspecies clonal experiments.

In October 2000, the first primate containing genes from another species was born—a monkey with a jellyfish gene. In 1995, researchers in Texas produced headless mice. In 1997, researchers in Britain produced headless tadpoles. In theory, headlessness might be useful for organ transplantation. One can envision, in a world in which embryos are routinely manufactured, the production of headless clones—subhuman creatures with usable human organs but no head, no brain, no consciousness to identify them with the human family.

The heart of the problem is this: Nature, through endless evolution, has produced cells with totipotent power. We are about to harness that power for crude human purposes. That should give us pause. Just around the corner lies the logical by-product of such power: human-animal hybrids, partly developed human bodies for use as parts, and other horrors imagined—Huxley's Deltas and Epsilons—and as yet unimagined. This is the Brave New World Factor. Its grounds for objecting to this research are not about the beginnings of life but about the ends; not the origin of these cells but their destiny; not where we took these magnificent cells from but where they are taking us.

OBJECTION III:
THE SLIPPERY SLOPE

The other prudential argument is that once you start tearing apart blastocysts, you get used to tearing apart blastocysts. And whereas now you'd only be doing that at the seven-day stage, when most people would look at this tiny clump of cells on the head of a pin and say it is not inviolable, it is inevitable that some scientist will soon say: Give me just a few more weeks to work with it and I could do wonders.

That will require quite a technological leap because the blastocyst will not develop as a human organism unless implanted in the uterus.

That means that to go beyond that seven-day stage you'd have to implant this human embryo either in an animal uterus or in some fully artificial womb.

Both possibilities may be remote, but they are real. And then we'll have a scientist saying: Give me just a few more months with this embryo, and I'll have actual kidney cells, brain cells, pancreatic cells that I can transplant back into the donor of the clone and cure him. Scientists at Advanced Cell Technology in Massachusetts have already gone past that stage in animals. They have taken cloned cow embryos past the blastocyst stage, taken tissue from the more developed cow fetus and reimplanted it back into the donor animal.

The scientists' plea to do the same in humans will be hard to ignore. Why grow the clone just to the blastocyst stage, destroy it, pull out the inner cell mass, grow stem cells out of that, propagate them in the laboratory and then try chemically or otherwise to tweak them into becoming kidney cells or brain cells or islet cells? This is Rube Goldberg. Why not just allow that beautiful embryonic machine, created by nature and far more sophisticated than our crude techniques, to develop unmolested? Why not let the blastocyst grow into a fetus that possesses the kinds of differentiated tissue that we could then use for curing the donor?

Scientifically, this would make sense. Morally, we will have crossed the line between tearing apart a mere clump of cells and tearing apart a recognizable human fetus. And at that point, it would be an even smaller step to begin carving up seven- and eight-month-old fetuses with more perfectly formed organs to alleviate even more pain and suffering among the living. We will, slowly and by increments, have gone from stem cells to embryo farms to factories with fetuses in various stages of development and humanness, hanging (metaphorically) on meat hooks waiting to be cut open to be used by the already born.

We would all be revolted if a living infant or developed fetus were carved up for parts. Should we build a fence around that possibility by prohibiting any research on even the very earliest embryonic clump of cells? Is the only way to avoid the slide never to mount the slippery slope at all? On this question, I am personally agnostic. If I were utterly convinced that we would never cross the seven-day line, then I would have no objection on these grounds to such research on the inner cell mass of a blastocyst. The question is: Can we be sure? This is not a question of principle; it is a question of prudence. It is almost a question of psychological probability. No one yet knows the answer.

OBJECTION IV:
MANUFACTURE

Note that while, up to now, I have been considering arguments against research cloning, they are all equally applicable to embryonic research done on a normal—i.e., noncloned—embryo. If the question is tearing up the blastocyst, there is no intrinsic moral difference between a two-parented embryo derived from a sperm and an egg and a single-parented embryo derived from a cloned cell. Thus the various arguments against this research—the intrinsic worth of the embryo, the prudential consideration that we might create monsters or the prudential consideration that we might *become* monsters in exploiting post-embryonic forms of human life (fetuses or even children)—are identical to the arguments for and against stem-cell research.

These arguments are serious—serious enough to banish the insouciance of the scientists who consider anyone questioning their work to be a Luddite—yet, in my view, insufficient to justify a legal ban on stem-cell research (as with stem cells from discarded embryos in fertility clinics). I happen not to believe that either personhood or ensoulment occurs at conception. I think we need to be apprehensive about what evil might arise from the power of stem-cell research, but that apprehension alone, while justifying vigilance and regulation, does not justify a ban on the practice. And I believe that given the good that might flow from stem-cell research, we should first test the power of law and custom to enforce the seven-day blastocyst line for embryonic exploitation before assuming that such a line could never hold.

This is why I support stem-cell research (using leftover embryos from fertility clinics) and might support research cloning were it not for one other aspect that is unique to it. In research cloning, the embryo is created with the explicit intention of its eventual destruction. That is a given because not to destroy the embryo would be to produce a cloned child. If you are not permitted to grow the embryo into a child, you are obliged at some point to destroy it.

Deliberately creating embryos for eventual and certain destruction means the launching of an entire industry of embryo manufacture. It means the routinization, the commercialization, the commodification of the human embryo. The bill that would legalize research cloning essentially sanctions, licenses and protects the establishment of a most ghoulish enterprise: the creation of nascent human life for the sole purpose of its exploitation and destruction.

How is this morally different from simply using discarded embryos from in vitro fertilization (IVF) clinics? Some have suggested that it is not, that to oppose research cloning is to oppose IVF and any stem-cell research that comes out of IVF. The claim is made that because in IVF there is a high probability of destruction of the embryo, it is morally equivalent to research cloning. But this is plainly not so. In research cloning there is not a high probability of destruction; there is 100% probability. Because every cloned embryo must be destroyed, it is nothing more than a means to someone else's end.

In IVF, the probability of destruction may be high, but it need not necessarily be. You could have a clinic that produces only a small number of embryos, and we know of many cases of multiple births resulting from multiple embryo implantation. In principle, one could have IVF using only a single embryo and thus involving no deliberate embryo destruction at all. In principle, that is impossible in research cloning.

Furthermore, a cloned embryo is created to be destroyed and used by others. An IVF embryo is created to develop into a child. One cannot disregard intent in determining morality. Embryos are created in IVF to serve reproduction. Embryos are created in research cloning to serve, well, research. If certain IVF embryos were designated as "helper embryos" that would simply aid an anointed embryo in turning into a child, then we would have an analogy to cloning. But, in fact, we don't know which embryo is anointed in IVF. They are all created to have a chance of survival. And they are all equally considered an end.

Critics counter that this ends-and-means argument is really obfuscation, that both procedures make an instrument of the embryo. In cloning, the creation and destruction of the embryo is a means to understanding or curing disease. In IVF, the creation of the embryo is a means of satisfying a couple's need for a child. They are both just means to ends.

But it makes no sense to call an embryo a means to the creation of a child. The creation of a child is the *destiny* of an embryo. To speak of an embryo as a means to creating a child empties the word *means* of content. The embryo in IVF is a stage in the development of a child; it is no more a means than a teenager is a means to the adult he or she later becomes. In contrast, an embryo in research cloning is pure means. Laboratory pure.

And that is where we must draw the line. During the great debate on stem-cell research, a rather broad consensus was reached (among those not committed to "intrinsic worth" rendering all embryos inviolable) that stem-cell research could be morally justified because the embryos destroyed for their possibly curative stem cells were derived from fertility clinics and thus were going to be discarded anyway. It was understood that human embryos should not be created solely for the purpose of being dismembered and then destroyed for the benefit of others. Indeed, when Senator Bill Frist made his impassioned presentation on the floor of the Senate supporting stem-cell research, he included among his conditions a total ban on creating human embryos just to be stem-cell farms.

Where cloning for research takes us decisively beyond stem-cell research is in sanctioning the manufacture of the human embryo. You can try to regulate embryonic research to prohibit the creation of Brave New World monsters; you can build fences on the slippery slope, regulating how many days you may grow an embryo for research; but once you countenance the very creation of human embryos for no other purpose than for their parts, you have crossed a moral frontier.

Research cloning is the ultimate in conferring thingness upon the human embryo. It is the ultimate in desensitization. And as such, it threatens whatever other fences and safeguards we might erect around embryonic research. The problem, one could almost say, is not what cloning does to the embryo, but what it does to us. Except that, once cloning has changed us, it will inevitably enable further assaults on human dignity. Creating a human embryo just so it can be used and then destroyed undermines the very foundation of the moral prudence that informs the entire enterprise of genetic research: the idea that, while a human embryo may not be a person, it is not nothing. Because if it is nothing, then everything is permitted. And if everything is permitted, then there are no fences, no safeguards, no bottom.

The New Republic, April 29, 2002

Adapted from the author's essay published in "Human Cloning and Human Dignity: An Ethical Inquiry," a report of the President's Council on Bioethics, Washington, D.C., July 2002.

CHAPTER 10

MAN AND GOD

THE REAL MESSAGE OF CREATIONISM

When the Kansas Board of Education voted recently to eliminate evolution from the state science curriculum, the sophisticates had quite a yuk. One editorial cartoon had an ape reclining in a tree, telling his mate, "We are descended from the Kansas School Board." The decision has been widely derided as a sign of resurgent Middle American obscurantism, a throwback to the Scopes "monkey trial."

Well, to begin with, the Scopes trial is not the great fable the rather fictional *Inherit the Wind* made it out to be. The instigators of the trial were not bluenosed know-nothings wanting to persecute some poor teacher for teaching evolution. They were officials of the American Civil Liberties Union so eager for a test case to overturn a new Tennessee law prohibiting the teaching of evolution that they promised to pay the expenses of the prosecution! The ACLU advertised for a volunteer and found one John Scopes, football coach and science teacher, willing to take the rap. He later said he was not sure whether he'd ever even taught any evolution.

Son of Scopes is not quite what it seems either. The twist in the modern saga is the injection of creationism as the scientific alternative to evolution. So, let's be plain. Creationism, which presents Genesis as literally and historically true, is not science. It is faith crudely disguised as science.

It is not science because it violates the central scientific canon that a theory must, at least in principle, be disprovable. Creationism is not. Any evidence that might be brought—fossil, geological, astronomical—to contradict the idea that the universe is no more than 6,000 years old is simply explained away as false clues deliberately created by God at the very beginning.

Why? To test our faith? To make fools of modern science? This is hardly even good religion. God may be mysterious, but he is certainly not malicious. And who but a malicious deity would have peppered the universe with endless phony artifacts designed to confound human reason?

Creationism has no part in the science curriculum of any serious country. Still, I see no reason why biblical creation could not to be taught in the schools—not as science, of course, but for its mythic grandeur and moral dimensions. If we can assign the *Iliad* and the *Odyssey*, we certainly ought to be able to assign Genesis.

But can we? There's the rub. It is very risky to assign Genesis today. The ACLU might sue. Ever since the Supreme Court decision of 1963 barring prayer from the public schools, any attempt to import not just prayer but biblical studies, religious tenets and the like into the schools is liable to end up in court.

That is why the Kansas school board decision on evolution is so significant. Not because Kansas is the beginning of a creationist wave—as science, creationism is too fundamentally frivolous and evolution too intellectually powerful—but because the Kansas decision is an important cultural indicator.

It represents the reaction of people of faith to the fact that all legitimate expressions of that faith in their children's public schooling are blocked by the new secular ethos. In a society in which it is unconstitutional to post the Ten Commandments in school, creationism is a back door to religion, brought in under the guise—the absurd yet constitutionally permitted guise—of science.

This pedagogic sleight of hand, by the way, did not originate with religious folk. Secularists have for years been using biology instruction as a back door for inculcating *their* values. A sex-ed class on the proper placement of a condom is more than instruction in reproductive mechanics. It is a seminar—unacknowledged and tacit but nonetheless powerful—on permissible sexual mores.

Religion—invaluable in America's founding, forming and flowering—deserves a place in the schools. Indeed, it had that place for almost 200 years. A healthy country would teach its children evolution—and the Ten Commandments. The reason that Kansas is going to have precisely the opposite—the worst of both worlds—is not because Kansans are primitives but because a religious people has tried to bring the fruits of faith, the teachings and higher values of religion, into the schools and been stymied.

The result is a kind of perverse Law of Conservation of Faith. Block all teaching of religious ideas? Okay, we'll sneak them in through biology.

This is nutty. It has kids looking for God in all the wrong places. For the purposes of a pluralist society, the Bible is not about fact. It is about values. If we were a bit more tolerant about allowing the teaching of biblical values as ethics, we'd find far less pressure for the teaching of biblical fables as science.

Time, November 22, 1999

GOD VS. CAESAR

In 1857, Chief Justice Roger B. Taney handed down the Dred Scott decision upholding and extending slavery. Taney's opinion was, it is generally agreed, "the worst constitutional decision of the 19th century" (the words are Robert Bork's). Yet there is a curious and little known fact about Judge Taney. More than 30 years earlier he had freed his own slaves. Today, therefore, we would say that while he was "personally" opposed to slavery he did not want to "impose" his views on others.

The Taney contradiction—privately opposed to but publicly tolerant of some widespread social practice—is the preferred position on abortion of pro-choice Catholic politicians today. This view does not sit well with the Catholic Church. It holds, quite plausibly, that the Taney position is as morally incoherent when applied to abortion as it was when applied to slavery.

At the center of the debate is New York governor Mario Cuomo, who personally believes that abortion is sinful but as governor has supported no abortion restrictions, indeed has advocated state funding of abortions for poor women. For this, one New York bishop has said that Cuomo is in danger of losing his soul and going to hell. Another New York bishop barred Cuomo from any church function in his diocese (later modified as a ban on discussing abortion at any church function). Cardinal John O'Connor of New York has backed up his two bishops, continuing the argument he started with Cuomo in 1984 about whether it is possible to have it both ways, Taney-like, on abortion.

Liberal commentary has rushed into the breach to argue not so much the merits of the issue but the propriety of the bishops' getting involved in the first place. The claim is that these clerical admonitions constitute an assault on the separation of church and state, a denial of religious pluralism, a form of religious tyranny. These prelates, writes Arthur Schlesinger, "seem to be doing their best to verify the fears long cherished by . . . a succession of anti-Catholic demagogues that the Roman Catholic Church would try to overrule the American democratic process."

This idea of overruling is outright nonsense. The Catholic Church is in no way compelling anyone to do anything, let alone interdicting the will of the majority. If it does manage to persuade a majority of Americans that abortion is wrong and ought to be banned, how is that different from any other group persuading a democratic majority to ban, say, polygamy or drug-taking?

As for the "threats" to Cuomo, they are entirely self-imposed. The force of the bishops' moral appeal derives exclusively from Cuomo's own freely offered profession that "I am a governor, I am a Democrat, but I am a Catholic first—my soul is more important to me than my body." Unlike President Kennedy, Cuomo is more than a nominal Catholic. His profession of faith makes him subject, voluntarily, to the teachings of his church. For the church to which he voluntarily adheres to repeat to him its position on abortion, as well as the penalties the church believes are due those who violate it, is hardly an act of imposition. It is an act of religious teaching that Cuomo himself invites when he says, "I—and many others like me—are eager for enlightenment, eager to learn new and better ways to manifest respect for the deep reverence for life that is our religion and our instinct."

The other liberal complaint is that since the Catholic position on abortion is religiously derived, if it ultimately becomes law, that constitutes an imposition of religion. This argument is nonsense too. Under American concepts of political pluralism, it makes no difference from where a belief comes. Whether it comes from church teaching, inner conviction or some trash novel, the legitimacy of any belief rests ultimately on its content, not on its origin. It is absurd to hold that a pro-abortion position derived from, say, Paul Ehrlich's overpopulation doomsday scenario is legitimate but an anti-abortion position derived from scripture is a violation of the First Amendment. The provenance of an opinion has nothing to do with its legitimacy as a contender for public opinion—and as candidate for becoming public law.

Moreover, it is particularly hypocritical for liberals to profess outrage at the involvement of the Catholic Church in this political issue, when only a few decades ago much of the civil rights and antiwar movements was run out of the churches. When Martin Luther King Jr. invoked scripture in support of his vision of racial equality and when the American Catholic Bishops invoked Augustine in their pastoral letter opposing nuclear deterrence, not a liberal in the land protested that this constituted a violation of the separation of church and state.

To his credit, Cuomo does not join the liberal chorus in denying the prelates a right to speak as they wish on abortion. Not so for many of his backers. When it suits their political purposes they approve, they demand, that the church stand up for right. When it does not suit them, Schlesinger comes forward to warn darkly that such outspokenness risks stirring up anti-Catholic bigotry.

On the face of it, I would say that it already has.

The Washington Post, March 23, 1990

BODY WORSHIP

For a long time—from the counterculture of the 1960s until, well, yesterday—it was pretty easy to tell conservatives from liberals. Conservatives were the folks who told you how to live your personal life. Liberals were the ones who told government and everybody else to lay off and leave you to your own space.

Conservatives went around promoting virtue and regulating vice: pornography, drugs, illegitimacy and the like. Liberals stood for self-expression and autonomy. The "right to choose" is quintessentially liberal, whether it be abortion or euthanasia or, as they say today, whatever.

Then came tobacco. Liberals, who had developed a 39-year reputation for being soft on drugs and crime and polymorphous perversities that even Freud could not have imagined, all of a sudden became caped crusaders. When it comes to smoking, they are bluenose prohibitionists.

True, the anti-smoking campaign has broad support. But liberal Democrats have labored mightily to make it their cause. It began with the famous hearings chaired by the pre-eminent California liberal, Henry Waxman, at which tobacco executives were made to line up and swear that nicotine is not addictive. Its apotheosis was Al Gore's 1996 convention speech with its lachrymose retelling of his sister's death and his solemn pledge "until I draw my last breath" to "pour my heart and soul" into carrying on the anti-smoking fight. War on tobacco would be the liberals' cause.

This seems odd. Liberals have always looked down their noses at any kind of prohibition, whether it was alcohol in the '20s or abortion today. They're for choice, are they not? But as smokers are chased out of their offices and banished from polite society, what little pro-smoking resistance there is comes from the right: from libertarians, from free-market conservatives and from traditionalists lamenting the state's forced extirpation of a venerable and private habit.

So what happened to liberals? My theory is this: Liberals have watched, astonished, as for decades conservatives thrived politically by showing concern for individual behavior. After years of deriding conservative "moralizing," liberals now are playing catch-up. Hence, for example, their slavish, often comical, adoption of the language of "family values."

Conservatives have made a political career out of showing concern for the soul. Liberals cannot quite bring themselves to support state regulation of the soul. (Indeed, by "family values," they mean not sexual morality but subsidized child care and a living wage.) So they have come up with their own alternative: not care for the soul but care for the body. Health is their religion, the body their temple.

Laissez-faire? No concern about right behavior? Not us, say the liberals. We too believe in virtue. No smoking! And that's just for starters. We are going to teach your kids safe sex, take Alar off their apples, feed them yogurt and broccoli for lunch and, for the ride home, lash them to their safety seats in cars with mandatory air bags.

Who says we don't care? Our motto: A healthy (multicultural) mind in a healthy body. Call it pagan if you like. We call it prudent.

Now, if you have any doubts about the liberals' newfound religion, take in a sex-education class at your kids' school. The hour is not devoted to biblical/Victorian/traditional morality. Sure, the kids are taught do's and don'ts. It's just that the don'ts are not actions that damn your eternal soul but behaviors that doom your precious body.

The core of the modern sexual code is disease prevention. The reason your little ones are taught the proper placement of a condom over a banana is to protect them from sexually transmitted diseases. With AIDS as a foil, sex-ed is not a form of moral education. It is a branch of hygiene.

As are the other liberal virtues. Like the mania for health foods. It feeds a nutritional fanaticism and fastidiousness that make Islamic and Jewish dietary prohibitions look positively, well, liberal. In elite society, thinness is not just attractive but virtuous, a sign of self-denial and strength of character. Fatness is not just unaesthetic; it is a moral failing. Temptation no longer comes in the form of the devil. It comes in the form of dessert.

This cult of the body is the perfect successor to the culture of narcissism of the Me Generation. Its genius is to take the stigma out of self-love and turn it into virtue. Its beauty is to take health and hygiene—perfectly good things, mind you—and make them a religion. In a political era demanding more public displays of piety and morality, liberals can now enthusiastically declare: We got religion too.

The Washington Post, September 26, 1997

CHERNENKO AND THE CASE
AGAINST ATHEISM

There have been many arguments made against atheism. The medieval philosophers divined a variety of proofs of God's existence. Aquinas had five. But the argument from Motion or the argument from Contingency is not the kind of thing we moderns talk about anymore. So for the definitive modern case against atheism, I suggest a radically modern experience: Watch a Soviet funeral.

I do it all the time. As Soviet state funerals have become regular events—Chernenko's was the third revival in 28 months of Death of a Helmsman—I have become a regular viewer. They mesmerize me, in a horrible sort of way. It is not just the music, the numbing repetition of Chopin's funeral march, but the massive, stone-cold setting. The Lenin Mausoleum, the focus of the ceremonies, is a model of socialist brutalist architecture. Cathedrals also remind us of the smallness of man, but poignantly, by comparing him to God. The Lenin Mausoleum has nothing to compare man to but its own squat vastness. The comparison is mocking.

Then there are the speeches, a jangle of empty phrases. Chernenko was eulogized for his "links to the masses," his "party principledness," his achievements in the fields of "ideology and propaganda." Was there a man behind—underneath—all this socialist realism? If so, not a word about him. The utter effacement of the person by the party reminded me of a response spokesman Vladimir Posner gave a few weeks ago to an American's question about Chernenko's health. "In this country," he said, annoyed, "the private lives of the leadership . . . are not subject to discussion." It was as if he had been asked to confirm Chernenko's sexual preferences, not his existence.

Finally, and to me most chilling, was the open casket displaying Chernenko's (and Andropov's and Brezhnev's) powdered body drowning in a sea of fresh flowers. The open bier is a mere variation on a communist theme: the mummification of the great leader. In believing cultures, where there is some sense of a surviving soul, this pathetic attachment to the body is unnecessary. In fact, it is discouraged. In the great monotheistic religions, the redeemer—Moses, Jesus, Mohammed—has no earthly resting place at all. In the great materialist religions, Soviet and Chinese communism, the resting place of the redeemer, indeed his frozen body, becomes a shrine. The result is the ultimate grotesquerie: after death, a fantastic assertion of the final primacy of man, even after he has become nothing more than embalmer's clay.

It turns out I'm not the only one to have been chilled by the barrenness of the Soviet way of death. Shortly after his return from Brezhnev's funeral, Vice President George Bush talked about what had struck him the most. He mentioned the austere pageantry, the goose-stepping soldiers, the music, "the body being drawn through Red Square—not, incidentally, by horses, but behind an armored personnel carrier. But what struck me most . . . was the fact that from start to finish there was not one mention of—God."

Why should that matter? you ask. After all, many of us are as tepid in our belief as the proverbial Unitarian who believes that there is, at most, one God. What is wrong with a society that believes in none? The usual answer follows the lines of an observation by Arthur Schlesinger (and others) that "the declining faith in the supernatural has been accompanied by the rise of the monstrous totalitarian creeds of the 20th century." Or as Chesterton put it, "The trouble when people stop believing in God is not that they thereafter believe in nothing; it is that they thereafter believe in anything." In this century, "anything" has included Hitler, Stalin and Mao, authors of the great genocidal madnesses of our time.

However, as the robotic orderliness of Chernenko's funeral demonstrates, the Soviet system is now anything but mad. The "monstrous creeds" have changed. Totalitarianism was once a truly crusading faith: messianic, hopeful, mobilized and marching. Now it is dead, burnt out. Classical totalitarianism has been replaced by what philosopher Michael Walzer calls "failed totalitarianism," the cold, empty shell of the old madness: The zeal, the energy, the purpose are gone; only bureaucracy and cynicism remain. Today the Soviet system, the greatest of all the failed totalitarianisms, no longer believes in "anything." It now believes in nothing. A nothing on eerie display at Wednesday's funeral.

Chesterton's case against atheism is that even if it is (God forbid) true, it is dangerous. Three hours of watching Chernenko placed in the Kremlin wall convinces me otherwise. The case against a public life bereft of all spirituality rests less on its danger than on its utter desolation.

The Washington Post, March 15, 1985

CHAPTER 11

MEMORY AND MONUMENTS

SWEET LAND OF LIBERTY

U niquely among the capitals of the world, Washington's monumental core pays homage to the word. The glory of the Jefferson Memorial is not the Founder's statue but, carved in stone
around him, his words on religious freedom, inalienable rights and
sacred honor. At the Lincoln Memorial, one cannot but be moved
by the eyes and grave bearing of the martyred president, but even
more moving are the surrounding words: the sublime cadences of the
Second Inaugural and the Gettysburg Address, both in their entirety.
(Lincoln's gift for concision helps. Castro, of the eight-hour speeches,
could not be so memorialized.)

Other capitals celebrate the *gloria* and *fortuna* of victory. No Arch
of Triumph here. True, in the last few decades the Mall has added
Vietnam and Korean memorials. But these are hardly glorifications
of battle. They are melancholy meditations upon wars of sorrow. The
very newest addition, the World War II memorial, is jarring and
deeply out of place precisely because its massive and pointless wreath-
bearing Teutonic columns represent European triumphalism disfig-
uring the heart of a Mall heretofore dedicated to the power and glory
of ideas.

But Washington has a second distinction, more subtle and even
more telling about the nature of America: its many public statues to

foreign liberators. I'm not talking about the statues of Churchill and Lafayette, great allies and participants in America's own epic struggles against tyranny. Everybody celebrates friends. I'm talking about the liberators who had nothing to do with us. Walk a couple of blocks from Dupont Circle at the heart of commercial Washington, and you come upon a tiny plaza graced by Gandhi, with walking stick. And perhaps 100 yards from him, within shouting distance, stands Tomas Masaryk, the great Czech patriot and statesman.

Masaryk, in formal dress and aristocratic demeanor, has nothing in common with the robed, slightly bent Gandhi with whom he shares the street—except that they were both great liberators—and except that they are honored by Americans precisely for their devotion to freedom.

Farther up the avenue stands Robert Emmet, the Irish revolutionary, while one block to the west of Masaryk looms a massive monument to a Ukrainian poet and patriot, Taras Shevchenko. And then gracing the avenues near the Mall are the Americans: great statues to Central and South American liberators, not just Juárez and Bolívar but even the more obscure, such as General José Artigas, father of modern Uruguay.

Discount if you will (as fashionable anti-Americanism does) the Statue of Liberty as ostentatious self-advertising or perhaps a relic of an earlier, more pure America. But as you walk the streets of Washington, it is harder to discount America's quiet homage to foreign liberators—statues built decades apart without self-consciousness and without any larger architectural (let alone political) plan. They have but one thing in common: They share America's devotion to liberty. Liberty not just here but everywhere. Indeed, liberty for its own sake.

America has long proclaimed this principle, but in the post-9/11 era, it has pursued it with unusual zeal and determination. Much of the world hears America declare the spread of freedom the centerpiece of its foreign policy and insists nonetheless that America's costly sacrifices in Iraq and even Afghanistan are nothing more than classic imperialism in search of dominion, oil, pipelines or whatever such commodity most devalues America's exertions. The overwhelming majority of Americans refuse to believe that. Whatever their misgivings about the cost and wisdom of these wars, they know how deep and authentic is the American devotion to liberty.

Many around the world find such sentiments and the accompanying declarations hard to credit. Europeans, in particular, with their long tradition of realpolitik, cannot conceive of a Great Power actually believing such hopeless idealism.

The skepticism is misplaced. It is not just that brave American soldiers die to permit Iraqis and Afghans to vote for the first time in their lives. There is evidence closer to home and of older pedigree. The skeptics might take a stroll through America's other great capital. Up New York's Sixth Avenue with its series of seven sculptures to Latin American leaders, culminating at Central Park with magnificent statues of Bolívar, Martí and San Martín. To Washington Square Park, where they will find the Italian revolutionary Garibaldi, while his more republican counterpart, Mazzini, resides along West Drive not very far from Lajos Kossuth, now of Riverside Drive, hero of the Hungarian revolution of 1848.

This is not for show. It is from the heart, the heart of a people conceived in liberty and still believing in liberty. How can they not? It is written in stone all around them.

The Washington Post, November 25, 2005

HOLOCAUST MUSEUM

I have long been uneasy about the idea of a Holocaust museum in Washington. If there is be to a showcase of the Jewish experience in the heart of America, why must it be the Holocaust? Why should Jews, a people with such an epic tradition, present themselves to America solely as victims of the greatest crime in history? The Jew as victim: Is this really what we want the visitor from Montana, who may not have met a Jew in his life, to carry home with him?

It was with these reservations that I visited the United States Holocaust Memorial Museum that was dedicated yesterday in Washington. The museum changed my mind.

Beginning with James Freed's severe, demanding building, it is a masterpiece. In the East Building of the National Gallery, the absence of right angles is a pleasant geometrical conceit; in the Holocaust Museum, the acute unforgiving angles, the sharp forced turns, are a powerful pedagogical device. This is the architecture of forced marches, of mechanized cruelty, of industrialized death. The building's texture of raw steel and brick and granite gives the feel of a factory, but its calculated irrationalities—cracked lines, dead ends, blotted windows, narrowing staircases—imply a machinery of derangement.

The details of that derangement are the subject of the permanent exhibit, three harrowing floors that take you step by step from the rise of Hitler in 1933 through the destruction of European Jewry 12 years later. Long before you reach the ovens of Majdanek, the shoes of Auschwitz, you feel you have had enough. But there is no escape, until the liberation at the end of the three floors and the emergence into a Hall of Remembrance, a stark, sky-lit hexagon, a chamber of reflection after a journey through absolute evil.

I know more about the Holocaust than I want to. Here I learned even more. I had, for example, made errors of scale. The cattle cars packed with Jews headed for death—you walk through one that took the doomed to Treblinka—were much smaller than I had imagined; the gas chambers of Auschwitz—a huge diorama depicts the actual machinery of scientific mass murder—were much larger. These were not rooms of death. These were auditoria of death. They took hundreds, thousands at a time for asphyxiation. I had imagined dozens.

Yet one of the triumphs of the museum is that it rises above numbers. It contains, for example, a three-story tower of photographs taken over a half century by the Jewish inhabitants of the village of Ejszyszki. Pictures of ordinary, flourishing life: a jaunty skater, a naughty smoker, bathers, lovers, mothers, cantors. These are the faces of the Jews of Ejszyszki, 3,500 in 1939.

A brief notation nearly buried in the wall text informs the visitor what he had feared upon entering this gallery of vibrant life. That in two days, Sept. 25 and 26, 1941, the Nazis and their Lithuanian collaborators herded and shot the Jews of Ejszyszki, leaving it forever Judenrein.

We return to the perennial problem of Holocaust remembrance: presenting Jews as victims. Does the Holocaust Museum solve it? No. But with the success (if one is permitted to use such a word in such a context) of the museum—its fidelity, its subtlety, its power—the problem loses its urgency.

Yes, dwelling on the Holocaust has its price. But a museum so miraculously executed is worth the price. Yes, the Holocaust is but one part of the Jewish experience. But it is a monumental part, and perishable. As this generation passes, the memory of the Holocaust will fade. This museum—immovable, irrefutable—will do much to guard the memory.

And it will do so not just by what it says and how well it says it but where it says it. The Hall of Remembrance has at each of its six corners a narrow vertical window. Through one you can see the Washington Monument, through another the Jefferson Memorial. The juxtaposition is not just redemptive. It is reassuring. The angels of democracy stand watch on this temple of evil. It is as if only in the heart of the world's most tolerant and most powerful democracy can such terrible testimony be safely contained. Only here will it remain secure and unmolested for the instruction of future generations.

Hitler boasted that his Reich would last 1,000 years. One has the feeling that in this building it will. One has the feeling that here the film (taken by the Nazis themselves) of the machine-gunning of the innocents of one Jewish town will run night and day until the end of time. Here, in such a building, in such a place, infamy will achieve the immortality to which it aspired.

Yes, there are Holocaust memorials in Poland and elsewhere. But these are not to be trusted. Who knows what Europe, birthplace of the Nazi plague, will one day say of or do with these monuments. There were anti-Jewish pogroms in Poland right after World War II, as if Hitler's job needed finishing.

Yes, there is a memorial in Israel. One might say that Israel itself is a memorial to the Holocaust. But there will be those in generations to come who will not trust the testimony of Jews.

With this building, America bears witness. The liberators have returned to finish the job. First rescue, then remembrance. Bless them.

The Washington Post, April 23, 1993

SACRILEGE AT GROUND ZERO

A place is made sacred by a widespread belief that it was visited by the miraculous or the transcendent (Lourdes, the Temple Mount), by the presence there once of great nobility and sacrifice (Gettysburg), or by the blood of martyrs and the indescribable suffering of the innocent (Auschwitz).

When we speak of Ground Zero as hallowed ground, what we mean is that it belongs to those who suffered and died there—and that such ownership obliges us, the living, to preserve the dignity and memory of the place, never allowing it to be forgotten, trivialized or misappropriated.

That's why Disney's 1993 proposal to build an American history theme park near Manassas Battlefield was defeated by a broad coalition that feared vulgarization of the Civil War (and that was wiser than me; at the time I obtusely saw little harm in the venture). It's why the commercial viewing tower built right on the border of Gettysburg was taken down by the Park Service. It's why, while no one objects to Japanese cultural centers, the idea of putting one up at Pearl Harbor would be offensive.

And why Pope John Paul II ordered the Carmelite nuns to leave the convent they had established at Auschwitz. He was in no way devaluing their heartfelt mission to pray for the souls of the dead. He was teaching them a lesson in respect: This is not your place; it belongs to others. However pure your voice, better to let silence reign.

Even New York mayor Michael Bloomberg, who denounced opponents of the proposed 15-story mosque and Islamic center near Ground Zero as tramplers on religious freedom, asked the mosque organizers "to show some special sensitivity to the situation." Yet, as columnist Rich Lowry pointedly noted, the government has no business telling churches how to conduct their business, shape their message or show "special sensitivity" to anyone about anything.

Bloomberg was thereby inadvertently conceding the claim of those he excoriates for opposing the mosque, namely that Ground Zero is indeed unlike any other place and therefore unique criteria govern what can be done there.

Bloomberg's implication is clear: If the proposed mosque were controlled by "insensitive" Islamist radicals either excusing or celebrating 9/11, he would not support its construction.

But then, why not? By the mayor's own expansive view of religious freedom, by what right do we dictate the message of any mosque? Moreover, as a practical matter, there's no guarantee that this couldn't happen in the future. Religious institutions in this country are autonomous. Who is to say that the mosque won't one day hire an Anwar al-Awlaki—spiritual mentor to the Fort Hood shooter and the Christmas Day bomber, and onetime imam at the Virginia mosque attended by two of the 9/11 terrorists?

An al-Awlaki preaching in Virginia is a security problem. An al-Awlaki preaching at Ground Zero is a sacrilege. Or would the mayor then step in—violating the same First Amendment he grandiosely pretends to protect from mosque opponents—and exercise a veto over the mosque's clergy?

Location matters. Especially this location. Ground Zero is the site of the greatest mass murder in American history—perpetrated by Muslims of a particular Islamist orthodoxy in whose cause they died and in whose name they killed.

Of course that strain represents only a minority of Muslims. Islam is no more intrinsically Islamist than present-day Germany is Nazi—yet despite contemporary Germany's innocence, no German of goodwill would even think of proposing a German cultural center at, say, Treblinka.

Which makes you wonder about the goodwill behind Imam Feisal Abdul Rauf's proposal. This is a man who has called U.S. policy "an accessory to the crime" of 9/11 and, when recently asked whether Hamas is a terrorist organization, replied, "I'm not a politician . . . . The issue of terrorism is a very complex question."

America is a free country where you can build whatever you want—but not anywhere. That's why we have zoning laws. No liquor store near a school, no strip malls where they offend local sensibilities and, if your house doesn't meet community architectural codes, you cannot build at all.

These restrictions are for reasons of aesthetics. Others are for more profound reasons of common decency and respect for the sacred. No commercial tower over Gettysburg, no convent at Auschwitz—and no mosque at Ground Zero.

Build it anywhere but there.

The governor of New York offered to help find land to build the mosque elsewhere. A mosque really seeking to build bridges, Rauf's ostensible hope for the structure, would accept the offer.

The Washington Post, August 13, 2010

FDR: THE DIGNITY OF DENIAL

Even as President Clinton officially opened the Franklin Roose-velt memorial last Friday in Washington, the great controversy raged: The memorial contains no statue of FDR in a wheel-chair. Should it?

The arguments pro and con are by now well known. One side points out that when a man has over 35,000 photographs taken of him and exactly two show him in a wheelchair, we can fairly conclude that he was intent upon concealing his disability. How odd, then, to honor a man by portraying him precisely opposite to the way he wanted to be seen.

The other side argues that Roosevelt was merely reflecting the prejudices of his time. He needed to hide his disability to achieve high office. Had he lived today, he would wear his wheels proudly.

However, the whole debate seems to miss the point. The very question of what Roosevelt would have wanted makes no sense. It depends on which Roosevelt. If the real Roosevelt, president of the United States, 1933–45, the answer is obvious: He would not—he did not—want his "splendid deception" undone.

And if by Roosevelt we mean Roosevelt today, i.e., a Roosevelt who had absorbed all the self-revelatory cultural conventions of our time, well then, of course he would bare everything. He would go on *Oprah*, indeed not just in a wheelchair but hand in hand with Lucy Mercer.

The point is not what some imaginary FDR would want, a question both indeterminate and unanswerable. The point is: Which of these competing ideals—the restraint and reticence of the historical FDR vs. the self-revelation and display of today's politicians that we would impute to a contemporary FDR—do we want to honor in a great national monument?

I vote for reticence. The current statue—FDR in his wooden

kitchen chair with casters, a great cape hiding the tiny wheels from all but the most observant visitor—captures perfectly Roosevelt's cloaking of his disability. At a time when our politicians are "stricken with self-pity and given to sniveling" (to quote Mary McGrory), what a balm is Roosevelt's attitude of defiant and dignified denial.

This is an age in which both the speaker of the House and the president of the United States cannot resist, in dramatic televised addresses, making pointed reference to their latest bereavement. This is an age in which the vice president, in consecutive convention speeches, makes lachrymose use, first, of a son's accident, then of a sister's death. (Noted one mordant wit: At this rate, his wife had better not walk near any plateglass windows.) In such an age, we can use the example of a man who through four presidential terms dealt with the agony of a nation while keeping his own agonies to himself.

In an age in which every celebrity finds it necessary to bare his soul and open her closet, we need a monument to a man who would have disdained such displays. Why, even poor Bob Dole found himself going up and down America for months talking about how reluctant he was to talk about the war injuries he could not stop talking about.

Such is the style of the '90s. Fine. But who dares argue that it can match Roosevelt's for nobility? It is not just that we have no right to impose our sensibility on Roosevelt. We should be ashamed to.

Leave Roosevelt out of a wheelchair. But not by saying, condescendingly: Well, he lived in a benighted time; let's make a concession to the attitudes he had to accommodate. After all, Roosevelt's deception did not reflect the attitudes just of his constituents. It reflected his own attitude to his disability. It is not just that he never discussed his paralysis with the voters. He never discussed it with his mother.

The critics say that to fail to portray FDR in a wheelchair is to give in to his false—i.e., nonmodern—consciousness about disability. On the contrary. It is to celebrate his ethos of bold denial.

Denial is not in great favor today. It is considered unhealthy, an almost cowardly psychic constriction. The mantra today is that all must be dealt with, talked out, coped with, opened up, faced squarely.

This may work for some. But it has become something of a religion. And if its priests are so correct about the joys of catharsis and the perils of denial, how do they explain how the champion denier of our century, Franklin Roosevelt, lived such a splendid life?

Roosevelt's denial of his disability was more than just a denial of crushing adversity, more than a jaunty, smiling, damn-the-torpedoes refusal to dwell upon—indeed, fully acknowledge—his physical reality. It was a denial of self, a strange notion for us living in this confessional age when self—self-exploration, self-expression, self-love—is paramount. Roosevelt's life had a grand outer directedness. He was not searching for the inner Franklin. He was reaching for a new America. It was the outer Franklin he cultivated, and it is that Franklin, the one who saved his country, that we honor and remember.

At a time like ours, when every cultural cue is an incitement to self-revelation, we can use a solitary monument to reticence. Leave FDR as he is.

Time, May 12, 1997

MARTIN LUTHER KING IN WORD AND STONE

It is one of the enduring mysteries of American history—so near-providential as to give the most hardened atheist pause—that it should have produced, at every hinge point, great men who matched the moment. A roiling, revolutionary 18th-century British colony gives birth to the greatest cohort of political thinkers ever: Jefferson, Adams, Madison, Hamilton, Washington, Franklin, Jay. The crisis of the 19th century brings forth Lincoln; the 20th, FDR.

Equally miraculous is Martin Luther King Jr. Black America's righteous revolt against a century of post-emancipation oppression could have gone in many bitter and destructive directions. It did not. This was largely the work of one man's leadership, moral imagination and strategic genius. He turned his own deeply Christian belief that "unearned suffering is redemptive" into a creed of nonviolence that he carved into America's political consciousness. The result was not just racial liberation but national redemption.

Such an achievement, such a life, deserves a monument alongside the other miracles of our history—Lincoln, Jefferson and FDR—which is precisely where stands the new Martin Luther King Jr. Memorial. It opened Monday on the Tidal Basin, adjacent to Roosevelt's seven acres, directly across from Jefferson's temple, and bisecting the invisible cartographic line connecting the memorials for Jefferson and Lincoln, authors of America's first two births of freedom, whose promises awaited fulfillment by King.

The new King memorial has its flaws, most notably its much-debated central element, the massive 30-foot stone carving of a standing, arms crossed, somewhat stern King. The criticism has centered on origins: The statue was made in China by a Chinese artist. The problem, however, is not ethnicity but sensibility. Lei Yixin, who receives a lifetime government stipend, has created 150 public monuments in the People's Republic, including several of Chairman Mao.

It shows. His flat, rigid, socialist realist King does not do justice to the supremely nuanced, creative, humane soul of its subject.

The artistic deficiencies, however, are trumped by placement. You enter the memorial through a narrow passageway, emerging onto a breathtaking opening to the Tidal Basin, a tranquil, tree-lined oasis with Jefferson at the far shore. Here stands King gazing across to the Promised Land—promised by that very same Jefferson—but whose shores King himself was never to reach. You are standing at America's Mount Nebo. You cannot but be deeply moved.

Behind the prophet, guarding him, is an arc of short quotations chiseled in granite. This is in keeping with that glorious feature of Washington's monumental core—the homage to words (rather than images of conquest and glory, as in so many other capitals), as befits a nation founded on an idea.

The choice of King quotations is not without problems, however. There are 14 quotes, but in no discernible order, chronological or thematic. None are taken from the "I Have a Dream" speech for understandable reasons of pedagogical redundancy. Nevertheless, some of the quotes are simply undistinguished, capturing none of the cadence and poetry of King's considerable canon.

More troubling, however, is the philosophical narrowness. The citations dwell almost exclusively on the universalist element of King's thought—exhortations, for example, that "our loyalties must transcend our race, our tribe, our class and our nation; and this means we must develop a world perspective," and "every nation must now develop an overriding loyalty to mankind as a whole in order to preserve the best in their individual societies."

Transcending all forms of sectarianism to achieve a common humanity was, of course, a major element of King's thought. But it was not the only one. Missing is any sense of King's Americanness. Indeed, the word *America* appears only once, and only in the context of stating his opposition to the Vietnam War. Yet as King himself insisted, his dream was "deeply rooted in the American dream." He consciously rooted civil rights in the American story, not just for tactical reasons of enlisting whites in the struggle but because he deeply believed that his movement, while fiercely adversarial, was quintessentially American, indeed a profound vindication of the American creed.

And yet, however much one wishes for a more balanced representation of King's own creed, there is no denying the power of this memorial. You must experience it. In the heart of the nation's capital, King now literally takes his place in the American pantheon, the only non-president to be so honored. As of Aug. 22, 2011, there is no room for anyone more on the shores of the Tidal Basin. This is as it should be.

The Washington Post, August 25, 2011

COLLECTIVE GUILT,
COLLECTIVE RESPONSIBILITY

No matter where you stand in the debate over the German cemetery at Bitburg—should President Reagan visit or should he not—everyone from Chancellor Helmut Kohl to Elie Wiesel seems to agree that there is, or ought to be, no such thing as collective responsibility. As Wiesel said in his White House address, "I do not believe in collective guilt nor in collective responsibility. Only the killers are guilty."

Can that be true? To start with, it is not the view of the common law. If you rob a bank and shoot the teller, you are not the only person guilty of murder. So is your unarmed accomplice. And the driver of the getaway car. In short, anyone who knowingly joined the criminal enterprise. The law spreads wide the net of guilt in order to express a moral truth: When you join a killing enterprise your private moral scruples do not limit your guilt. You may not be a killer, but if you sign up with killers, you are party to the deed.

In fact, Wiesel's own argument against the Bitburg visit rests (correctly) on the idea of collective guilt. Wiesel implored the president not to go because of "the presence of SS graves." He did not inquire into the individual deeds of these SS men. He did not need to. To be a member of the SS is enough. Did any of these men pull the trigger at Malmedy, where the Waffen SS murdered 71 American POWs? Or at Oradour, where they murdered 642 Frenchmen? Or was it their comrades? It hardly matters. These crimes would simply compound the guilt; to be a member of the SS is guilt enough. When you join the most monstrous of killing organizations, when you carry its seal, you become responsible for its crimes.

The collective guilt of the German Army is of a different order. The SS was designed to kill, the Wehrmacht to defend the killers and conquer at their command. This does not make the ordinary German soldier a mass murderer. But that said, he does not become the moral equivalent of, say, an American soldier. Between mass murder and ordinary soldierhood lies a vast moral no-man's-land, and in that no-man's-land lies Bitburg. Soldiers who die defending a regime of incomprehensible criminality are not criminals, but they bear—let us be charitable—a taint. (Which is why even without the SS, Bitburg's dead are far down any list of those deserving to be graced by the presence of an American president.) A soldier cannot totally divorce himself from his cause.

When Lord Mountbatten died, he left instructions that the Japanese not be invited to his funeral. He could not forgive the way they had treated his men as prisoners in Southeast Asia during the war. Now, certainly only those Japanese who tortured his men were torturers. But just as certainly, the nation that produced these torturers and produced the war in which the tortures took place bears some taint. Not enough, by any means, to warrant a trial. But enough, certainly, to warrant exclusion from a funeral.

We apply the same logic of collective guilt (and measured response) to white South Africans. Why, after all, are they banned from civilized international life (such as sports), if not for the feeling that by acquiescing to apartheid, they bear some guilt—for which ostracism is not too disproportionate a penalty.

But what about those with no conceivable connection to a historical crime? Two-thirds of Germans today, Helmut Kohl likes to remind us, are too young to remember the war. Surely they do not bear collective responsibility for Germany's past.

Surely they do. They bear, of course, no guilt. But they bear responsibility. The distinction is important.

Ask yourself: None of us was around when treaties were made and broken with the Indians a hundred years ago; we bear no guilt; are we absolved of responsibility to make redress today for the sins of our fathers?

I wasn't born when Japanese-Americans were interned during

World War II. If Congress decides to apologize or to compensate the victims with my tax dollars (Sen. Spark Matsunaga introduced the resolution yesterday), will I have suffered an injustice?

I think not. The point is this. There is such a thing as a corporate identity. My American identity entitles me to certain corporate privileges: life, liberty, happiness pursued, columns uncensored. These benefits I receive wholly undeserved. They are mine by accident of birth. So are America's debts. I cannot claim one and disdain the other.

During the centuries of slavery in America, my ancestors were being chased by unfriendly authorities across Eastern Europe. I feel, and bear, no guilt for the plight of blacks. But America's life is longer than mine. America has sins, and obligations that flow from those sins. To be American today is to share in those obligations.

Or are my children going to default on Treasury bonds issued today on the grounds that they were not yet born when these collective obligations were incurred?

It is good politics around V-E Day to deny the notion of collective responsibility. Only, it is nonsense. Collective responsibility is an elementary principle of national life. It is not just that without that principle there would be no national apologies such as that proposed by Matsunaga or war reparations such as those given by democratic Germany to Nazi Germany's victims. There would be no bond market.

The Washington Post, May 3, 1985

PART THREE

HISTORICAL

CHAPTER 12

THE JEWISH QUESTION, AGAIN

THOSE TROUBLESOME JEWS

The world is outraged at Israel's blockade of Gaza. Turkey denounces its illegality, inhumanity, barbarity, etc. The usual UN suspects, Third World and European, join in. The Obama administration dithers.

But as Leslie Gelb, former president of the Council on Foreign Relations, writes, the blockade is not just perfectly rational, it is perfectly legal. Gaza under Hamas is a self-declared enemy of Israel—a declaration backed up by more than 4,000 rockets fired at Israeli civilian territory. Yet having pledged itself to unceasing belligerency, Hamas claims victimhood when Israel imposes a blockade to prevent Hamas from arming itself with still more rockets.

In World War II, with full international legality, the United States blockaded Germany and Japan. And during the October 1962 missile crisis, we blockaded ("quarantined") Cuba. Arms-bearing Russian ships headed to Cuba turned back because the Soviets knew that the U.S. Navy would either board them or sink them. Yet Israel is accused of international criminality for doing precisely what John Kennedy did: impose a naval blockade to prevent a hostile state from acquiring lethal weaponry.

Oh, but weren't the Gaza-bound ships on a mission of humanitarian relief? No. Otherwise they would have accepted Israel's offer

to bring their supplies to an Israeli port, be inspected for military
matériel and have the rest trucked by Israel into Gaza—as every week
10,000 tons of food, medicine and other humanitarian supplies are
sent by Israel to Gaza.

Why was the offer refused? Because, as organizer Greta Berlin
admitted, the flotilla was not about humanitarian relief but about
breaking the blockade, i.e., ending Israel's inspection regime, which
would mean unlimited shipping into Gaza and thus the unlimited
arming of Hamas.

Israel has already twice intercepted ships laden with Iranian arms
destined for Hezbollah and Gaza. What country would allow that?

But even more important, why did Israel even have to resort to
blockade? Because blockade is Israel's fallback as the world systematically de-legitimizes its traditional ways of defending itself—forward
and active defense.

(1) *Forward defense:* As a small, densely populated country surrounded by hostile states, Israel had, for its first half-century, adopted
forward defense—fighting wars on enemy territory (such as the Sinai
and Golan Heights) rather than its own.

Where possible (Sinai, for example), Israel has traded territory for
peace. But where peace offers were refused, Israel retained the territory as a protective buffer zone. Thus Israel retained a small strip of
southern Lebanon to protect the villages of northern Israel. And it
took many losses in Gaza, rather than expose Israeli border towns to
Palestinian terror attacks. It is for the same reason America wages a
grinding war in Afghanistan: You fight them there, so you don't have
to fight them here.

But under overwhelming outside pressure, Israel gave it up. The
Israelis were told the occupations were not just illegal but at the root
of the anti-Israel insurgencies—and therefore withdrawal, by remov-
ing the cause, would bring peace.

Land for peace. Remember? Well, during the past decade, Israel
gave the land—evacuating South Lebanon in 2000 and Gaza in 2005.
What did it get? An intensification of belligerency, heavy militariza-

tion of the enemy side, multiple kidnappings, cross-border attacks and, from Gaza, years of unrelenting rocket attack.

(2) *Active defense:* Israel then had to switch to active defense—military action to disrupt, dismantle and defeat (to borrow President Obama's description of our campaign against the Taliban and al-Qaeda) the newly armed terrorist mini-states established in southern Lebanon and Gaza after Israel withdrew.

The result? The Lebanon war of 2006 and Gaza operation of 2008–09. They were met with yet another avalanche of opprobrium and calumny by the same international community that had demanded the land-for-peace Israeli withdrawals in the first place. Worse, the UN Goldstone report, which essentially criminalized Israel's defensive operation in Gaza while whitewashing the *casus belli*—the preceding and unprovoked Hamas rocket war—effectively de-legitimized any active Israeli defense against its self-declared terror enemies.

(3) *Passive defense:* Without forward or active defense, Israel is left with but the most passive and benign of all defenses—a blockade to simply prevent enemy rearmament. Yet, as we speak, this too is headed for international de-legitimation. Even the United States is now moving toward having it abolished.

But, if none of these is permissible, what's left?

Ah, but that's the point. It's the point understood by the blockade-busting flotilla of useful idiots and terror sympathizers, by the Turkish front organization that funded it, by the automatic anti-Israel Third World chorus at the United Nations, and by the supine Europeans who've had quite enough of the Jewish problem.

What's left? Nothing. The whole point of this relentless international campaign is to deprive Israel of *any* legitimate form of self-defense. Why, just last week, the Obama administration joined the jackals, and reversed four decades of U.S. practice, by signing on to a consensus document that singles out Israel's possession of nuclear weapons—thus de-legitimizing Israel's very last line of defense: deterrence.

The world is tired of these troublesome Jews, 6 million hard by the Mediterranean, refusing every invitation to national suicide. For which they are relentlessly demonized, ghettoized and constrained from defending themselves, even as the more committed anti-Zionists—Iranian in particular—openly prepare a more final solution.

The Washington Post, June 4, 2010

LAND WITHOUT PEACE

While diplomatically inconvenient for the Western powers, Palestinian Authority president Mahmoud Abbas' attempt to get the United Nations to unilaterally declare a Palestinian state has elicited widespread sympathy. After all, what choice did he have? According to the accepted narrative, Middle East peace is made impossible by a hard-line Likud-led Israel that refuses to accept a Palestinian state and continues to build settlements.

It is remarkable how this gross inversion of the truth has become conventional wisdom. In fact, Benjamin Netanyahu brought his Likud-led coalition to open recognition of a Palestinian state, thereby creating Israel's first national consensus for a two-state solution. He is also the only prime minister to agree to a settlement freeze—10 months—something no Labor or Kadima government has ever done.

To which Abbas responded by boycotting the talks for nine months, showing up in the 10th, then walking out when the freeze expired. Last week he reiterated that he will continue to boycott peace talks unless Israel gives up—in advance—claim to any territory beyond the 1967 lines. Meaning, for example, that the Jewish Quarter in Jerusalem is Palestinian territory. This is not just absurd. It violates every prior peace agreement. They all stipulate that such demands are to be the *subject* of negotiations, not their precondition.

Abbas unwaveringly insists on the so-called "right of return," which would demographically destroy Israel by swamping it with millions of Arabs, thereby turning the world's only Jewish state into the world's 23rd Arab state. And he has repeatedly declared, as recently as last week in New York: "We shall not recognize a Jewish state."

Nor is this new. It is perfectly consistent with the long history of Palestinian rejectionism. Consider:

- Camp David, 2000. At a U.S.-sponsored summit, Prime Minister Ehud Barak offers Yasser Arafat a Palestinian state on the West Bank and Gaza—and, astonishingly, the previously inconceivable division of Jerusalem. Arafat refuses. And makes no counteroffer, thereby demonstrating his unseriousness about making *any* deal. Instead, within two months, he launches a savage terror war that kills a thousand Israelis.

- Taba, 2001. An even sweeter deal—the Clinton Parameters—is offered. Arafat walks away again.
- Israel, 2008. Prime Minister Ehud Olmert makes the ultimate capitulation to Palestinian demands—100% of the West Bank (with land swaps), Palestinian statehood, the division of Jerusalem with the Muslim parts becoming the capital of the new Palestine. And incredibly, he offers to turn over the city's holy places, including the Western Wall—Judaism's most sacred site, its Kaaba—to an international body on which sit Jordan and Saudi Arabia.

Did Abbas accept? Of course not. If he had, the conflict would be over and Palestine would already be a member of the United Nations.

This is not ancient history. All three peace talks occurred over the past decade. And every one completely contradicts the current mindless narrative of Israeli "intransigence" as the obstacle to peace.

Settlements? Every settlement remaining within the new Palestine would be destroyed and emptied, precisely as happened in Gaza.

So why did the Palestinians say no? Because saying yes would have required them to sign a final peace agreement that accepted a Jewish state on what they consider the Muslim patrimony.

The key word here is *final*. The Palestinians are quite prepared to sign interim agreements, like Oslo. Framework agreements, like Annapolis. Cease-fires, like the 1949 armistice. Anything but a final deal. Anything but a final peace. Anything but a treaty that ends the conflict once and for all—while leaving a Jewish state still standing.

After all, why did Abbas go to the United Nations last week? For nearly half a century, the United States has pursued a Middle East settlement on the basis of the formula of land for peace. Land for peace produced the Israel-Egypt peace of 1979 and the Israel-Jordan peace of 1994. Israel has offered the Palestinians land for peace three times since. And been refused every time.

Why? For exactly the same reason Abbas went to the United Nations last week: to get land *without* peace. Sovereignty with no reciprocal recognition of a Jewish state. Statehood without negotiations. An independent Palestine in a continued state of war with Israel.

Israel gave up land without peace in South Lebanon in 2000 and, in return, received war—the Lebanon war of 2006—and 50,000 Hezbollah missiles now targeted on the Israeli homeland. In 2005, Israel gave up land without peace in Gaza, and again was rewarded with war—and constant rocket attack from an openly genocidal Palestinian mini-state.

Israel is prepared to give up land, but never again without peace. A final peace. Which is exactly what every Palestinian leader from Haj Amin al-Husseini to Yasser Arafat to Mahmoud Abbas has refused to accept. Which is why, regardless of who is governing Israel, there has never been peace. Territorial disputes are solvable; existential conflicts are not.

Land for peace, yes. Land without peace is nothing but an invitation to national suicide.

The Washington Post, September 29, 2011

BORAT THE FEARFUL

B orat is many things: a sidesplitting triumph of slapstick and scatology, a runaway moneymaker and budding franchise, the worst thing to happen to Kazakhstan since the Mongol hordes and, as columnist David Brooks astutely points out, a supreme display of elite snobbery reveling in the humiliation of the hoaxed hillbilly.

But it is one thing more, something Brooks alluded to in passing but that requires at least one elaboration: an unintentionally revealing demonstration of the unfortunate attitude many liberal Jews have toward working-class American Christians, especially evangelicals.

You know the shtick. Borat goes around America making antisemitic remarks in order to elicit a nodding antisemitic response. And with enough liquor and cajoling, he succeeds. In the most notorious such scene (on *Da Ali G Show*, where the character was born), Borat sings "Throw the Jew Down the Well" in an Arizona bar as the local rubes join in.

Sacha Baron Cohen, the creator of *Borat*, revealed his purpose for doing that in a rare out-of-character interview he granted *Rolling Stone* in part to counter charges that he was promoting antisemitism. On the face of it, this would be odd, given that Cohen is himself a Sabbath-observing Jew. His defense is that he is using Borat's antisemitism as a "tool" to expose it in others. And that his Arizona bar stunt revealed, if not antisemitism, then "indifference" to antisemitism. And that, he maintains, was the path to the Holocaust.

Whoaaaa. Does he really believe such rubbish? Can a man that smart (Cambridge, investment banker and now brilliant filmmaker) really believe that indifference to antisemitism and the road to the Holocaust are to be found in a country-and-western bar in Tucson?

Of all the gin joints in all the towns in all the world.

With antisemitism reemerging in Europe and rampant in the Islamic world; with Iran acquiring the ultimate weapon of genocide and proclaiming its intention to wipe out the world's largest Jewish community (Israel); with America and, in particular, its Christian evangelicals the only remaining Gentile constituency anywhere willing to defend that besieged Jewish outpost—is the American heartland really the locus of antisemitism? Is this the one place to go to find it?

In Venezuela, Hugo Chávez says that the "descendants of the same ones that crucified Christ" have "taken possession of all the wealth in the world." Just this month, Tehran hosted an international festival of Holocaust cartoons featuring enough hooked noses and horns to give Goebbels a posthumous smile. Throughout the Islamic world, newspapers and television, schoolbooks and sermons are filled with the most vile antisemitism.

Baron Cohen could easily have found what he seeks closer to home. He is, after all, from Europe, where synagogues are torched and cemeteries desecrated in a revival of antisemitism—not "indifference" to but active—unseen since the Holocaust. Where a Jew is singled out for torture and death by French-African thugs. Where a leading Norwegian intellectual—*et tu*, Norway?—mocks "God's Chosen People" ("We laugh at this people's capriciousness and weep at its misdeeds") and calls for the destruction of Israel, the "state founded . . . on the ruins of an archaic national and warlike religion."

Yet, amid this gathering darkness, an alarming number of liberal Jews are seized with the notion that the real threat lurks deep in the hearts of American Protestants, most specifically southern evangelicals. Some fear that their children are going to be converted; others, that below the surface lies a pogrom waiting to happen; still others, that the evangelicals will take power in Washington and enact their own sharia law.

This is all quite crazy. America is the most welcoming, religiously tolerant, philo-semitic country in the world. No nation since Cyrus the Great's Persia has done more for the Jews. And its reward is to be exposed as latently antisemitic by an itinerant Jew looking for laughs and, he solemnly assures us, for the path to the Holocaust?

Look. It is very hard to be a Jew today, particularly in Baron Cohen's Europe, where Jew-baiting is once again becoming acceptable. But it is a sign of the disorientation of a distressed and confused people that we should find it so difficult to distinguish our friends from our enemies.

The Washington Post, November 24, 2006

JUDGING ISRAEL

Jews are news. It is an axiom of journalism. An indispensable axiom, too, because it is otherwise impossible to explain why the deeds and misdeeds of dot-on-the-map Israel get an absurdly disproportionate amount of news coverage around the world. If you are trying to guess how much coverage any Middle East event received, and you are permitted but one question, the best question you can ask about the event is: Were there any Jews in the vicinity? The paradigmatic case is the page in the *International Herald Tribune* that devoted seven of its eight columns to the Palestinian uprising. Among the headlines: "Israeli Soldier Shot to Death; Palestinian Toll Rises to 96." The eighth column carried a report that 5,000 Kurds died in an Iraqi gas attack.

Whatever the reason, it is a fact that the world is far more interested in what happens to Jews than to Kurds. It is perfectly legitimate, therefore, for journalists to give the former more play. But that makes it all the more incumbent to be fair in deciding how to play it.

How should Israel be judged? Specifically: Should Israel be judged by the moral standards of its neighborhood or by the standards of the West?

The answer, unequivocally, is: the standards of the West. But the issue is far more complicated than it appears.

The first complication is that although the neighborhood standard ought not to be Israel's, it cannot be ignored when judging Israel. Why? It is plain that compared with the way its neighbors treat protest, prisoners and opposition in general, Israel is a beacon of human rights. The salient words are Hama, the town where Syria dealt with an Islamic uprising by killing perhaps 20,000 people in two weeks and then paving the dead over; and Black September (1970), during which enlightened Jordan dealt with its Palestinian intifada by killing at least 2,500 Palestinians in ten days, a toll that the Israeli intifada would need ten years to match.

Any moral judgment must take into account the alternative. Israel cannot stand alone, and if it is abandoned by its friends for not meeting Western standards of morality, it will die. What will replace it? The neighbors: Syria, Jordan, the PLO, Hamas, Islamic Jihad, Ahmed Jabril, Abu Nidal (if he is still around) or some combination of these—an outcome that will induce acute nostalgia for Israel's human-rights record.

Any moral judgment that refuses to consider the alternative is merely irresponsible. That is why Israel's moral neighborhood is important. It is not just the neighborhood, it is the alternative and, if Israel perishes, the future. It is morally absurd, therefore, to reject Israel for failing to meet Western standards of human rights when the consequence of that rejection is to consign the region to neighbors with considerably less regard for human rights.

Nevertheless, Israel cannot be judged by the moral standards of the neighborhood. It is part of the West. It bases much of its appeal to Western support on shared values, among which is a respect for human rights. The standard for Israel must be Western standards.

But what exactly does "Western standards" mean? Here we come to complication No. 2. There is not a single Western standard, there are two: what we demand of Western countries at peace and what we demand of Western countries at war. It strains not just fairness but also logic to ask Israel, which has known only war for its 40 years' existence, to act like a Western country at peace.

The only fair standard is this one: How have the Western democracies reacted in similar conditions of war, crisis and insurrection? The morally relevant comparison is not with an American police force reacting to violent riots, say, in downtown Detroit. (Though even by this standard—the standard of America's response to the urban riots of the '60s—Israel's handling of the intifada has been measured.) The relevant comparison is with Western democracies at war: to, say, the

U.S. during the Civil War, the British in Mandatory Palestine, the French in Algeria.

Last fall Anthony Lewis excoriated Israel for putting down a tax revolt in the town of Beit Sahour. He wrote: "Suppose the people of some small American town decided to protest federal government policy by withholding their taxes. The government responded by sending in the Army. . . . Unthinkable? Of course it is in this country. But it is happening in another . . . Israel."

Middle East scholar Clinton Bailey tried to point out just how false this analogy is. Protesting federal government policy? The West Bank is not Selma. Palestinians are not demanding service at the lunch counter. They demand a flag and an army. This is insurrection for independence. They are part of a movement whose covenant explicitly declares its mission to be the abolition of the State of Israel.

Bailey tried manfully for the better analogy. It required him to posit (1) a pre-glasnost Soviet Union, (2) a communist Mexico demanding the return of "occupied Mexican" territory lost in the Mexican War (Texas, New Mexico, Arizona, Utah, Nevada and California) and (3) insurrection by former Mexicans living in these territories demanding secession from the Union. Then imagine, Bailey continued, that the insurrectionists, supported and financed by Mexico and other communist states in Latin America, obstruct communications; attack civilians and police with stones and firebombs; kill former Mexicans holding U.S. government jobs ("collaborators") and then begin a tax revolt. Now you have the correct analogy. Would the U.S., like Israel, then send in the army? Of course.

But even this analogy falls flat because it is simply impossible to imagine an America in a position of conflict and vulnerability analogous to Israel's. America's condition is so radically different, so far from the brink. Yet when Western countries have been in conditions approximating Israel's, when they have faced comparable rebellions, they have acted not very differently.

We do not even have to go back to Lincoln's Civil War suspension of habeas corpus, let alone Sherman's march through Georgia. Consider that during the last Palestinian intifada, the Arab Revolt of 1936–39, the British were in charge of Palestine. They put down the revolt "without mercy, without qualms," writes Middle East scholar Fouad Ajami. Entire villages were razed. More than 3,000 Palestinians were killed. In 1939 alone, the British hanged 109. (Israel has no death penalty.)

French conduct during the Algerian war was noted for its indiscriminate violence and systematic use of torture. In comparison, Israeli behavior has been positively restrained. And yet Israel faces a far greater threat. All the Algerians wanted, after all, was independence. They were not threatening the extinction of France. If Israel had the same assurance as France that its existence was in no way threatened by its enemies, the whole Arab-Israeli conflict could have been resolved decades ago.

Or consider more contemporary democracies. A year ago, when rioting broke out in Venezuela over government-imposed price increases, more than 300 were killed in less than one week. In 1984 the army of democratic India attacked rebellious Sikhs in the Golden Temple, killing 300 in one day. And yet these democracies were not remotely as threatened as Israel. Venezuela was threatened with disorder; India, at worst, with secession. The Sikhs have never pledged themselves to throw India into the sea.

"Israel," opined the *Economist,* "cannot in fairness test itself against a standard set by China and Algeria while still claiming to be part of the West." This argument, heard all the time, is a phony. Israel asks to be judged by the standard not of China and Algeria but of Britain and France, of Venezuela and India. By that standard, the standard of democracies facing similar disorders, Israel's behavior has been measured and restrained.

Yet Israel has been treated as if this were not true. The thrust of the reporting and, in particular, the commentary is that Israel has failed dismally to meet Western standards, that it has been particularly barbaric in its treatment of the Palestinian uprising. No other country is repeatedly subjected to Nazi analogies. In no other country is the death or deportation of a single rioter the subject (as it was for the first year of the intifada, before it became a media bore) of front-page news, of emergency Security Council meetings, of full-page ads in the *New York Times*, of pained editorials about Israel's lost soul, etc., etc.

Why is that so? Why is it that of Israel a standard of behavior is demanded that is not just higher than its neighbors', not just equal to that of the West, but in fact far higher than that of any Western country in similar circumstances? Why the double standard?

For most, the double standard is unconscious. Critics simply assume it appropriate to compare Israel with a secure and peaceful America. They ignore the fact that there are two kinds of Western standards and that fairness dictates subjecting Israel to the standard of a Western country at war.

But other critics openly demand higher behavior from the Jewish state than from other states. Why? Jews, it is said, have a long history of oppression. They thus have a special vocation to avoid oppressing others. This dictates a higher standard in dealing with others.

Note that this reasoning is applied only to Jews. When other people suffer—Vietnamese, Algerians, Palestinians, the French Maquis—they are usually allowed a grace period during which they are judged by a somewhat lower standard. The victims are, rightly or wrongly (in my view, wrongly), morally indulged. A kind of moral affirmative action applies. We are asked to understand the former victims' barbarities because of how they themselves suffered. There has, for example, been little attention to and less commentary on the 150 Palestinians lynched by other Palestinians during the intifada. How many know that this year as many Palestinians have died at the hands of Palestinians as at the hands of Israelis?

With Jews, that kind of reasoning is reversed: Jewish suffering does not entitle them to more leeway in trying to prevent a repetition of their tragedy, but to less. Their suffering requires them, uniquely among the world's sufferers, to bend over backward in dealing with their enemies.

Sometimes it seems as if Jews are entitled to protection and equal moral consideration only insofar as they remain victims. Oriana Fallaci once said plaintively to Ariel Sharon, "You are no more the nation of the great dream, the country for which we cried." Indeed not. In establishing a Jewish state, the Jewish people made a collective decision no longer to be cried for. They chose to become actors in history and not its objects. Historical actors commit misdeeds and should be judged like all nation-states when they commit them. It is perverse to argue that because this particular nation-state is made up of people who have suffered the greatest crime in modern history, they, more than any other people on earth, have a special obligation to be delicate with those who would bring down on them yet another national catastrophe.

That is a double standard. What does double standard mean? To call it a higher standard is simply a euphemism. That makes it sound like a compliment. In fact, it is a weapon. If I hold you to a higher standard of morality than others, I am saying that I am prepared to denounce you for things I would never denounce anyone else for.

If I were to make this kind of judgment about people of color—say, if I demanded that blacks meet a higher standard in their dealings with others—that would be called racism.

Let's invent an example. Imagine a journalistic series on cleanliness in neighborhoods. A city newspaper studies a white neighborhood and a black neighborhood and finds that while both are messy, the black neighborhood is cleaner. But week in, week out, the paper runs front-page stories comparing the garbage and graffiti in the black neighborhood to the pristine loveliness of Switzerland—then chips in an op-ed piece deploring, more in sadness than in anger, the irony that blacks, who for so long had degradation imposed on them, should now impose degradation on themselves.

Something is wrong here. To denounce blacks for misdemeanors that we overlook in whites—that is a double standard. It is not a compliment. It is racism.

The conscious deployment of a double standard directed at the Jewish state and at no other state in the world, the willingness systematically to condemn the Jewish state for things others are not condemned for—this is not a higher standard. It is a discriminatory standard. And discrimination against Jews has a name too. The word for it is antisemitism.

Time, February 26, 1990

ESSAY: ZIONISM AND THE
FATE OF THE JEWS

I. A SMALL NATION

Milan Kundera once defined a small nation as "one whose very existence may be put in question at any moment; a small nation can disappear, and it knows it."

The United States is not a small nation. Neither is Japan. Or France. These nations may suffer defeats. They may even be occupied. But they cannot disappear. Kundera's Czechoslovakia could—and once did. Prewar Czechoslovakia is the paradigmatic small nation: a liberal democracy created in the ashes of war by a world determined to let little nations live free; threatened by the covetousness and sheer mass of a rising neighbor; compromised fatally by a West grown weary "of a quarrel in a far-away country between people of whom we know nothing"; left truncated and defenseless, succumbing finally to conquest. When Hitler entered Prague in March 1939, he declared, "Czechoslovakia has ceased to exist."

Israel too is a small country. This is not to say that extinction is its fate. Only that it can be.

Moreover, in its vulnerability to extinction, Israel is not just any small country. It is the only small country—the only country, period—whose neighbors publicly declare its very existence an affront to law, morality and religion and make its extinction an explicit, paramount national goal. Nor is the goal merely declarative. Iran, Libya and Iraq conduct foreign policies designed for the killing of Israelis and the destruction of their state. They choose their allies (Hamas, Hezbollah) and develop their weapons (suicide bombs, poison gas, anthrax, nuclear missiles) accordingly. Countries as far away as Malaysia will not allow a representative of Israel on their soil or even permit the showing of *Schindler's List* lest it engender sympathy for Zion.

Others are more circumspect in their declarations. No longer is the destruction of Israel the unanimous goal of the Arab League, as it was for the 30 years before Camp David. Syria, for example, no longer explicitly enunciates it. Yet Syria would destroy Israel tomorrow if it had the power. (Its current reticence on the subject is largely due to its post–Cold War need for the American connection.)

Even Egypt, first to make peace with Israel and the presumed model for peacemaking, has built a vast U.S.-equipped army that conducts military exercises obviously designed for fighting Israel. Its huge "Badr '96" exercises, for example, Egypt's largest since the 1973 war, featured simulated crossings of the Suez Canal.

And even the PLO, which was forced into ostensible recognition of Israel in the Oslo Agreements of 1993, is still ruled by a national charter that calls in at least 14 places for Israel's eradication. The fact that after five years and four specific promises to amend the charter it remains unamended is a sign of how deeply engraved the dream of eradicating Israel remains in the Arab consciousness.

II. THE STAKES

The contemplation of Israel's disappearance is very difficult for this generation. For 50 years, Israel has been a fixture. Most people cannot remember living in a world without Israel.

Nonetheless, this feeling of permanence has more than once been rudely interrupted—during the first few days of the Yom Kippur War when it seemed as if Israel might be overrun, or those few weeks in May and early June 1967 when Nasser blockaded the Straits of Tiran and marched 100,000 troops into Sinai to drive the Jews into the sea.

Yet Israel's stunning victory in 1967, its superiority in conventional weaponry, its success in every war in which its existence was at stake, has bred complacency. Some ridicule the very idea of Israel's impermanence. Israel, wrote one diaspora intellectual, "is fundamentally indestructible. Yitzhak Rabin knew this. The Arab leaders on Mount Herzl [at Rabin's funeral] knew this. Only the land-grabbing, trigger-happy saints of the right do not know this. They are animated by the imagination of catastrophe, by the thrill of attending the end."

Thrill was not exactly the feeling Israelis had when during the Gulf War they entered sealed rooms and donned gas masks to protect themselves from mass death—in a war in which Israel was not even engaged. The feeling was fear, dread, helplessness—old existential Jewish feelings that post-Zionist fashion today deems anachronistic, if not reactionary. But wish does not overthrow reality. The Gulf War reminded even the most wishful that in an age of nerve gas, missiles and nukes, an age in which no country is completely safe from weapons of mass destruction, Israel with its compact population and tiny area is particularly vulnerable to extinction.

Israel is not on the edge. It is not on the brink. This is not '48 or '67 or '73. But Israel is a small country. It can disappear. And it knows it.

It may seem odd to begin an examination of the meaning of Israel and the future of the Jews by contemplating the end. But it does concentrate the mind. And it underscores the stakes. The stakes could not be higher. It is my contention that on Israel—on its existence and survival—hangs the very existence and survival of the Jewish people. Or, to put the thesis in the negative, that the end of Israel means the end of the Jewish people. They survived destruction and exile at the hands of Babylon in 586 B.C. They survived destruction and exile at the hands of Rome in A.D. 70, and finally in A.D. 135. They cannot survive another destruction and exile. The Third Commonwealth—modern Israel, born just 50 years ago—is the last.

The return to Zion is now the principal drama of Jewish history. What began as an experiment has become the very heart of the Jewish people—its cultural, spiritual and psychological center, soon to become its demographic center as well. Israel is the hinge. Upon it rest the hopes—the only hope—for Jewish continuity and survival.

III. THE DYING DIASPORA

In 1950, there were 5 million Jews in the United States. In 1990, the number was a slightly higher 5.5 million. In the intervening decades, overall U.S. population rose 65%. The Jews essentially tread water. In fact, in the last half-century Jews have shrunk from 3% to 2% of the American population. And now they are headed for not just relative but absolute decline. What sustained the Jewish population at its current level was, first, the post-war baby boom, then the influx of 400,000 Jews, mostly from the Soviet Union.

Well, the baby boom is over. And Russian immigration is drying up. There are only so many Jews where they came from. Take away these historical anomalies, and the American Jewish population would be smaller today than yesterday. In fact, it is now headed for catastrophic decline. Steven Bayme, director of Jewish Communal Affairs at the American Jewish Committee, flatly predicts that in 20 years the Jewish population will be down to 4 million, a loss of nearly 30%. In 20 years. Projecting just a few decades further yields an even more chilling future.

How does a community decimate itself in the benign conditions of the United States? Easy: low fertility and endemic intermarriage.

The fertility rate among American Jews is 1.6 children per woman. The replacement rate (the rate required for the population to remain constant) is 2.1. The current rate is thus 20% below what is needed for zero growth. Thus fertility rates alone would cause a 20% decline in every generation. In three generations, the population would be cut in half.

The low birth rate does not stem from some peculiar aversion of Jewish women to children. It is merely a striking case of the well-known and universal phenomenon of birth rates declining with rising education and socioeconomic class. Educated, successful working women tend to marry late and have fewer babies.

Add now a second factor, intermarriage. In the United States today more Jews marry Christians than marry Jews. The intermarriage rate is 52%. (A more conservative calculation yields 47%; the demographic effect is basically the same.) In 1970, the rate was 8%.

Most important for Jewish continuity, however, is the ultimate identity of the children born to these marriages. Only about one in four is raised Jewish. Thus two-thirds of Jewish marriages are producing children three-quarters of whom are lost to the Jewish people. Intermarriage rates alone would cause a 25% decline in population in every generation. (Math available upon request.) In two generations, half the Jews would disappear.

Now combine the effects of fertility and intermarriage and make the overly optimistic assumption that every child raised Jewish will grow up to retain his Jewish identity (i.e., a zero dropout rate). You can start with 100 American Jews; you end up with 60. In one generation, more than a third have disappeared. In just two generations, two out of every three will vanish.

One can reach this same conclusion by a different route (bypassing the intermarriage rates entirely). A *Los Angeles Times* poll of American Jews conducted in March 1998 asked a simple question: Are you raising your children as Jews? Only 70% said yes. A population in which the biological replacement rate is 80% and the cultural replacement rate is 70% is headed for extinction. By this calculation, every 100 Jews are raising 56 Jewish children. In just two generations, 7 out of every 10 Jews will vanish.

The demographic trends in the rest of the Diaspora are equally unencouraging. In Western Europe, fertility and intermarriage rates mirror those of the United States. Take Britain. Over the last generation, British Jewry has acted as a kind of controlled experiment: a Diaspora community living in an open society, but, unlike that in the United States, not artificially sustained by immigration. What happened? Over the last quarter-century, the number of British Jews declined by over 25%.

Over the same interval, France's Jewish population declined only slightly. The reason for this relative stability, however, is a onetime factor: the influx of North African Jewry. That influx is over. In

France today only a minority of Jews between the ages of 20 and 44 live in a conventional family with two Jewish parents. France, too, will go the way of the rest.

"The dissolution of European Jewry," observes Bernard Wasserstein in *Vanishing Diaspora: The Jews in Europe Since 1945,* "is not situated at some point in the hypothetical future. The process is taking place before our eyes and is already far advanced." Under present trends, "the number of Jews in Europe by the year 2000 would then be not much more than 1 million—the lowest figure since the last Middle Ages."

In 1900, there were 8 million.

The story elsewhere is even more dispiriting. The rest of what was once the diaspora is now either a museum or a graveyard. Eastern Europe has been effectively emptied of its Jews. In 1939, Poland had 3.2 million Jews. Today it is home to 3,500. The story is much the same in the other capitals of Eastern Europe.

The Islamic world, cradle to the great Sephardic Jewish tradition and home to one-third of world Jewry three centuries ago, is now practically *Judenrein.* Not a single country in the Islamic world is home to more than 20,000 Jews. After Turkey with 19,000 and Iran with 14,000, the country with the largest Jewish community in the entire Islamic world is Morocco with 6,100. There are more Jews in Omaha, Nebraska.

These communities do not figure in projections. There is nothing to project. They are fit subjects not for counting but for remembering. Their very sound has vanished. Yiddish and Ladino, the distinctive languages of the European and Sephardic diasporas, like the communities that invented them, are nearly extinct.

IV. THE DYNAMICS OF ASSIMILATION

Is it not risky to assume that current trends will continue? No. Nothing will revive the Jewish communities of Eastern Europe and the

Islamic world. And nothing will stop the rapid decline by assimilation of Western Jewry. On the contrary. Projecting current trends—assuming, as I have done, that rates remain constant—is rather conservative: It is risky to assume that assimilation will not accelerate. There is nothing on the horizon to reverse the integration of Jews into Western culture. The attraction of Jews *to* the larger culture and the level of acceptance of Jews *by* the larger culture are historically unprecedented. If anything, the trends augur an intensification of assimilation.

It stands to reason. As each generation becomes progressively more assimilated, the ties to tradition grow weaker (as measured, for example, by synagogue attendance and number of children receiving some kind of Jewish education). This dilution of identity, in turn, leads to a greater tendency to intermarriage and assimilation. Why not? What, after all, are they giving up? The circle is complete and self-reinforcing.

Consider two cultural artifacts. With the birth of television a half-century ago, Jewish life in America was represented by *The Goldbergs:* urban Jews, decidedly ethnic, heavily accented, socially distinct. Forty years later *The Goldbergs* begat *Seinfeld,* the most popular entertainment in America today. The Seinfeld character is nominally Jewish. He might cite his Jewish identity on occasion without apology or self-consciousness—but, even more important, without consequence. It has not the slightest influence on any aspect of his life.

Assimilation of this sort is not entirely unprecedented. In some ways, it parallels the pattern in Western Europe after the emancipation of the Jews in the late 18th and 19th centuries. The French Revolution marks the turning point in the granting of civil rights to Jews. As they began to emerge from the ghetto, at first they found resistance to their integration and advancement. They were still excluded from the professions, higher education and much of society. But as these barriers began gradually to erode and Jews advanced socially, Jews began a remarkable embrace of European culture and, for many, Christianity. In *A History of Zionism,* Walter Laqueur notes the view of Gabriel Riesser, an eloquent and courageous mid-19th-century advocate of emancipation, that a Jew who preferred the non-existent state and nation of Israel to Germany should be put under police protection not because he was dangerous but because he was obviously insane.

Moses Mendelssohn (1729–1786) was a harbinger. Cultured, cosmopolitan, though firmly Jewish, he was the quintessence of early emancipation. Yet his story became emblematic of the rapid historical progression from emancipation to assimilation: Four of his six children and eight of his nine grandchildren were baptized.

In that more religious, more Christian age, assimilation took the form of baptism, what Henrich Heine called the admission ticket to European society. In the far more secular late 20th century, assimilation merely means giving up the quaint name, the rituals and the other accouterments and identifiers of one's Jewish past. Assimilation today is totally passive. Indeed, apart from the trip to the county courthouse to transform, say, (*shmattes* by) Ralph Lifshitz into (Polo by) Ralph Lauren, it is marked by an absence of actions rather than the active embrace of some other faith. Unlike Mendelssohn's children, Seinfeld required no baptism.

We now know, of course, that in Europe, emancipation through assimilation proved a cruel hoax. The rise of antisemitism, particularly late 19th-century racial antisemitism culminating in Nazism, disabused Jews of the notion that assimilation provided escape from the liabilities and dangers of being Jewish. The saga of the family of Madeleine Albright is emblematic. Of her four Jewish grandparents— highly assimilated, with children some of whom actually converted and erased their Jewish past—three went to their deaths in Nazi concentration camps *as Jews*.

Nonetheless, the American context is different. There is no American history of antisemitism remotely resembling Europe's. The American tradition of tolerance goes back 200 years to the very founding of the country. Washington's letter to the synagogue in Newport pledges not tolerance—tolerance bespeaks non-persecution bestowed as a favor by the dominant upon the deviant—but equality. It finds no parallel in the history of Europe. In such a country, assimilation seems a reasonable solution to one's Jewish problem. One could do worse than merge one's destiny with that of a great and humane nation dedicated to the proposition of human dignity and equality.

Nonetheless, while assimilation may be a solution for individual Jews, it clearly is a disaster for Jews as a collective with a memory, a language, a tradition, a liturgy, a history, a faith, a patrimony that will all perish as a result.

Whatever value one might assign to assimilation, one cannot deny its reality. The trends, demographic and cultural, are stark. Not just in the long-lost outlands of the Diaspora, not just in its erstwhile European center, but even in its new American heartland, the future will be one of diminution, decline and virtual disappearance. This will not occur overnight. But it will occur soon—in but two or three generations, a time not much further removed from ours today than the founding of Israel 50 years ago.

V. ISRAELI EXCEPTIONALISM

Israel is different. In Israel the great temptation of modernity—assimilation—simply does not exist. Israel is the very embodiment of Jewish continuity: It is the only nation on earth that inhabits the same land, bears the same name, speaks the same language and worships the same God that it did 3,000 years ago. You dig the soil and you find pottery from Davidic times, coins from Bar Kokhba and 2,000-year-old scrolls written in a script remarkably like the one that today advertises ice cream at the corner candy store.

Because most Israelis are secular, however, some ultra-religious Jews dispute Israel's claim to carry on an authentically Jewish history. So do some secular Jews. A French critic (sociologist Georges Friedmann) once called Israelis "Hebrew-speaking gentiles." In fact, there was once a fashion among a group of militantly secular Israeli intellectuals to call themselves "Canaanites," i.e., people rooted in the land but entirely denying the religious tradition from which they came.

Well then, call these people what you will. *Jews*, after all, is a relatively recent name for this people. They started out as Hebrews, then became Israelites. Jew—derived from the Kingdom of Judah, one of the two successor states to the Davidic and Solomonic Kingdom of Israel—is the post-exilic term for Israelite. It is a latecomer to history.

What to call the Israeli who does not observe the dietary laws, has no use for the synagogue and regards the Sabbath as the day for a drive to the beach—a fair description, by the way, of most of the prime ministers of Israel? It does not matter. Plant a Jewish people in a country that comes to a standstill on Yom Kippur; speaks the language of the Bible; moves to the rhythms of the Hebrew (lunar) calendar; builds cities with the stones of its ancestors; produces Hebrew poetry and literature, Jewish scholarship and learning unmatched anywhere in the world—and you have continuity.

Israelis could use a new name. Perhaps we will one day relegate the word *Jew* to the 2,000-year exilic experience and once again call these people Hebrews. The term has a nice historical echo, being the name by which Joseph and Jonah answered the question: "Who are you?"

In the cultural milieu of modern Israel, assimilation is hardly the problem. Of course Israelis eat McDonald's and watch *Dallas* reruns. But so do Russians and Chinese and Danes. To say that there are heavy Western (read: American) influences on Israeli culture is to say nothing more than that Israel is as subject to the pressures of globalization as any other country. But that hardly denies its cultural distinctiveness, a fact testified to by the great difficulty immigrants have in adapting to Israel.

In the Israeli context, assimilation means the reattachment of Russian and Romanian, Uzbeki and Iraqi, Algerian and Argentinian Jews to a distinctively Hebraic culture. It means the exact opposite of what it means in the diaspora: It means *giving up* alien languages, customs, and traditions. It means giving up Christmas and Easter for Hanukkah and Passover. It means giving up ancestral memories of the steppes and the pampas and the savannas of the world for Galilean hills and Jerusalem stone and Dead Sea desolation. That is what these new Israelis learn. That is what is transmitted to their children. That is why their survival as Jews is secure. Does anyone doubt that the near-million Soviet immigrants to Israel would have been largely lost to the Jewish people had they remained in Russia—and that now they will not be lost?

Some object to the idea of Israel as carrier of Jewish continuity because of the myriad splits and fractures among Israelis: Orthodox versus secular, Ashkenazi versus Sephardi, Russian versus sabra, and so on. Israel is now engaged in bitter debates over the legitimacy of Conservative and Reform Judaism and the encroachment of Orthodoxy upon the civic and social life of the country.

So what's new? Israel is simply recapitulating the Jewish norm. There are equally serious divisions in the diaspora, as there were within the last Jewish Commonwealth: "Before the ascendancy of the Pharisees and the emergence of Rabbinic orthodoxy after the fall of the Second Temple," writes Harvard Near East scholar Frank Cross, "Judaism was more complex and variegated than we had supposed." The Dead Sea Scrolls, explains Hershel Shanks, "emphasize a hitherto unappreciated variety in Judaism of the late Second Temple period, so much so that scholars often speak not simply of Judaism but of Judaisms."

The Second Commonwealth was a riot of Jewish sectarianism: Pharisees, Sadducees, Essenes, apocalyptics of every stripe, sects now lost to history, to say nothing of the early Christians. Those concerned about the secular-religious tensions in Israel might contemplate the centuries-long struggle between Hellenizers and traditionalists during the Second Commonwealth. The Maccabean revolt of 167–4 B.C., now celebrated as Hanukkah, was, among other things, a religious civil war among Jews.

Yes, it is unlikely that Israel will produce a single Jewish identity. But that is unnecessary. The relative monolith of Rabbinic Judaism in the Middle Ages is the exception. Fracture and division are facts of life during the modern era, as during the First and Second Commonwealths. Indeed, during the period of the First Temple, the people of Israel were actually split into two often warring states. The current divisions within Israel pale in comparison.

Whatever identity or identities are ultimately adopted by Israelis, the fact remains that for them the central problem of diaspora Jewry—suicide by assimilation—simply does not exist. Blessed with this security of identity, Israel is growing. As a result, Israel is not just the cultural center of the Jewish world, it is rapidly becoming its demographic center as well. The relatively high birth rate yields a natural increase in population. Add a steady net rate of immigration (nearly a million since the late 1980s), and Israel's numbers rise inexorably even as the diaspora declines.

Within a decade Israel will pass the United States as the most populous Jewish community on the globe. Within our lifetime a majority of the world's Jews will be living in Israel. That has not happened since well before Christ.

A century ago, Europe was the center of Jewish life. More than 80% of world Jewry lived there. The Second World War destroyed European Jewry and dispersed the survivors to the New World (mainly the United States) and to Israel. Today, 80% of world Jewry lives either in the United States or in Israel. Today we have a bipolar Jewish universe with two centers of gravity of approximately equal size. It is a transitional stage, however. One star is gradually dimming, the other brightening.

Soon and inevitably the cosmology of the Jewish people will have been transformed again, turned into a single-star system with a dwindling diaspora orbiting around. It will be a return to the ancient norm: The Jewish people will be centered—not just spiritually but physically—in their ancient homeland.

VI. THE END OF DISPERSION

The consequences of this transformation are enormous. Israel's centrality is more than just a question of demography. It represents a bold and dangerous new strategy for Jewish survival.

For two millennia, the Jewish people survived by means of dispersion and isolation. Following the first exile in 586 B.C. and the second exile in A.D. 70 and A.D. 135, Jews spread first throughout Mesopotamia and the Mediterranean Basin, then to northern and eastern Europe and eventually west to the New World, with communities in practically every corner of the earth, even unto India and China.

Throughout this time, the Jewish people survived the immense pressures of persecution, massacre and forced conversion not just by faith and courage but by geographic dispersion. Decimated here, they would survive there. The thousands of Jewish villages and towns spread across the face of Europe, the Islamic world and the New World provided a kind of demographic insurance. However many Jews were massacred in the First Crusade along the Rhine, however many villages were destroyed in the 1648–1649 pogroms in Ukraine, there were always thousands of others spread around the globe to carry on.

This dispersion made for weakness and vulnerability for individual Jewish communities. Paradoxically, however, it made for endurance and strength for the Jewish people as a whole. No tyrant could amass enough power to threaten Jewish survival everywhere.

Until Hitler. The Nazis managed to destroy most everything Jewish from the Pyrenees to the gates of Stalingrad, an entire civilization a thousand years old. There were 9 million Jews in Europe when Hitler came to power. He killed two-thirds of them. Fifty years later, the Jews have yet to recover. There were 16 million Jews in the world in 1939. Today, there are 13 million.

The effect of the Holocaust was not just demographic, however. It was psychological, indeed ideological, as well. It demonstrated once and for all the catastrophic danger of powerlessness. The solution was self-defense, and that meant a demographic reconcentration in a place endowed with sovereignty, statehood and arms.

Before World War II there was great debate in the Jewish world over Zionism. Reform Judaism, for example, was for decades anti-Zionist. The Holocaust resolved that debate. Except for those at the extremes—the ultra-Orthodox right and far left—Zionism became the accepted solution to Jewish powerlessness and vulnerability. Amid the ruins, Jews made a collective decision that their future lay in self-defense and territoriality, in the ingathering of the exiles to a place where they could finally acquire the means to defend themselves.

It was the right decision, the only possible decision. But oh so perilous. What a choice of place to make one's final stand: a dot on the map, a tiny patch of near desert, a thin ribbon of Jewish habitation behind the flimsiest of natural barriers (which the world demands that Israel relinquish). One determined tank thrust can tear it in half. One small battery of nuclear-tipped Scuds can obliterate it entirely.

To destroy the Jewish people, Hitler needed to conquer the world. All that is needed today is to conquer a territory smaller than Vermont. The terrible irony is that in solving the problem of powerlessness, the Jews have necessarily put all their eggs in one basket, a small basket hard by the waters of the Mediterranean. And on its fate hinges everything Jewish.

VII. THINKING THE UNTHINKABLE

What if the Third Jewish Commonwealth meets the fate of the first two? The scenario is not that far-fetched: A Palestinian state is born, arms itself, concludes alliances with, say, Iraq and Syria. War breaks out between Palestine and Israel (over borders or water or terrorism). Syria and Iraq attack from without. Egypt and Saudi Arabia join the battle. The home front comes under guerrilla attack from Palestine. Chemical and biological weapons rain down from Syria, Iraq and Iran. Israel is overrun.

Why is this the end? Can the Jewish people not survive as they did when their homeland was destroyed and their political independence extinguished twice before? Why not a new exile, a new diaspora, a new cycle of Jewish history?

First, because the cultural conditions of exile would be vastly different. The first exiles occurred at a time when identity was nearly coterminous with religion. An expulsion two millennia later into a secularized world affords no footing for a reestablished Jewish identity.

But more important: Why retain such an identity? Beyond the dislocation would be the sheer demoralization. Such an event would simply break the spirit. No people could survive it. Not even the Jews. This is a people that miraculously survived two previous destructions and two millennia of persecution in the hope of ultimate return and restoration. Israel is that hope. To see it destroyed, to have Isaiahs and Jeremiahs lamenting the widows of Zion once again amid the ruins of Jerusalem is more than one people could bear.

Particularly coming after the Holocaust, the worst calamity in Jewish history. To have survived it is miracle enough. Then to survive the destruction of that which arose to redeem it—the new Jewish state—is to attribute to Jewish nationhood and survival supernatural power.

Some Jews and some scattered communities would, of course, survive. The most devout, already a minority, would carry on—as an exotic tribe, a picturesque Amish-like anachronism, a dispersed and pitied remnant of a remnant. But the Jews as a people would have retired from history.

We assume that Jewish history is cyclical: Babylonian exile in 586 B.C., followed by return in 538 B.C. Roman exile in A.D. 135, followed by return, somewhat delayed, in 1948. We forget a linear part of Jewish history: There was one other destruction, a century and a half before the fall of the First Temple. It went unrepaired. In 722 B.C., the Assyrians conquered the other, larger Jewish state, the northern kingdom of Israel. (Judah, from which modern Jews are descended, was the southern kingdom.) This is the Israel of the Ten Tribes, exiled and lost forever.

So enduring is their mystery that when Lewis and Clark set off on their expedition, one of the many questions prepared for them by Dr. Benjamin Rush at Jefferson's behest was this: "What Affinity between their [the Indians'] religious Ceremonies & those of the Jews?" "Jefferson and Lewis had talked at length about these tribes," explains Stephen Ambrose. "They speculated that the lost tribes of Israel could be out there on the Plains."

Alas, not. The Ten Tribes had melted away into history. As such, they represent the historical norm. Every other people so conquered and exiled has in time disappeared. Only the Jews defied the norm. Twice. But never, I fear, again.

The Weekly Standard, May 11, 1998

CHAPTER 13

THE GOLDEN AGE

THE '80S: REVIVAL

R arely does history respect the calendar, but this time events have conspired to demarcate precisely the 1980s. Christmas, 1979, the day of the Soviet invasion of Afghanistan, marks the apogee of the Soviet empire. November of 1989, with the communist crackup in Eastern Europe, marks its nadir. What happened in the interval defines the '80s. They will be remembered—long after the avarice, the corruption and the other delightful excesses of the time are forgotten—as the decade of the revival and triumph of the West.

Nineteen seventy-nine was the annus mirabilis of the Soviet imperium. In that one year, Iran turned fanatically anti-American, and the Soviets or their clients seized Afghanistan, Nicaragua, Cambodia and, just to rub it in, Grenada. It was also the West's post-war low, as oil shocks, inflation and the hostage crisis completed America's post-Vietnam demoralization.

Then, the great turn, which came not with Reagan's inaugural but, in the interest of historical neatness, in 1980, the last year of the Carter administration. It was a post-Afghanistan Jimmy Carter who reasserted a foreign policy hard line (arming the mujahidin, embargoing Soviet grain, cutting off aid to the Sandinistas). It was then too that Carter's Federal Reserve chairman, Paul Volcker, began squeezing the economy to break inflation.

Reagan finished the job with a vengeance. He let Volcker's cruel but inflation-breaking recession proceed through the 1982 election year. He challenged the Soviets to an all-out arms race with which they could not keep up. He brandished SDI (Strategic Defense Initiative), which the Soviets read as a sign that the United States was prepared to use its technological superiority to trump Soviet military power, their one claim to superpower status.

NATO then held together for the most overlooked geopolitical victory of the '80s: the successful deployment of the intermediate-range nuclear missiles (INF) in Europe, thus facing down both Soviet threats and the West's peace movement. The final straw was the Reagan Doctrine, which put American arms and money behind a worldwide anti-communist guerrilla campaign that gave the Soviets bleeding wounds on three continents.

And just when they thought they had America down, the combination of INF, SDI, the Reagan Doctrine and the huge defense buildup made it clear to the Soviets that they were facing a future that they could only lose. American resilience in this decade came as a shock to the Soviets. Their new foreign policy is the residue of that shock.

After all, the Soviets had achieved something astonishing: For 40 years they had single-handedly taken on the most formidable alliance of great powers in history—the United States, Britain, France, Japan, two-thirds of Germany and a host of other highly industrialized countries—and held it to a draw. At the end of the '80s, it became clear to Gorbachev that this could not continue. In July of 1988, Eduard Shevardnadze before his own Foreign Ministry workers scornfully rejected "the idea, which gained a firm hold in the minds and deeds of certain strategists, that the Soviet Union could be as strong as any possible coalition of states opposing it." Their only hope was to abandon a losing contest. They sued for peace.

Who killed communism? There is a lot of credit to go around. But certainly none goes to those who since 1972 have urged, "Come home, America." Who opposed the defense buildup. Who inflamed the nuclear hysteria of the early '80s and joined its panicked, now merely quaint, call for a nuclear freeze. Who called for a moratorium on INF, i.e., a surrender to the street. Who denounced the Reagan Doctrine on the grounds that it was the road to Vietnam, when, in fact, it turned Brezhnev's empire into a Soviet Vietnam.

Wrong on every count. Now foreign policy liberals are reduced to arguing that the monumental collapse of the Soviet empire is the work of one man whose rise is some complicated accident of Russian history. The Gorbachev reversal is no accident. It was the premise and the goal of the entire policy of containment, as outlined by George Kennan in 1947. "It would be an exaggeration to say that American behavior unassisted and alone could . . . bring about the early fall of Soviet power in Russia," he wrote. "But the United States has it in its power to increase enormously the strains under which Soviet policy must operate . . . and in this way to promote tendencies which must eventually find their outlet in either the breakup or the gradual mellowing of Soviet power." The '80s represent the final fulfillment of that policy.

Which is why with the waning of the decade the conservatives' time might soon be up. Voters are not sentimental. They don't give points for past achievement. They turned out Winston Churchill less than three months after V-E Day.

The rule is: What have you done for me lately? After the Democratic Party built the magnificent structure of the New Deal, it ran out of ideas, and the voters threw the rascals out. Conservatives have done what they were asked to do in 1980: break inflation and restore Western power. Their job is done.

The voters sense it. The Republicans took a whipping in the 1989 elections. Their social agenda (most prominently, abortion) proved unenactable. And that was the fallback for a party whose economic and foreign policy agenda has already been enacted.

There is another turn ahead. Democrats will do everything in their power to blow it, but one new idea and the '90s belongs to them.

The Washington Post, November 24, 1989

THE '90S: SERENITY

What does it mean when the major item in the president's end-of-year news conference is a puppy-naming? It means we should be wistful at the passing of 1997. We may never see another year like it. When a chocolate Lab leads the news, we know times are good.

How good? Look at the numbers. Unemployment is at its lowest in two decades. Inflation hovers at 2%, early 1960s numbers. That is not supposed to happen. We have been bred on the axiom that unemployment and inflation are mutually contradictory, that when one form of social misery declines, the other must rise. Well, not anymore.

The economy is growing at more than 3%. Hourly wages are up 4%. Factories are producing at that perfect knife-edge of near capacity, but not quite so much as to create industrial bottlenecks (and thus shortages and inflation).

Even more amazing are the indices of social pathology, which we once assumed must inexorably get worse. They have reversed course. Crime is down, dramatically. Rape, for example, is down 45% since 1993; murder about 30%. In New York City, the crime rate has not been this low in 30 years. The unlivable has become livable again.

Welfare rolls are down, too. After just 12 months of welfare reform (August 1996–July 1997), one in every six welfare recipients has gone off the dole. That is almost 2 million people. In places with aggressive anti-welfare programs such as Wisconsin, rolls have been cut by a third. Even such recalcitrant indices as abortion are down.

Nor are the good times just economic and social. Geopolitically, we are enjoying the fruits of victory in the Cold War. At no time in the past 500 years has the gap in power between the No. 1 nation and its nearest rival been as great as it is today. While the critics had conceded America's military and cultural hegemony—a carrier in every ocean, a Big Mac in every pot—they had long clung to the idea of American economic decline.

And look what happened. We are now riding a productivity and growth spurt that has left the rest of the world in our dust. Europe lives with double-digit unemployment and almost total economic stagnation. Asia, the rising tiger, is now in the throes of a collapse so great that its ripples, ironically, constitute the one major threat to our current prosperity.

Now the puzzle: If this is a golden age, why doesn't it feel like a golden age? I recently told an assembly at my son's high school that they were living through a time so blessed they would tell their grandchildren about it. They looked at me uncomprehendingly. First, because they have known little else but good times. And second, because it is hard for anyone to apprehend the sheer felicity of one's own time until it is gone.

But I suspect there is a third reason: We live in gold—but without glory. We associate golden ages with heroic times like that of Pericles. Our triumphs, in contrast, are of the domestic variety. This is the age of Seinfeld, life in miniature. No great battles, no great art, no great triumphs. We know these are diminished times when our most recent military hero is a pilot who, shot down by ragtag Serbs, manages to survive by hiding in the forests of Bosnia like a "scared little bunny rabbit" (his words: Scott O'Grady's heroism is his honesty).

No matter. Who needs wars? Who needs heroes? Who needs glory? These things are not sought; they are thrust upon a nation, unwillingly. Britain's finest hour was 1940. Would you choose for your child to live in London during the blitz or in Lansing under Clinton? By any historical standard, life has never been so good. Why, the news has gotten so absurdly good we have to cast our net very far to find the bad. El Niño is about the best we can do.

Does this mean that the news will only get better? On the contrary. With every passing month of such profound tranquillity and prosperity, the implausibility of these times becomes all the more striking.

Golden ages never last. There might be a sudden crisis, perhaps a collapse of economic confidence coming from the Asian contagion. Or perhaps just a gradual undoing of all the self-reinforcing good news: a spike of inflation, a little recession, a rise in welfare, and the whole cycle slowly reverses itself.

I hold with those who say this lovely world will end in ice, not fire. But either way, it must surely end. So enjoy it while it lasts. Because it won't.

The Washington Post, December 19, 1997

COLD WAR NOSTALGIA

*We look back to that era now, and we long for a—I even made a
crack the other day. I said, "Gosh, I miss the Cold War." It was a
joke, I mean, I don't really miss it, but you get the joke.*
                            —President Bill Clinton, interview with
                                  the *Washington Post*, Oct. 15, 1993

I t is not really a joke. It is an alibi. When the Clinton administration runs into trouble abroad—debacle in Somalia, humiliation in
Haiti, dithering over Bosnia—it likes to preface its list of extenu-
ations with: Of course, we no longer have the easy divisions of the
Cold War to make things clear and crisp and simple. Things are so
much harder now.

So clear and crisp and simple? Curious. During the Cold War,
especially during its last two decades, liberals claimed that things
were not so simple, that only ideologues and dimwits—Ronald Reagan, for example—insisted on seeing the world through the prism of
the Cold War.

Now they tell us how clear and clarifying it was. "We had an
intellectually coherent thing," said Clinton of the Cold War era.
"The American people knew what the rules were and when we did
whatever." How about when we did Vietnam? Vietnam, fought under
the theory of containment enunciated first by Harry Truman in 1947,
was the quintessential Cold War engagement. It was also the most
divisive.

At the time, Bill Clinton called it "a war I opposed and despised
with a depth of feeling I have reserved solely for racism in America."
Yet it was prosecuted by two successive administrations. In the 1972
election, the winner by a landslide was Richard Nixon, war president.
Same war. Clinton had a clarity of vision about the war no less certain than Nixon's—only diametrically opposed.

Vietnam rent the nation because it presented the basic dilemmas of the Cold War period: Was containment the paramount American foreign policy goal? Was it worth the risk of military intervention? Where? At what cost? There were no easy answers. There was certainly none of the unanimity that nostalgics now pretend there was.

To hear the blather about Cold War consensus, one would think that the '80s never happened. At every turn, on every issue for which there presumably was one simple, knee-jerk, anti-Soviet answer—the MX, El Salvador, Nicaragua, Grenada, "Euromissile" deployment—there was deep division. And practically every time, liberals, so wistful now for the easy choices of yore, made the wrong choice.

In the late '70s, for example, the Soviets aggressively deployed medium-range Euromissiles designed to intimidate and neutralize Western Europe. It was a clear-cut challenge. The correct response was equally clear-cut: a NATO counterdeployment of comparable medium-range missiles.

Reagan and Thatcher and Kohl pulled it off. But not without enormous resistance from Western liberals and leftists. In America the resistance took the form of a nuclear-freeze movement that would have frozen Soviet missiles in place and frozen NATO's out.

Where were the Democrats on this one? They forced a nuclear-freeze resolution through the House of Representatives, 278 to 149. Their central idea—if one can speak of a hysteria in terms of ideas—was that Reagan was blinded by his Cold War anti-Sovietism. The real enemy, they insisted, was not communism but the nuclear weapons themselves.

Similarly on the other great Cold War issue, Third World revolution: The real enemy, the Democrats protested, was not communism but deprivation. In the great debates over El Salvador and Nicaragua, liberals insisted that to see these conflicts in Cold War, East-West terms was again to miss the point.

"If Central America were not racked with injustices, there would be no revolution," said the Democrats in a 1983 televised address opposing military aid to El Salvador. "There would be nothing for the Soviets to exploit. But unless those oppressive conditions change, that region will continue to seethe with revolution—with or without the Soviets."

As history has demonstrated: wrong. No one would dare claim that in Central America poverty and injustice are gone. But the region no longer seethes with revolution. What happened? Injustice did not disappear. The Soviets did, and with them the sinews and romance of socialist revolution.

The evil empire was the enemy. That was the central tenet of American cold warriors. Liberals deplored such talk as crude Manichaeism. Now, after 20 years of deriding anti-communists for being blinded by the Soviet threat, they wistfully recall how the Soviet threat brilliantly illuminated the foreign policy landscape—and lament how obscure it all is with the lodestar gone. Ah, the Golden Age when everything was easy and we all joined hands in the Cold War battles of Vietnam and Nicaragua and the Euromissiles.

Yesterday, *cold warrior* was a liberal epithet. Today everyone pretends to have been one. My father, who had a Frenchman's appreciation for cynicism, had a term for this kind of after-battle résumé revision. *Maquis d'après-guerre:* resistance fighter, post-war.

Time, November 29, 1993

CHAPTER 14

THE AGE OF HOLY TERROR

SEPTEMBER 11, 2001

This is not crime. This is war. One of the reasons there are terrorists out there capable and audacious enough to carry out the deadliest attack on the United States in its history is that, while they have declared war on us, we have in the past responded—with the exception of a few useless cruise missile attacks on empty tents in the desert—by issuing subpoenas.

Secretary of State Colin Powell's first reaction to the day of infamy was to pledge to "bring those responsible to justice." This is exactly wrong. Franklin Roosevelt did not respond to Pearl Harbor by pledging to bring the commander of Japanese naval aviation to justice. He pledged to bring Japan to its knees.

You bring criminals to justice; you rain destruction on combatants. This is a fundamental distinction that can no longer be avoided. The bombings of Sept. 11, 2001, must mark a turning point. War was long ago declared on us. Until we declare war in return, we will have thousands of more innocent victims.

We no longer have to search for a name for the post–Cold War era. It will henceforth be known as the age of terrorism. Organized terror has shown what it can do: execute the single greatest massacre in American history, shut down the greatest power on the globe and send its leaders into underground shelters. All this, without even resorting to chemical, biological or nuclear weapons of mass destruction.

This is a formidable enemy. To dismiss it as a bunch of cowards perpetrating senseless acts of violence is complacent nonsense. People willing to kill thousands of innocents while they kill themselves are not cowards. They are deadly, vicious warriors and need to be treated as such. Nor are their acts of violence senseless. They have a very specific aim: to avenge alleged historical wrongs and to bring the great American satan to its knees.

Nor is the enemy faceless or mysterious. We do not know for sure who gave the final order but we know what movement it comes from. The enemy has identified itself in public and openly. Our delicate sensibilities have prevented us from pronouncing its name.

Its name is radical Islam. Not Islam as practiced peacefully by millions of the faithful around the world. But a specific fringe political movement, dedicated to imposing its fanatical ideology on its own societies and destroying the society of its enemies, the greatest of which is the United States.

Israel, too, is an affront to radical Islam, and thus of course must be eradicated. But it is the smallest of fish. The heart of the beast—with its military in Saudi Arabia, Kuwait, Turkey and the Persian Gulf; with a culture that "corrupts" Islamic youth; with an economy and technology that dominate the world—is the United States. That is why we were struck so savagely.

How do we know? Who else trains cadres of fanatical suicide murderers who go to their deaths joyfully? And the average terrorist does not coordinate four hijackings within one hour. Nor fly a plane into the tiny silhouette of a single building. For that you need skilled pilots seeking martyrdom. That is not a large pool to draw from.

These are the shock troops of the enemy. And the enemy has many branches. Hezbollah in Lebanon, Hamas and Islamic Jihad in Israel, the Osama bin Laden organization headquartered in Afghanistan, and various Arab "liberation fronts" based in Damascus. And then there are the governments: Iran, Iraq, Syria and Libya among them. Which one was responsible? We will find out soon enough.

But when we do, there should be no talk of bringing these people to "swift justice," as Karen Hughes dismayingly promised mid-afternoon yesterday. An open act of war demands a military response, not a judicial one.

Military response against whom? It is absurd to make war on the individuals who send these people. The terrorists cannot exist in a vacuum. They need a territorial base of sovereign protection. For 30 years we have avoided this truth. If bin Laden was behind this, then Afghanistan is our enemy. *Any* country that harbors and protects him is our enemy. We must carry their war to them.

We should seriously consider a congressional declaration of war. That convention seems quaint, unused since World War II. But there are two virtues to declaring war: It announces our seriousness both to our people and to the enemy, and it gives us certain rights as belligerents (of blockade, for example).

The "long peace" is over. We sought this war no more than we sought war with Nazi Germany and Imperial Japan or Cold War with the Soviet Union. But when war was pressed upon the greatest generation, it rose to the challenge. The question is: Will we?

The Washington Post, September 12, 2001

WHEN IMAGINATION FAILS

A few men with knives. Why didn't the passengers, numbering in the dozens, just overpower them? Of the four hijacked planes, only one failed to reach its terror destination. Why just one? The question seems unfair, even disrespectful. But its answer illuminates the deepest problem in facing terrorism: failure of the imagination. The passengers' seeming passivity is reminiscent of the Holocaust. We ask, with trepidation: How could Jews have allowed themselves to be herded into gas chambers by just a few people carrying machine guns? Because it was inconceivable—six decades later it remains inconceivable—that the men carrying the weapons would do what they, in fact, did do. The victims were told these were showers. Who could imagine herding children into gas chambers? In all of human history, no people had ever done that. The victims could not plumb the depths of their enemy's evil.

I suspect the same happened to the doomed passengers on the hijacked planes. After all, hijackings have been going on for 40 years. Almost invariably, everybody ends up okay. The hijacker wants to go to Cuba, or make a political point, or get the world's attention. Never in history had hijackers intentionally turned a passenger plane into a flying bomb, killing everyone aboard, including themselves. Decades of experience teach us that if you simply do what the hijackers say, they'll eventually get tired and give up. That's the rule.

But when the rules don't apply, when inconceivably cold-blooded evil is in command, the victims are truly helpless. In the face of unfathomable evil, decent people are psychologically disarmed. What is so striking—and so alien to civilized sensibilities—about the terrorists of radical Islam is their cult of death. Their rhetoric is soaked in the glory of immolation: immolation of the infidel and self-immolation of the avenger. Not since the Nazi rallies of the 1930s has the world witnessed such celebration of blood and soil, of killing and dying. What Western TV would feature, as does Palestinian TV, a children's song with the lyric "How pleasant is the smell of martyrs . . . the land enriched by the blood, the blood pouring out of a fresh body"?

The most chilling detail of the 1983 marine barracks bombing in Beirut is that in his last seconds the suicide bomber was smiling. *Bassamat al-farah*, it is called. The smile of joy. Suicide bombers are taught that they are guaranteed immediate admission to paradise, where 72 black-eyed virgins await their pleasure.

The West has not known such widespread, murderous perversion of religion since the religious wars of the 17th century. Who could have imagined deliberately flying into a building? The FBI didn't. The FAA didn't. We could hardly believe it as we saw it happening. What hijacked passenger could possibly imagine such a scenario? Why then did the passengers on the plane that went down near Pittsburgh decide to resist the hijackers and prevent them from completing their mission? Because they knew: Their relatives had told them by cell phone that the World Trade Center had already been attacked by hijacked planes. They were armed with final awareness of the nature of the evil they faced.

So armed, they could act. So armed, they did.

Time, September 24, 2001

"THE BORDERS OF ISLAM ARE BLOODY"

We've had unintended wars. We've had phony wars. We've had a Soccer War (Honduras–El Salvador, 1969). But not since the War of Jenkins' Ear—sparked by Spanish mistreatment of British seamen, including one Capt. Robert Jenkins, whose display to the House of Commons of his severed ear launched a war on the Spanish nasties in October 1739—have we had anything quite as, well, idiosyncratic as the War of Parsley Point.

What else to call the conflict over Perejil (Spanish for *parsley*), a god-forsaken rocky island the size of a soccer field a few hundred yards off the Moroccan coast that technically belongs to Spain and that Morocco seized July 11, 2002, by force: a dozen soldiers, two tents and a flag?

More farce than force. The reaction was something worthy of *The Mouse That Roared*. You half expected Peter Sellers, dressed in drag, to be leading the Spanish invasion force to kick the Moroccans out. In fact, Spain sent what, by current end-of-history European standards, was quite an armada: two frigates, three patrol boats, a helicopter and a boatload of threats. On Wednesday, Spain cashed in the threats, retaking the island with ridiculous overkill: warships, special ground forces, helicopters and combat aircraft. The remaining six Moroccans surrendered.

It is hard to take all of this seriously, since it comes on the heels of the accidental British invasion of Spain earlier this year. Royal Marines in Gibraltar went out to practice beach landings but missed by a couple of miles and stormed a beach in neighboring Spain. "They landed on our coast with typical commando tactics," said the mayor of La Linea de la Concepcion proudly. "But we managed to hold them on the beach."

After Morocco's non-accidental "invasion" of Perejil, everybody got into the act. The European Union declared "its full solidarity with Spain." NATO, which could not even use this worthless rock for target practice, weighed in on Spain's side, too. The Arab League predictably lined up with its fellow Arabs, declaring Perejil "a Moroccan island."

Not exactly *The Guns of August,* although the way far-flung allies, who had not even heard of this misbegotten rock till last week, lined up instantly behind one or the other of the aggrieved parties had an eerie, ghostly echo.

Now, Morocco will hardly go to war over Parsley Point. For one thing, Morocco is no match for Spain. For another, the timing of the whole stunt, during the three-day wedding of the Moroccan king, Mohammed VI, turned the invasion into a cheap, if bizarre, wedding present to himself and the nation.

Nonetheless, this comedy holds some serious lessons. Europe berates the United States for holding on to primitive notions of sovereignty at a time when the sophisticated Europeans are yielding sovereignty to Brussels, adopting the euro, wallowing in Kyoto and, most recently, genuflecting to the newly established International Criminal Court. Yet here they are lining up in lockstep to defend Spanish sovereignty over a piece of worthless rock that only dubiously belongs to Spain, by supposed attachment to the other dubiously claimed Spanish enclaves of Ceuta and Melilla, that in turn are little more than colonial anachronisms on the coast of North Africa. This same Europe heaps scorn on the United States for defending an infinitely more serious sovereign claim—to democratic legal jurisdiction over its own citizens and soldiers rather than yielding it to the arbitrariness of the new criminal court.

Even more important, however, is that the War of Parsley Point reminds us of the corrosive irredentism for Islamic lands long ago taken by the sword and then lost to the sword. We forget Islam's astonishing early successes. From a standing start in the early seventh century, it conquered Arabia, North Africa and Spain within 100 years. Muslims have not forgotten. The later loss of Spain, to say nothing of European colonialism in the Arab world (including what remains of Spanish sovereignty in Morocco), still burns. After all, how did Ayman al-Zawahiri, Osama bin Laden's deputy, begin that first post–Sept. 11 celebratory videotape? By invoking the loss of "Andalusia"—southern Iberia, lost to the Christian infidel the year Columbus sailed the Atlantic. For many in the Islamic world, it happened yesterday.

Much of the conflict in the world today—the Philippines, Kashmir, Chechnya, the West Bank, Sudan, Nigeria and now on this ridiculous little rock in the Mediterranean—represents the Islamic world, once expanding, long contracting, pushing out once again to reclaim its place in the sun.

As Samuel Huntington has written, the borders of Islam are bloody. At least in the War of Parsley Point, no one has been killed and no one is likely to be. It will all end with the game's being called on account of silliness. The game goes on everywhere else, however, not as farce but as tragedy.

The Washington Post, July 19, 2002

To War or Not to War?

There are two logically coherent positions one can take on war with Iraq.

Hawks favor war on the grounds that Saddam Hussein is reckless, tyrannical and instinctively aggressive, and that if he comes into possession of nuclear weapons in addition to the weapons of mass destruction he already has, he is likely to use them or share them with terrorists. The threat of mass death on a scale never before seen residing in the hands of an unstable madman is intolerable—and must be preempted.

Doves oppose war on the grounds that the risks exceed the gains. War with Iraq could be very costly, possibly degenerating into urban warfare. It likely would increase the chances of weapons of mass destruction being loosed by a Saddam Hussein facing extinction and with nothing to lose. Moreover, Saddam Hussein has as yet never used these weapons against America and its allies because he is deterred by our overwhelming power. Why disturb the status quo? Deterrence served us well against such monsters as Stalin and Mao. It will serve us just as well in containing a much weaker Saddam Hussein.

Preemption is the position of the Bush administration hawks. Deterrence is advanced by a small number of congressional Democratic doves. But, ah, there is a third way. It is the position of Democratic Party elders Al Gore, Ted Kennedy (both of whom delivered impassioned speeches attacking the president's policy) and, as far as can be determined, Senate Majority Leader Tom Daschle. This third way accepts all the premises of the antiwar camp. It gives us all the reasons why war could be catastrophic: chemical or bio-weapon attacks, door-to-door fighting in Baghdad, alienating allies, destroying the worldwide coalition of the war on terror, encouraging the recruitment of new terrorists, etc.

Moreover, they argue, deterrence works. "I have seen no persuasive evidence," said Kennedy, "that Saddam would not be deterred from attacking U.S. interests by America's overwhelming military superiority." So far, so good. But then these senior Democratic critics, having eviscerated the president's premises, proceed to enthusiastically endorse his conclusion—that Saddam Hussein's weapons facilities must be subjected to the most intrusive and far-reaching inspection, and that if he cheats and refuses to cooperate, we must go to war against him.

This is utterly incoherent. In principle, a search for genocidal weapons that can be hidden in a basement or even a closet cannot possibly succeed without the full cooperation of the host government. Not a serious person on the planet believes that Saddam Hussein will give it.

More important, why are these critics insisting on inspection and disarmament anyway? They have elucidated all the various costs of attempting to disarm Iraq forcibly, and told us that deterrence has worked just fine to keep Saddam Hussein from doing us any harm. If deterrence works, by what logic does Kennedy insist that Saddam Hussein "must be disarmed"?

The enthusiasm of these senior Democrats for inspections is really nothing more than an argument for delay. Yet what advantage is there to delay? The war will be just as costly tomorrow as today. Even assuming that delay gets us a few extra allies, how does that prevent Saddam Hussein from launching his awful weapons or resorting to urban warfare?

The virtue of delay is that it gives Democrats political cover. Ever since George McGovern, Democrats have been trying to escape their reputation for being soft, indeed unserious, on foreign policy. The last time Saddam Hussein threatened the peace (by invading Kuwait), 7 out of 10 Democrats in Congress voted against authorizing the use of force and in favor of the useless pseudo-solution of sanctions. So this time, the Democrats' leaders make the antiwar argument but have the political savvy to conclude by running up the flag and sounding the bugle.

I happen to believe that the preemption school is correct, that the risks of allowing Saddam Hussein to acquire his weapons will only grow with time. Nonetheless, I can both understand and respect those few Democrats who make the principled argument against war with Iraq on the grounds of deterrence, believing that safety lies in reliance on a proven (if perilous) balance of terror rather than the risky innovation of forcible disarmament by preemption.

What is hard both to understand and to respect, however, is the delay school. They tell us that this war will be both terrible and unnecessary—and then come out foursquare in support of starting it later, after Saddam Hussein has refused to play nice with inspectors. They manage to criticize the war, and still come out in favor of it. A neat trick—and, given the gravity of the issue, an unseemly one.

The Washington Post, October 7, 2002

THE SURGE, DENIED

No one can spend some 10 days visiting the battlefields in Iraq without seeing major progress in every area. . . . If the U.S. provides sustained support to the Iraqi government—in security, governance, and development—there is now a very real chance that Iraq will emerge as a secure and stable state.

—Anthony Cordesman, "The Situation in Iraq:
A Briefing from the Battlefield," Feb. 13, 2008

This from a man who was a severe critic of the post-war occupation of Iraq and who, as author Peter Wehner points out, is no wide-eyed optimist. In fact, in May 2006 Cordesman had written that "no one can argue that the prospects for stability in Iraq are good." Now, however, there is simply no denying the remarkable improvements in Iraq since the surge began a year ago.

Unless you're a Democrat. As Joe Lieberman (I-Conn.) put it, "Democrats have remained emotionally invested in a narrative of defeat and retreat in Iraq." Their Senate leader, Harry Reid, declares the war already lost. Their presidential candidates (eight of them at the time) unanimously oppose the surge. Then the evidence begins trickling in.

We get news of the Anbar Awakening, which has now spread to other Sunni areas and Baghdad. The sectarian civil strife that the Democrats insisted was the reason for us to leave dwindles to the point of near disappearance. Much of Baghdad is returning to normal. There are 90,000 neighborhood volunteers—ordinary citizens who act as auxiliary police and vital informants on terrorist activity—starkly symbolizing the insurgency's loss of popular support. Captured letters of al-Qaeda leaders reveal despair as they are driven—mostly by Iraqi Sunnis, their own Arab co-religionists—to flight and into hiding.

After agonizing years of searching for the right strategy and the right general, we are winning. How do Democrats react? From Nancy Pelosi to Barack Obama, the talking point is the same: Sure, there is military progress. We could have predicted that. (They in fact had predicted the opposite, but no matter.) But it's all pointless unless you get national reconciliation.

"National" is a way to ignore what is taking place at the local and provincial level, such as Shiite cleric Ammar al-Hakim, scion of the family that dominates the largest Shiite party in Iraq, traveling last October to Anbar in an unprecedented gesture of reconciliation with the Sunni sheiks.

Doesn't count, you see. Democrats demand nothing less than federal-level reconciliation, and it has to be expressed in actual legislation.

The objection was not only highly legalistic but also politically convenient: Very few (including me) thought this would be possible under the Maliki government. Then last week, indeed on the day Cordesman published his report, it happened. Mirabile dictu, the Iraqi parliament approved three very significant pieces of legislation.

First, a provincial powers law that turns Iraq into arguably the most federal state in the entire Arab world. The provinces get not only power but also elections by Oct. 1. U.S. ambassador Ryan Crocker has long been calling this the most crucial step to political stability. It will allow, for example, the pro-American Anbar sheiks to become the legitimate rulers of their province, exercise regional autonomy and forge official relations with the Shiite-dominated central government.

Second, parliament passed a partial amnesty for prisoners, 80% of whom are Sunni. Finally, it approved a $48 billion national budget that allocates government revenue—about 85% of which is from oil—to the provinces. Kurdistan, for example, gets one-sixth.

What will the Democrats say now? They will complain that there is still no oil-distribution law. True. But oil revenue is being distributed to the provinces in the national budget. The fact that parliament could not agree on a permanent formula for the future simply means that it will be allocating oil revenue year by year as part of the budget process. Is that a reason to abandon Iraq to al-Qaeda and Iran?

Despite all the progress, military and political, the Democrats remain unwavering in their commitment to withdrawal on an artificial timetable that inherently jeopardizes our "very real chance that Iraq will emerge as a secure and stable state."

Why? Imagine the transformative effects in the region, and indeed in the entire Muslim world, of achieving a secure and stable Iraq, friendly to the United States and victorious over al-Qaeda. Are the Democrats so intent on denying George Bush retroactive vindication for a war they insist is his that they would deny their own country a now-achievable victory?

The Washington Post, February 22, 2008

WHO LOST IRAQ?

Barack Obama was a principled opponent of the Iraq War from its beginning. But when he became president in January 2009, he was handed a war that was won. The surge had succeeded. Al-Qaeda in Iraq had been routed, driven to humiliating defeat by an Anbar Awakening of Sunnis fighting side by side with the infidel Americans. Even more remarkably, the Shiite militias had been taken down, with U.S. backing, by the forces of Shiite prime minister Nouri al-Maliki. They crushed the Sadr militias from Basra to Sadr City.

Al-Qaeda decimated. A Shiite prime minister taking a decisively nationalist line. Iraqi Sunnis ready to integrate into a new national government. U.S. casualties at their lowest ebb in the entire war. Elections approaching. Obama was left with but a single task: Negotiate a new status-of-forces agreement (SOFA) to reinforce these gains and create a strategic partnership with the Arab world's only democracy.

He blew it. Negotiations, such as they were, finally collapsed last month. There is no agreement, no partnership. As of Dec. 31, the U.S. military presence in Iraq will be liquidated.

And it's not as if that deadline snuck up on Obama. He had three years to prepare for it. Everyone involved, Iraqi and American, knew that the 2008 SOFA calling for full U.S. withdrawal was meant to be renegotiated. And all major parties but one (the Sadr faction) had an interest in some residual stabilizing U.S. force, like the post-war deployments in Japan, Germany and Korea.

Three years, two abject failures. The first was the administration's inability, at the height of American post-surge power, to broker a centrist nationalist coalition governed by the major blocs—one predominantly Shiite (Maliki's), one predominantly Sunni (Ayad Allawi's), one Kurdish—that among them won a large majority (69%) of seats in the 2010 election.

Vice President Biden was given the job. He failed utterly. The government ended up effectively being run by a narrow sectarian coalition where the balance of power is held by the relatively small (12%) Iranian-client Sadr faction.

The second failure was the SOFA itself. U.S. commanders recommended nearly 20,000 troops, considerably fewer than our 28,500 in Korea, 40,000 in Japan and 54,000 in Germany. The president rejected those proposals, choosing instead a level of 3,000 to 5,000 troops.

A deployment so risibly small would have to expend all its energies simply protecting itself—the fate of our tragic, missionless 1982 Lebanon deployment—with no real capability to train the Iraqis, build their U.S.-equipped air force, mediate ethnic disputes (as we have successfully done, for example, between local Arabs and Kurds), operate surveillance and special-ops bases and establish the kind of close military-to-military relations that undergird our strongest alliances.

The Obama proposal was an unmistakable signal of unseriousness. It became clear that he simply wanted out, leaving any Iraqi foolish enough to maintain a pro-American orientation exposed to Iranian influence, now unopposed and potentially lethal. Message received. Just this past week, Massoud Barzani, leader of the Kurds—for two decades the staunchest of U.S. allies—visited Tehran to bend a knee to both President Mahmoud Ahmadinejad and Ayatollah Ali Khamenei.

It didn't have to be this way. Our friends did not have to be left out in the cold to seek Iranian protection. Three years and a won war had given Obama the opportunity to establish a lasting strategic alliance with the Arab world's second most important power.

He failed, though he hardly tried very hard. The excuse is Iraqi refusal to grant legal immunity to U.S. forces. But the Bush administration encountered the same problem and overcame it. Obama had little desire to. Indeed, he portrays the evacuation as a success, the fulfillment of a campaign promise.

But surely the obligation to defend the security and the interests of the nation supersede personal vindication. Obama opposed the war, but when he became commander in chief the terrible price had already been paid in blood and treasure. His obligation was to make something of that sacrifice, to secure the strategic gains that sacrifice had already achieved.

He did not, failing at precisely what this administration so flatters itself for doing so well: diplomacy. After years of allegedly clumsy brutish force, Obama was to usher in an era of not hard power, not soft power, but smart power.

Which turns out in Iraq to be . . . no power. Years from now, we will be asking not "Who lost Iraq?"—that already is clear—but "Why?"

The Washington Post, November 3, 2011

From Freedom Agenda to
Freedom Doctrine

Today, everyone and his cousin supports the "freedom agenda." Of course, yesterday it was just George W. Bush, Tony Blair and a band of neocons with unusual hypnotic powers who dared challenge the received wisdom of Arab exceptionalism—the notion that Arabs, as opposed to East Asians, Latin Americans, Europeans and Africans, were uniquely allergic to democracy. Indeed, the left spent the better part of the Bush years excoriating the freedom agenda as either fantasy or yet another sordid example of U.S. imperialism.

Now it seems everyone, even the left, is enthusiastic for Arab democracy. Fine. Fellow travelers are welcome. But simply being in favor of freedom is not enough. With Egypt in turmoil and in the midst of a perilous transition, we need foreign-policy principles to ensure democracy for the long run.

No need to reinvent the wheel. We've been through something analogous before. After World War II, Western Europe was newly freed but unstable, in ruin—and in play. The democracy we favored for the continent faced internal and external threats from communist totalitarians. The United States adopted the Truman Doctrine that declared America's intention to defend these newly free nations.

This meant not just protecting allies at the periphery, such as Greece and Turkey, from insurgency and external pressure, but supporting democratic elements within Western Europe against powerful and determined domestic communist parties.

Powerful they were. The communists were not just the most organized and disciplined. In France, they rose to largest postwar party; in Italy, to second largest. Under the Truman Doctrine, U.S. presidents used every instrument available, including massive assistance—

covert and overt, financial and diplomatic—to democratic parties to
keep the communists out of power.

As the states of the Arab Middle East throw off decades of dictatorship, their democratic future faces a major threat from the new
totalitarianism: Islamism. As in Soviet days, the threat is both internal and external. Iran, a mini-version of the old Soviet Union, has its
own allies and satellites—Syria, Lebanon and Gaza—and its own
Comintern, with agents operating throughout the region to extend
Islamist influence and undermine pro-Western secular states. That's
precisely why in this revolutionary moment, Iran boasts of an Islamist
wave sweeping the Arab world.

We need a foreign policy that not only supports freedom in the
abstract but is guided by long-range practical principles to achieve
it—a Freedom Doctrine composed of the following elements:

(1) The United States supports democracy throughout the Middle
East. It will use its influence to help democrats everywhere
throw off dictatorial rule.

(2) Democracy is more than just elections. It requires a free
press, the rule of law, the freedom to organize, the establishment of independent political parties and the peaceful transfer of power. Therefore, the transition to democracy and initial
elections must allow time for these institutions, most notably
political parties, to establish themselves.

(3) The only U.S. interest in the internal governance of these new
democracies is to help protect them against totalitarians, foreign and domestic. The recent Hezbollah coup in Lebanon
and the Hamas dictatorship in Gaza dramatically demonstrate
how anti-democratic elements that achieve power democratically can destroy the very democracy that empowered them.

(4) Therefore, just as during the Cold War the United States
helped keep European communist parties out of power (to see
them ultimately wither away), it will be U.S. policy to oppose
the inclusion of totalitarian parties—the Muslim Brotherhood

or, for that matter, communists—in any government, whether
provisional or elected, in newly liberated Arab states.

We may not have the power to prevent this. So be it. The Brotherhood may today be so relatively strong in Egypt, for example, that
a seat at the table is inevitable. But under no circumstances should
a presidential spokesman say, as did Robert Gibbs, that the new
order "has to include a whole host of important non-secular actors."
Why gratuitously legitimize Islamists? Instead, Americans should
be urgently supporting secular democratic parties in Egypt and elsewhere with training, resources and diplomacy.

We are, unwillingly again, parties to a long twilight struggle, this
time with Islamism—most notably Iran, its proxies and its potential
allies, Sunni and Shiite. We should be clear-eyed about our preferred
outcome—real democracies governed by committed democrats—and
develop policies to see this through.

A freedom doctrine is a freedom agenda given direction by guiding principles. Truman did it. So can we.

The Washington Post, February 11, 2011

LANGUAGE AND LEADERSHIP

Jen Psaki, blameless State Department spokeswoman, explained that the hasty evacuation of our embassy in Yemen was not an evacuation but "a reduction in staff." This proved a problem because the Yemeni government had already announced (and denounced) the "evacuation"—the word normal folks use for the panicky ordering of people onto planes headed out of the country.

Thus continues the administration's penchant for wordplay, the bending of language to fit a political need. In Janet Napolitano's famous formulation, terror attacks are now "man-caused disasters." And the "global war on terror" is no more. It's now an "overseas contingency operation."

Nidal Hasan proudly tells a military court that he, a soldier of Allah, killed 13 American soldiers in the name of jihad. But the massacre remains officially classified as an act not of terrorism but of "workplace violence."

The U.S. ambassador to Libya and three others are killed in an al-Qaeda–affiliated terror attack—and for days it is waved off as nothing more than a spontaneous demonstration gone bad. After all, famously declared Hillary Clinton, what difference does it make?

Well, it makes a difference, first, because truth is a virtue. Second, because if you keep lying to the American people, they may seriously question whether anything you say—for example, about the benign nature of NSA surveillance—is not another self-serving lie.

And third, because leading a country through yet another long twilight struggle requires not just honesty but clarity. This is a president who to this day cannot bring himself to identify the enemy as radical Islam. Just Tuesday night, explaining the U.S. embassy closures across the Muslim world, he cited the threat from "violent extremism."

The word *extremism* is meaningless. People don't devote themselves to being extreme. Extremism has no content. The extreme of what? In this war, an extreme devotion to the supremacy of a radically fundamentalist vision of Islam and to its murderous quest for dominion over all others.

But for President Obama, the word *Islamist* may not be uttered. Language must be devised to disguise the unpleasantness.

Result? The world's first lexicological war. Parry and thrust with linguistic tricks, deliberate misnomers and ever more transparent euphemisms. Next: armor-piercing onomatopoeias and amphibious synecdoches.

This would all be comical and merely peculiar if it didn't reflect a larger, more troubling reality: The confusion of language is a direct result of a confusion of policy—which is served by constant obfuscation.

Obama doesn't like this terror war. He particularly dislikes its unfortunate religious coloration, which is why "Islamist" is banished from his lexicon. But soothing words, soothing speeches in various Muslim capitals, soothing policies—"open hand," "mutual respect"— have yielded nothing. The war remains. Indeed, under his watch, it has spread. And as commander in chief he must defend the nation.

He must. But he desperately wants to end the whole struggle. This is no secret wish. In a major address to the National Defense University just three months ago he declared, "This war, like all wars, must end." The plaintive cry of a man hoping that saying so makes it so.

The result is visible ambivalence that leads to vacillating policy reeking of incoherence. Obama defends the vast NSA data dragnet because of the terrible continuing threat of terrorism. Yet at the same time, he calls for not just amending but actually repealing the legal basis for the entire war on terror, the 2001 Authorization for Use of Military Force.

Well, which is it? If the tide of war is receding, why the giant NSA snooping programs? If al-Qaeda is on the run, as he incessantly assured the nation throughout 2012, why is America cowering in 19 closed-down embassies and consulates? Why was Boston put on an unprecedented full lockdown after the marathon bombings? And from Somalia to Afghanistan, why are we raining death by drone on "violent extremists"? Every target, amazingly, a jihadist. What a coincidence.

This incoherence of policy and purpose is why an evacuation from Yemen must be passed off as "a reduction in staff." Why the Benghazi terror attack must be blamed on some hapless Egyptian-American videographer. Why the Fort Hood shooting is nothing but some loony Army doctor gone postal.

In the end, this isn't about language. It's about leadership. The wordplay is merely cover for uncertain policy embedded in confusion and ambivalence about the whole enterprise.

This is not leading from behind. This is not leading at all.

The Washington Post, August 9, 2013

CHAPTER 15

THE AGE TO COME

HYPERPROLIFERATION:
CAN WE SURVIVE IT?

Like many physicists who worked on the Manhattan Project, Richard Feynman could not get the Bomb out of his mind after the war. "I would see people building a bridge," he wrote. "And I thought, they're crazy, they just don't understand, they don't understand. Why are they making new things? It's so useless."

Feynman was convinced man had finally invented something that he could not control and that would ultimately destroy him. For six decades we have suppressed that thought and built enough history to believe Feynman's pessimism was unwarranted. After all, soon afterward, the most aggressive world power, Stalin's Soviet Union, acquired the Bomb yet never used it. Seven more countries have acquired it since and never used it either. Even North Korea, which huffs and puffs and threatens every once in a while, dares not use it. Even Kim Jong Il is not suicidal.

But that's the point. We're now at the dawn of an era in which an extreme and fanatical religious ideology, undeterred by the usual calculations of prudence and self-preservation, is wielding state power and will soon be wielding nuclear power.

We have difficulty understanding the mentality of Iran's newest rulers. Then again, we don't understand the mentality of the men who flew into the World Trade Center or the mobs in Damascus and Tehran who chant "Death to America"—and Denmark (!)—and embrace the glory and romance of martyrdom.

This atavistic love of blood and death and, indeed, self-immolation in the name of God may not be new—medieval Europe had an abundance of millennial Christian sects—but until now it has never had the means to carry out its apocalyptic ends.

That is why Iran's arriving at the threshold of nuclear weaponry is such a signal historical moment. It is not just that its president says crazy things about the Holocaust. It is that he is a fervent believer in the imminent reappearance of the 12th Imam, Shi'ism's version of the Messiah. President Mahmoud Ahmadinejad has been reported as saying in official meetings that the end of history is only two or three years away. He reportedly told an associate that on the podium of the General Assembly last September, he felt a halo around him and for "those 27 or 28 minutes, the leaders of the world did not blink . . . as if a hand was holding them there and opened their eyes to receive" his message. He believes that the Islamic revolution's raison d'être is to prepare the way for the messianic redemption, which in his eschatology is preceded by worldwide upheaval and chaos. How better to light the fuse for eternal bliss than with a nuclear flame?

Depending on your own beliefs, Ahmadinejad is either mystical or deranged. In either case, he is exceedingly dangerous. And Iran is just the first. With infinitely accelerated exchanges of information helping develop whole new generations of scientists, extremist countries led by similarly extreme men will be in a position to acquire nuclear weaponry. If nothing is done, we face not proliferation but hyperproliferation. Not just one but many radical states will get weapons of mass extinction, and then so will the fanatical and suicidal terrorists who are their brothers and clients.

That will present the world with two futures. The first is Feynman's vision of human destruction on a scale never seen. The second, perhaps after one or two cities are lost with millions killed in a single day, is a radical abolition of liberal democracy as the species tries to maintain itself by reverting to strict authoritarianism—a self-imposed expulsion from the Eden of post-Enlightenment freedom.

Can there be a third future? That will depend on whether we succeed in holding proliferation at bay. Iran is the test case. It is the most dangerous political entity on the planet, and yet the world response has been catastrophically slow and reluctant. Years of knowingly useless negotiations, followed by hesitant international resolutions, have brought us to only the most tentative of steps—referral to a Security Council that lacks unity and resolve. Iran knows this and therefore defiantly and openly resumes its headlong march to nuclear status. If we fail to prevent an Iranian regime run by apocalyptic fanatics from going nuclear, we will have reached a point of no return. It is not just that Iran might be the source of a great conflagration but that we will have demonstrated to the world that for those similarly inclined there is no serious impediment.

Our planet is 4,500,000,000 years old, and we've had nukes for exactly 61. No one knows the precise prospects for human extinction, but Feynman was a mathematical genius who knew how to calculate odds. If he were to watch us today about to let loose the agents of extinction, he'd call a halt to all bridge building.

Time, March 26, 2006

DEATH BY DRONE

The nation's vexation over the morality and legality of President Obama's drone war has produced a salutary but hopelessly confused debate. Three categories of questions are being asked. They must be separated to be clearly understood.

1. By what right does the president order the killing by drone of enemies abroad? What criteria justify assassination?

Answer: (a) imminent threat, under the doctrine of self-defense, and (b) affiliation with al-Qaeda, under the laws of war.

Imminent threat is obvious. If we know a freelance jihadist cell in Yemen is actively plotting an attack, we don't have to wait until after the fact. Elementary self-defense justifies attacking first.

Al-Qaeda is a different matter. We are in a mutual state of war. Osama bin Laden issued his fatwa declaring war on the United States in 1996; we reciprocated three days after 9/11 with Congress' Authorization for Use of Military Force—against al-Qaeda and those who harbor and abet it. (Such resolutions are the contemporary equivalent of a declaration of war, as evidenced in the 1991 Persian Gulf War and the 2003 Iraq War.)

Regarding al-Qaeda, therefore, imminence is not required. Its members are legitimate targets, day or night, awake or asleep. Nothing new here. In World War II, we bombed German and Japanese barracks without hesitation.

Unfortunately, Obama's Justice Department memos justifying the drone attacks are hopelessly muddled. They imply that the sole justification for drone attack is imminent threat—and whereas al-Qaeda is plotting all the time, an al-Qaeda honcho sleeping in his bed is therefore a legitimate target.

Nonsense. Slippery nonsense. It gives the impression of an administration making up criteria to fit the president's kill list. No need to confuse categories. A sleeping Anwar al-Awlaki could lawfully be snuffed not because of imminence but because he was self-declared al-Qaeda and thus an enemy combatant as defined by congressional resolution and the laws of war.

2. But al-Awlaki was no ordinary enemy. He was a U.S. citizen. By what right does the president order the killing by drone of an American? Where's the due process?

Answer: Once you take up arms against the United States, you become an enemy combatant, thereby forfeiting the privileges of citizenship and the protections of the Constitution, including due process. You retain only the protection of the laws of war—no more and no less than those of your foreign comrades-in-arms. (Indeed, David French, senior counsel at the American Center for Law and Justice, suggests stripping such traitors of their citizenship, thereby formalizing their extra-constitutional status.)

Lincoln steadfastly refused to recognize the Confederacy as a separate nation. The soldiers that his Union army confronted at Antietam were American citizens (in rebellion)—killed without due process. Nor did the Americans storming German bunkers at Normandy inquire before firing whether there were any German Americans among them—to be excused for gentler treatment while the other Germans were mowed down.

3. Who has the authority to decide life-and-death targeting?

In war, the ultimate authority is always the commander in chief and those in the lawful chain of command to whom he has delegated such authority.

This looks troubling. Obama sitting alone in the Oval Office deciding which individuals to kill. But how is that different from Lyndon Johnson sitting in his office choosing bombing targets in North Vietnam?

Moreover, we firebombed entire cities in World War II. Who chose? Commanders under the ultimate authority of the president.

No judicial review, no outside legislative committee, no secret court, no authority above the president.

Okay, you say. But today's war is entirely different: no front line, no end in sight.

So what? It's the jihadists who decided to make the world a battle-field and to wage war in perpetuity. Until they abandon the field, what choice do we have but to carry the fight to them?

We have our principles and precedents for lawful warmaking, and a growing body of case law for the more vexing complexities of the present war—for example, the treatment of suspected terrorists apprehended on U.S. soil. The courts having granted them varying degrees of habeas corpus protection, it is clear that termination by drone (a measure far more severe than detention) would be forbidden—unless Congress and the courts decide otherwise, which, short of a Taliban invasion from New Brunswick, is inconceivable.

Now, for those who believe that the war on terror is not war but law enforcement, (a) I concede that they will find the foregoing analysis to be useless and (b) I assert that they are living on a different and distant planet.

For us earthlings, on the other hand, the case for Obama's drone war is strong. Pity that his Justice Department couldn't make it.

The Washington Post, February 14, 2013

No Hiding from History

The war in Syria, started by locals, is now a regional conflict, the meeting ground of two warring blocs. On one side, the radical Shiite bloc led by Iran, which overflies Iraq to supply Bashar al-Assad and sends Hezbollah to fight for him. Behind them lies Russia, which has stationed ships offshore, provided the regime with tons of weaponry and essentially claimed Syria as a Russian protectorate.

And on the other side are the Sunni Gulf states terrified of Iranian hegemony (territorial and soon nuclear); non-Arab Turkey, now convulsed by an internal uprising; and fragile Jordan, dragged in by geography.

And behind them? No one. It's the Spanish Civil War except that only one side—the fascists—showed up. The natural ally of what began as a spontaneous, secular, liberationist uprising in Syria was the United States. For two years, it did nothing.

President Obama's dodge was his chemical-weapons "red line." In a conflict requiring serious statecraft, Obama chose to practice forensics instead, earnestly agonizing over whether reported poison-gas attacks reached the evidentiary standards of *CSI: Miami*.

Obama talked "chain of custody," while Iran and Russia, hardly believing their luck, reached for regional dominance—the ayatollahs solidifying their "Shiite crescent," Vladimir Putin seizing the opportunity to dislodge America as regional hegemon, a position the United States achieved four decades ago under Henry Kissinger.

And when finally forced to admit that his red line had been crossed—a "game changer," Obama had gravely warned—what did he do? Promise the rebels small arms and ammunition.

That's it? It's meaningless: The rebels are already receiving small arms from the Gulf states.

Compounding the halfheartedness, Obama transmitted his new

"calculus" through his deputy national security adviser. Deputy, mind you. Obama gave 39 (or was it 42?) speeches on health-care reform. How many on the regional war in Syria, in which he has now involved the United States, however uselessly? Zero.

Serious policy making would dictate that we either do something that will alter the course of the war, or do nothing. Instead, Obama has chosen to do just enough to give the appearance of having done something.

But it gets worse. Despite his commitment to steadfast inaction, Obama has been forced by events to send F-16s, Patriot missiles and a headquarters unit of the 1st Armored Division (indicating preparation for a possible "larger force," explains the *Washington Post*)—to Jordan. America's most reliable Arab ally needs protection. It is threatened not just by a flood of refugees but also by the rise of Iran's radical Shiite bloc with ambitions far beyond Syria, beyond even Jordan and Lebanon to Yemen, where, it was reported just Wednesday, Iran is arming and training separatists.

Obama has thus been forced back into the very vacuum he created—but at a distinct disadvantage. We are now scrambling to put together some kind of presence in Jordan as a defensive counterweight to the Iran-Hezbollah-Russia bloc.

The tragedy is that we once had a counterweight and Obama threw it away. Obama still thinks the total evacuation of Iraq is a foreign-policy triumph. In fact, his inability—unwillingness?—to negotiate a Status of Forces Agreement that would have left behind a small but powerful residual force in Iraq is precisely what compels him today to re-create in Jordan a pale facsimile of that regional presence.

Whatever the wisdom of the Iraq War in the first place, when Obama came to office in January 2009 the war was won. We had a golden opportunity to reap the rewards of this too-bloody war by establishing a strategic relationship with an Iraq that was still under American sway. Iraqi airspace, for example, was under U.S. control as we prepared to advise and rebuild Iraq's nonexistent air force.

With our evacuation, however, Iraqi airspace today effectively belongs to Iran—over which it is flying weapons, troops and advisers to turn the tide in Syria. The U.S. air bases, the vast military equipment, the intelligence sources available in Iraq were all abandoned. Gratis. Now we're trying to hold the line in Jordan.

Obama is learning very late that, for a superpower, inaction is a form of action. You can abdicate, but you really can't hide. History will find you. It has now found Obama.

The Washington Post, June 21, 2013

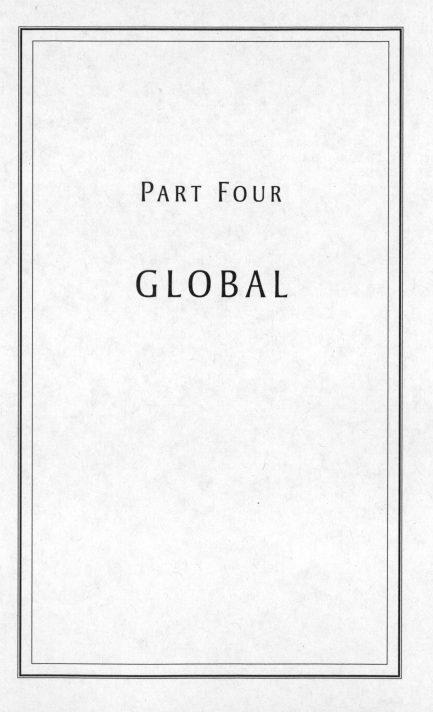

PART FOUR

GLOBAL

CHAPTER 16

THREE ESSAYS ON AMERICA
AND THE WORLD

THE UNIPOLAR MOMENT (1990)

I

Ever since it became clear that an exhausted Soviet Union was calling off the Cold War, the quest has been on for a new American role in the world. Roles, however, are not invented in the abstract; they are a response to a perceived world structure. Accordingly, thinking about post–Cold War American foreign policy has been framed by several conventionally accepted assumptions about the shape of the post–Cold War environment.

First, it has been assumed that the old bipolar world would beget a multipolar world with power dispersed to new centers in Japan, Germany (and/or "Europe"), China and a diminished Soviet Union/ Russia. Second, that the domestic American consensus for an internationalist foreign policy, a consensus radically weakened by the experience in Vietnam, would substantially be restored now that policies and debates inspired by "an inordinate fear of communism" could be safely retired. Third, that in the new post-Soviet strategic environment the threat of war would be dramatically diminished.

All three of these assumptions are mistaken. The immediate post–

Cold War world is not multipolar. It is unipolar. The center of world power is an unchallenged superpower, the United States, attended by its Western allies. Second, the internationalist consensus is under renewed assault. The assault this time comes not only from the usual pockets of post-Vietnam liberal isolationism (e.g., the churches) but from a resurgence of 1930s-style conservative isolationism. And third, the emergence of a new strategic environment, marked by the rise of small aggressive states armed with weapons of mass destruction and possessing the means to deliver them (what might be called Weapon States), makes the coming decades a time of heightened, not diminished, threat of war.

II

The most striking feature of the post–Cold War world is its unipolarity. No doubt, multipolarity will come in time. In perhaps another generation or so there will be great powers coequal with the United States, and the world will, in structure, resemble the pre–World War I era. But we are not there yet, nor will we be for decades. Now is the unipolar moment.

There is today no lack of second-rank powers. Germany and Japan are economic dynamos. Britain and France can deploy diplomatic and to some extent military assets. The Soviet Union possesses several elements of power—military, diplomatic and political—but all are in rapid decline. There is but one first-rate power and no prospect in the immediate future of any power to rival it.

Only a few months ago it was conventional wisdom that the new rivals, the great pillars of the new multipolar world, would be Japan and Germany (and/or Europe). How quickly a myth can explode. The notion that economic power inevitably translates into geopolitical influence is a materialist illusion. Economic power is a necessary condition for great power status. But it certainly is not sufficient, as has been made clear by the recent behavior of Germany and Japan, which have generally hidden under the table since the first shots rang out in Kuwait. And while a unified Europe may sometime in the next century act as a single power, its initial disarray and disjointed national responses to the crisis in the Persian Gulf again illustrate that "Europe" does not yet qualify even as a player on the world stage.

Which leaves us with the true geopolitical structure of the post–Cold War world, brought sharply into focus by the Gulf crisis: a single pole of world power that consists of the United States at the apex of the industrial West. Perhaps it is more accurate to say the United States and behind it the West, because where the United States does not tread, the alliance does not follow. That was true for the reflagging of Kuwaiti vessels in 1987. It has been all the more true of the world's subsequent response to the invasion of Kuwait.

American preeminence is based on the fact that it is the only country with the military, diplomatic, political and economic assets to be a decisive player in any conflict in whatever part of the world it chooses to involve itself. In the Persian Gulf, for example, it was the United States, acting unilaterally and with extraordinary speed, that in August 1990 prevented Iraq from taking effective control of the entire Arabian Peninsula.

Iraq, having inadvertently revealed the unipolar structure of today's world, cannot stop complaining about it. It looks at allied and Soviet support for American action in the Gulf and speaks of a conspiracy of North against South. Although it is perverse for Iraqi leader Saddam Hussein to claim to represent the South, his analysis does contain some truth. The unipolar moment means that with the close of the century's three great Northern civil wars (World War I, World War II and the Cold War) an ideologically pacified North seeks security and order by aligning its foreign policy behind that of the United States. That is what is taking shape now in the Persian Gulf. And for the near future, it is the shape of things to come.

The Iraqis are equally acute in demystifying the much celebrated multilateralism of this new world order. They charge that the entire multilateral apparatus (United Nations resolutions, Arab troops,

European Community pronouncements and so on) established in the Gulf by the United States is but a transparent cover for what is essentially an American challenge to Iraqi regional hegemony.

But of course. There is much pious talk about a new multilateral world and the promise of the United Nations as guarantor of a new post–Cold War order. But this is to mistake cause and effect, the United States and the United Nations. The United Nations is guarantor of nothing. Except in a formal sense, it can hardly be said to exist. Collective security? In the Gulf, without the United States leading and prodding, bribing and blackmailing, no one would have stirred. Nothing would have been done: no embargo, no Desert Shield, no threat of force. The world would have written off Kuwait the way the last body pledged to collective security, the League of Nations, wrote off Abyssinia.

There is a sharp distinction to be drawn between real and apparent multilateralism. True multilateralism involves a genuine coalition of coequal partners of comparable strength and stature—the World War II Big Three coalition, for example. What we have today is pseudo-multilateralism: A dominant great power acts essentially alone but, embarrassed at the idea and still worshipping at the shrine of collective security, recruits a ship here, a brigade there and blessings all around to give its unilateral actions a multilateral sheen. The Gulf is no more a collective operation than was Korea, still the classic case study in pseudo-multilateralism.

Why the pretense? Because a large segment of American opinion doubts the legitimacy of unilateral American action but accepts quite readily actions undertaken by the "world community" acting in concert. Why it should matter to Americans that their actions get a Security Council nod from, say, Deng Xiaoping and the butchers of Tiananmen Square is beyond me. But to many Americans it matters. It is largely for domestic reasons, therefore, that American political leaders make sure to dress unilateral action in multilateral clothing. The danger, of course, is that they might come to believe their own pretense.

But can America long sustain its unipolar preeminence? The spec-

tacle of secretaries of state and treasury flying around the world rat-
tling tin cups to support America's Persian Gulf deployment exposed
the imbalance between America's geopolitical reach and its resources.
Does that not imply that the theorists of American decline and
"imperial overstretch" are right and that unipolarity is unsustainable?

It is, of course, true that if America succeeds in running its economy into the ground, it will not be able to retain its unipolar role for
long. In which case the unipolar moment will be brief indeed (one
decade, perhaps, rather than, say, three or four). But if the economy
is run into the ground it will not be because of imperial overstretch,
i.e., because America has overreached abroad and drained itself with
geopolitical entanglements. The United States today spends 5.4% of
its GNP on defense. Under John F. Kennedy, when the United States
was at its economic and political apogee, it spent almost twice as
much. Administration plans have U.S. defense spending on a trajectory down to 4% by 1995, the lowest since Pearl Harbor.

An American collapse to second-rank status will be not for foreign
but for domestic reasons. This is not the place to engage in extended
debate about the cause of America's economic difficulties. But the
notion that we have spent ourselves into penury abroad is simply
not sustainable. America's low savings rate, poor educational system, stagnant productivity, declining work habits, rising demand for
welfare-state entitlements and new taste for ecological luxuries have
nothing at all to do with engagement in Europe, Central America or
the Middle East. Over the last 30 years, while taxes remained almost
fixed (rising from 18.3% to 19.6%) and defense spending declined,
domestic entitlements nearly doubled. What created an economy of
debt unrivaled in American history is not foreign adventures but the
low tax ideology of the 1980s, coupled with America's insatiable desire
for yet higher standards of living without paying any of the cost.

One can debate whether America is in true economic decline. Its
percentage of world GNP is roughly where it has been throughout
the 20th century (between 22% and 26%), excepting the aberration
of the immediate post–World War II era when its competitors were

digging out from the rubble of war. But even if one does argue that America is in economic decline, it is simply absurd to imply that the road to solvency is to, say, abandon El Salvador, evacuate the Philippines or get out of the Gulf. There may be other good reasons for doing all of these. But it is nonsense to suggest doing them as a way to get at the root of America's economic problems.

It is, moreover, a mistake to view America's exertions abroad as nothing but a drain on its economy. As can be seen in the Gulf, America's involvement abroad is in many ways an essential pillar of the American economy. The United States is, like Britain before it, a commercial, maritime, trading nation that needs an open, stable world environment in which to thrive. In a world of Saddams, if the United States were to shed its unique superpower role, its economy would be gravely wounded. Insecure sea-lanes, impoverished trading partners, exorbitant oil prices, explosive regional instability are only the more obvious risks of an American abdication. Foreign entanglements are indeed a burden. But they are also a necessity. The cost of ensuring an open and safe world for American commerce—5.4% of GNP and falling—is hardly exorbitant.

III

Can America support its unipolar status? Yes. But *will* Americans support such unipolar status? That is a more problematic question. For a small but growing chorus of Americans this vision of a unipolar world led by a dynamic America is a nightmare. Hence the second major element of the post–Cold War reality: the revival of American isolationism.

I have great respect for American isolationism. First, because of its popular appeal and, second, because of its natural appeal. On the face of it, isolationism seems the logical, God-given foreign policy for the United States. It is not just geography that inclines us to it—we are an island continent protected by two vast oceans, bordered by two neighbors that could hardly be friendlier—but history. America was founded on the idea of cleansing itself of the intrigues and irrationalities, the dynastic squabbles and religious wars of the Old World. One must have respect for a strain of American thinking so powerful that four months before Pearl Harbor the vote to extend draft enlistments passed the House of Representatives by a single vote.

Isolationists say rather unobjectionably that America should confine its attentions in the world to defending vital national interests. But the more extreme isolationists define vital national interests to mean the physical security of the United States, and the more elusive isolationists take care never to define them at all.

Isolationists will, of course, say that this is unfair, that they do believe in defending vital national interests beyond the physical security of the United States. We have a test case. Iraq's invasion of Kuwait and hegemonic designs on Arabia posed as clear a threat to American interests as one can imagine—a threat to America's oil-based economy, to its close allies in the region and ultimately to American security itself. The rise of a hostile power, fueled by endless oil income, building weapons of mass destruction and the means to deliver them regionally and eventually intercontinentally (Saddam has already tested a three-stage rocket) can hardly be a matter of indifference to the United States.

If under these conditions a cadre of influential liberals and conservatives finds that upon reflection (and in contradiction to the doctrine enunciated by the most dovish president of the post-war era, Jimmy Carter) the Persian Gulf is not, after all, a vital American interest, then it is hard to see what "vital interest" can mean. If the Persian Gulf is not a vital interest, then nothing is. All that is left is preventing an invasion of the Florida Keys. And for that you need a Coast Guard—you do not need a Pentagon and you certainly do not need a State Department.

Isolationism is the most extreme expression of the American desire to return to tend its vineyards. But that desire finds expression in another far more sophisticated and serious foreign policy school:

not isolationism but realism, the school that insists that American foreign policy be guided solely by interests and that generally defines these interests in a narrow and national manner.

Many of realism's practitioners were heroic in the heroic struggles against fascism and communism. Now, however, some argue that the time for heroism is passed. For example, Jeane J. Kirkpatrick wrote, to be sure before the Gulf crisis, that "It is time to give up the dubious benefits of superpower status," time to give up the "unusual burdens" of the past and "return to 'normal' times." That means taking "care of pressing problems of education, family, industry and technology" at home. That means that we should not try to be the balancer of power in Europe or in Asia, or try to shape the political evolution of the Soviet Union. We should aspire instead to be "a normal country in a normal time."

This is a rather compelling vision of American purpose. But I am not sure there is such a thing as normal times. If a normal time is a time when there is no evil world empire on the loose, when the world is in ideological repose, then even such a time is not necessarily peacetime. Saddam has made this point rather emphatically. If a normal time is a time when the world sorts itself out on its own, leaving America relatively unmolested—say, for America, the 19th century—then I would suggest that there are no normal times. The world does not sort itself out on its own. In the 19th century, for example, international stability was not achieved on its own but, in large part, as the product of Britain's unrelenting exertions on behalf of the balance of power. America tended her vineyards, but only behind two great ocean walls patrolled by the British navy. Alas, the British navy is gone.

International stability is never a given. It is never the norm. When achieved, it is the product of self-conscious action by the great powers, and most particularly of the greatest power, which now and for the foreseeable future is the United States. If America wants stability, it will have to create it. Communism is indeed finished; the last of the messianic creeds that have haunted this century is quite dead. But there will constantly be new threats disturbing our peace.

IV

What threats? Everyone recognizes one great change in the international environment, the collapse of communism. If that were the only change, then this might be a normal time and the unipolar vision I have outlined would seem at once unnecessary and dangerous.

But there is another great change in international relations. And here we come to the third and most crucial new element in the post–Cold War world: the emergence of a new strategic environment marked by the proliferation of weapons of mass destruction. It is a certainty that in the near future there will be a dramatic increase in the number of states armed with biological, chemical and nuclear weapons and the means to deliver them anywhere on earth. "By the year 2000," estimates Defense Secretary Dick Cheney, "more than two dozen developing nations will have ballistic missiles, 15 of those countries will have the scientific skills to make their own and half of them either have or are near getting nuclear capability, as well. Thirty countries will have chemical weapons and ten will be able to deploy biological weapons."

It is of course banal to say that modern technology has shrunk the world. But the obvious corollary, that in a shrunken world the divide between regional superpowers and great powers is radically narrowed, is rarely drawn. Missiles shrink distance. Nuclear (or chemical or biological) devices multiply power. Both can be bought at market. Consequently the geopolitical map is irrevocably altered. Fifty years ago, it took a Germany—centrally located, highly industrial and heavily populated—to pose a threat to world security and to the other great powers. It was inconceivable that a relatively small Middle Eastern state with an almost entirely imported industrial base could do anything more than threaten its neighbors. The central truth of the coming era is that this is no longer the case: Relatively small, peripheral and backward states will be able to emerge rapidly as threats not only to regional, but to world, security.

Iraq, which (unless disarmed by Desert Storm) will likely be in possession of intercontinental missiles within the decade, is the prototype of this new strategic threat, what might be called the "Weapon State." The Weapon State is an unusual international creature marked by several characteristics:

- It is not much of a nation-state. Iraq, for example, is a state of recent vintage with arbitrary borders whose ruling party explicitly denies that Iraq is a nation. (It refers to Iraq and Syria as regions, part of the larger Arab nation for which it reserves the term.)

- In the Weapon State, the state apparatus is extraordinarily well developed and completely dominates civil society. The factor that permits most Weapon States to sustain such a structure is oil. Normally a state needs some kind of tacit social contract with the civil society because ultimately the state must rely on society to support it with taxes. The oil states are in an anomalous position: They do not need a social contract because national wealth comes from oil and oil is wholly controlled by the state. Oil states are peculiarly distributive states. Government distributes goods to society rather than the other way around. It is therefore the source not only of power but of wealth. This makes possible an extraordinary degree of social control exercised by a powerful, often repressive state apparatus.

- The current Weapon States have deep grievances against the West and the world order that the West has established and enforces. The Weapon States are therefore subversive of the international status quo, which they see as a residue of colonialism. These resentments fuel an obsessive drive to high-tech military development as the only way to leapfrog history and to place themselves on a footing from which to challenge a Western-imposed order.

The Weapon States need not be an oil state. North Korea, hard at work on nuclear technology, is a candidate Weapon State. It has about as much legitimacy as a nation-state as the German Democratic Republic. Its state apparatus totally dominates civil society by virtue not of oil but of an exquisitely developed Stalinism. Its anti-Western grievances run deep.

The danger from the Weapon State is posed today by Iraq, tomorrow perhaps by North Korea or Libya. In the next century, however, the proliferation of strategic weapons will not be restricted to Weapon States. Windfall wealth allows oil states to import high-technology weapons in the absence of a mature industrial base. However, it is not hard to imagine maturer states—say, Argentina, Pakistan, Iran, South Africa—reaching the same level of weapons development by means of ordinary industrialization. (Today most of these countries are friendly, but some are unstable and potentially hostile.)

The post–Cold War era is thus perhaps better called the era of weapons of mass destruction. The proliferation of weapons of mass destruction and their means of delivery will constitute the greatest single threat to world security for the rest of our lives. That is what makes a new international order not an imperial dream or a Wilsonian fantasy but a matter of the sheerest prudence. It is slowly dawning on the West that there is a need to establish some new regime to police these weapons and those who brandish them.

In parliamentary debate on the Gulf crisis even British Labour Party leader Neil Kinnock has emphasized that it is not enough to get Iraq out of Kuwait. Iraq's chemical stocks, he said, must be destroyed and its nuclear program internationally controlled. When the Labour Party, hardly a home for hawks, speaks thus, we have the makings, the beginnings, of a new Western consensus.

To do what exactly? There is no definite answer, but any solution will have to include three elements: denying, disarming and defending. First, we will have to develop a new regime, similar to COCOM (Coordinating Committee on Export Controls) to deny yet more high technology to such states. Second, those states that acquire such weapons anyway will have to submit to strict outside control or risk being physically disarmed. A final element must be the development of antiballistic missile and air defense systems to defend against those weapons that do escape Western control or preemption.

There might be better tactics but the overall strategy is clear. With the rise of the Weapon State, there is no alternative to confronting, deterring and, if necessary, disarming states that brandish and use weapons of mass destruction. And there is no one to do that but the United States, backed by as many allies as will join the endeavor.

The alternative to such robust and difficult interventionism—the alternative to unipolarity—is not a stable, static multipolar world. It is not an 18th-century world in which mature powers like Europe, Russia, China, America and Japan jockey for position in the game of nations. The alternative to unipolarity is chaos.

I do not mean to imply that weapons of mass destruction are the only threat facing the post–Cold War world. They are only the most obvious. Other threats exist, but they are more speculative and can be seen today only in outline: the rise, for example, of intolerant aggressive nationalism in a disintegrating communist bloc (in one extreme formulation, the emergence of a reduced but resurgent, xenophobic and resentful "Weimar" Russia). And some threats to the peace of the 21st century are as invisible today as was, say, Nazism in 1920. They will make themselves known soon enough. Only a hopeless utopian can believe otherwise.

We are in for abnormal times. Our best hope for safety in such times, as in difficult times past, is in American strength and will— the strength and will to lead a unipolar world, unashamedly laying down the rules of world order and being prepared to enforce them. Compared to the task of defeating fascism and communism, averting chaos is a rather subtle call to greatness. It is not a task we are any more eager to undertake than the great twilight struggle just concluded. But it is just as noble and just as necessary.

Foreign Affairs, Winter 1990/1991
Adapted from the author's Jackson Memorial Lecture to the Henry M. Jackson Foundation, Washington, D.C., September 18, 1990.

DEMOCRATIC REALISM (2004)

A UNIPOLAR WORLD

Americans have a healthy aversion to foreign policy. It stems from a sense of thrift: Who needs it? We're protected by two great oceans. We have this continent practically to ourselves. And we share it with just two neighbors, both friendly, one so friendly that its people seem intent upon moving in with us.

It took three giants of the 20th century to drag us into its great battles: Wilson into World War I, Roosevelt into World War II, Truman into the Cold War. And then it ended with one of the great anticlimaxes in history. Without a shot fired, without a revolution, without so much as a press release, the Soviet Union simply gave up and disappeared.

It was the end of everything—the end of communism, of socialism, of the Cold War, of the European wars. But the end of everything was also a beginning. On December 26, 1991, the Soviet Union died and something new was born, something utterly new—a unipolar world dominated by a single superpower unchecked by any rival and with decisive reach in every corner of the globe.

This is a staggering new development in history, not seen since the fall of Rome. It is so new, so strange, that we have no idea how to deal with it. Our first reaction—the 1990s—was utter confusion.

The next reaction was awe. When Paul Kennedy, who had once popularized the idea of American decline, saw what America did in the Afghan war—a display of fully mobilized, furiously concentrated unipolar power at a distance of 8,000 miles—he not only recanted, he stood in wonder: "Nothing has ever existed like this disparity of power," he wrote, "nothing. . . . No other nation comes close. . . . Charlemagne's empire was merely western European in its reach. The Roman empire stretched farther afield, but there was another great empire in Persia, and a larger one in China. There is, therefore, no comparison."

Even Rome is no model for what America is today. First, because we do not have the imperial culture of Rome. We are an Athenian republic, even more republican and infinitely more democratic than Athens. And this American Republic has acquired the largest seeming empire in the history of the world—acquired it in a fit of absentmindedness greater even than Britain's. And it was not just absentmindedness; it was sheer inadvertence. We got here because of Europe's suicide in the world wars of the 20th century, and then the death of its Eurasian successor, Soviet Russia, for having adopted a political and economic system so inhuman that, like a genetically defective organism, it simply expired in its sleep, leaving us with global dominion.

Second, we are unlike Rome, unlike Britain and France and Spain and the other classical empires of modern times, in that *we do not hunger for territory*. The use of the word *empire* in the American context is ridiculous. It is absurd to apply the word to a people whose first instinct upon arriving on anyone's soil is to demand an exit strategy. I can assure you that when the Romans went into Gaul and the British into India, they were not looking for exit strategies. They were looking for entry strategies.

In David Lean's *Lawrence of Arabia,* King Faisal says to Lawrence, "I think you are another of these desert-loving English. . . . The English have a great hunger for desolate places." Indeed, for five centuries, the Europeans did hunger for deserts and jungles and oceans and new continents.

Americans do not. We like it here. We like our McDonald's. We like our football. We like our rock and roll. We've got the Grand Canyon and Graceland. We've got Silicon Valley and South Beach. We've got everything. And if that's not enough, we've got Vegas—which is a facsimile of everything. What could we possibly need anywhere else? We don't like exotic climates. We don't like exotic languages—lots of declensions and moods. We don't even know what a mood is. We like Iowa corn and New York hot dogs, and if we want Chinese or Indian or Italian, we go to the food court. We don't send the marines for takeout.

That's because we are not an imperial power. We are a commercial republic. We don't take food; we trade for it. Which makes us something unique in history, an anomaly, a hybrid: a commercial republic with overwhelming global power. A commercial republic that, by pure accident of history, has been designated custodian of the international system. The eyes of every supplicant from East Timor to Afghanistan, from Iraq to Liberia, Arab and Israeli, Irish and British, North and South Korean are upon us.

That is who we are. That is where we are.

Now the question is: What do we do? What is a unipolar power to do?

I. ISOLATIONISM

The oldest and most venerable answer is to hoard that power and retreat. This is known as isolationism. Of all the foreign policy schools in America, it has the oldest pedigree, not surprising in the only great power in history to be isolated by two vast oceans.

Isolationism originally sprang from a view of America as spiritually superior to the Old World. We were too good to be corrupted by its low intrigues, entangled by its cynical alliances.

Today, however, isolationism is an ideology of fear. Fear of trade. Fear of immigrants. Fear of the Other. Isolationists want to cut off trade and immigration and withdraw from our military and strategic commitments around the world. Even isolationists, of course, did not oppose the war in Afghanistan, because it was so obviously an act of self-defense—only a fool or a knave or a Susan Sontag could oppose that. But anything beyond that, isolationists oppose.

They are for a radical retrenchment of American power—for pulling up the drawbridge to Fortress America.

Isolationism is an important school of thought historically but not today. Not just because of its brutal intellectual reductionism, but because it is so obviously inappropriate to the world of today—a world of export-driven economies, of massive population flows and of 9/11, the definitive demonstration that the combination of modern technology and transnational primitivism has erased the barrier between "over there" and over here.

Classical isolationism is not just intellectually obsolete, it is politically bankrupt as well. Four years ago, its most public advocate, Pat Buchanan, ran for president of the United States and carried Palm Beach. By accident.

Classic isolationism is moribund and marginalized. Who then rules America?

II. LIBERAL INTERNATIONALISM

In the 1990s, it was liberal internationalism. Liberal internationalism is the foreign policy of the Democratic Party and the religion of the foreign policy elite. It has a peculiar history. It traces its pedigree to Woodrow Wilson's utopianism, Harry Truman's anti-communism, and John Kennedy's militant universalism. But after the Vietnam War, it was transmuted into an ideology of passivity, acquiescence and almost reflexive anti-interventionism.

Liberals today proudly take credit for Truman's and Kennedy's roles in containing communism, but they prefer to forget that, for the last half of the Cold War, liberals used "cold warrior" as an epithet. In the early 1980s, they gave us the nuclear freeze movement, a form of unilateral disarmament in the face of Soviet nuclear advances. Today, John Kerry boasts of opposing, during the 1980s, what he calls Ronald Reagan's "illegal war in Central America"—and oppose he did what was, in fact, an indigenous anti-communist rebellion that ultimately succeeded in bringing down Sandinista rule and ushering in democracy in all of Central America.

That boast reminds us how militant was liberal passivity in the last half of the Cold War. But that passivity outlived the Cold War. When Kuwait was invaded, the question was: Should the United States go to war to prevent the Persian Gulf from falling into hostile hands? The Democratic Party joined the Buchananite isolationists in saying no. The Democrats voted no overwhelmingly—two to one in the House, more than four to one in the Senate.

And yet, quite astonishingly, when liberal internationalism came to power just two years later in the form of the Clinton administration, it turned almost hyperinterventionist. It involved us four times in military action: deepening intervention in Somalia, invading Haiti, bombing Bosnia, and finally going to war over Kosovo. How to explain the amazing transmutation of Cold War and Gulf War doves into Haiti and Balkan hawks? The crucial and obvious difference is this: Somalia, Haiti, Bosnia and Kosovo were humanitarian ventures—fights for right and good, devoid of raw national interest. And only humanitarian interventionism—disinterested interventionism devoid of national interest—is morally pristine enough to justify the use of force. The history of the 1990s refutes the lazy notion that liberals have an aversion to the use of force. They do not. They have an aversion to using force for reasons of pure national interest.

And by national interest I do not mean simple self-defense. Everyone believes in self-defense, as in Afghanistan. I am talking about national interest as defined by a Great Power: shaping the international environment by projecting power abroad to secure economic, political and strategic goods. Intervening militarily for *that* kind of national interest, liberal internationalism finds unholy and unsupportable. It sees that kind of national interest as merely self-interest writ large, in effect, a form of grand national selfishness. Hence Kuwait, no; Kosovo, yes.

The other defining feature of the Clinton foreign policy was multilateralism, which expressed itself in a mania for treaties. The Clinton administration negotiated a dizzying succession of parchment promises on bio-weapons, chemical weapons, nuclear testing, carbon emissions, antiballistic missiles, etc.

Why? No sentient being could believe that, say, the chemical or biological weapons treaties were anything more than transparently useless. Senator Joseph Biden once defended the Chemical Weapons Convention, which even its proponents admitted was unenforceable, on the grounds that it would "provide us with a valuable tool"—the "moral suasion of the entire international community."

Moral suasion? Was it moral suasion that made Qaddafi see the wisdom of giving up his weapons of mass destruction? Or Iran agree for the first time to spot nuclear inspections? It was the suasion of the bayonet. It was the ignominious fall of Saddam—and the desire of interested spectators not to be next on the list. The whole point of this treaty was to keep *rogue states* from developing chemical weapons. Rogue states are, by definition, impervious to moral suasion.

Moral suasion is a farce. Why then this obsession with conventions, protocols, legalisms? Their obvious net effect is to temper American power. Who, after all, was really going to be most constrained by these treaties? The Anti-Ballistic Missile Treaty amendments were aimed squarely at American advances and strategic defenses, not at Russia, which lags hopelessly behind. The Kyoto Protocol exempted India and China. The nuclear test ban would have seriously degraded the American nuclear arsenal. And the land mine treaty (which the Clinton administration spent months negotiating but, in the end, met so much Pentagon resistance that even Clinton could not initial it) would have had a devastating impact on U.S. conventional forces, particularly at the DMZ in Korea.

But that, you see, is the whole point of the multilateral enterprise: to reduce American freedom of action by making it subservient to, dependent on, constricted by the will—and interests—of other nations. To tie down Gulliver with a thousand strings. To domesticate the most undomesticated, most outsized, national interest on the planet—ours.

Today, multilateralism remains the overriding theme of liberal internationalism. When in power in the 1990s, multilateralism expressed itself as a mania for treaties. When out of power in this decade, multilateralism manifests itself in the slavish pursuit of "international legitimacy"—and opposition to any American action undertaken without universal foreign blessing.

Which is why the Democratic critique of the war in Iraq is so peculiarly one of process and not of policy. The problem was that we did not have the permission of the UN; we did not have a large enough coalition; we did not have a second Security Council resolution. Kofi Annan was unhappy and the French were cross.

The Democratic presidential candidates all say that we should have internationalized the conflict, brought in the UN, enlisted the allies. Why? Two reasons: assistance and legitimacy. First, they say, we could have used these other countries to help us in the reconstruction.

This is rich. Everyone would like to have more help in reconstruction. It would be lovely to have the Germans and the French helping reconstruct Baghdad. But the question is moot, and the argument is cynical: France and Germany made absolutely clear that they would never support the overthrow of Saddam. So, accommodating them was not a way to get them into the reconstruction, it was a way to ensure that there would never be any reconstruction because Saddam would still be in power.

Of course it would be nice if we had more allies rather than fewer. It would also be nice to be able to fly. But when some nations are not with you on your enterprise, including them in your coalition is not a way to broaden it; it's a way to abolish it.

At which point, liberal internationalists switch gears and appeal to legitimacy—on the grounds that multilateral action has a higher moral standing. I have always found this line of argument incomprehensible. By what possible moral calculus does an American intervention to liberate 25 million people forfeit moral legitimacy because it lacks the blessing of the butchers of Tiananmen Square or the cynics of the Quai d'Orsay?

Which is why it is hard to take these arguments at face value. Look: We know why liberal internationalists demanded UN sanction for the war in Iraq. It was a way to stop the war. It was the Gulliver effect. Call a committee meeting of countries with hostile or contrary interests—i.e., the Security Council—and you have guaranteed yourself another twelve years of inaction.

Historically, multilateralism is a way for weak countries to multiply their power by attaching themselves to stronger ones. But multilateralism imposed on Great Powers, and particularly on a unipolar power, is intended to *restrain* that power. Which is precisely why France is an ardent multilateralist. But why should America be?

Why, in the end, *does* liberal internationalism want to tie down Gulliver, to blunt the pursuit of American national interests by making them subordinate to a myriad of other interests?

In the immediate post-Vietnam era, this aversion to national interest might have been attributed to self-doubt and self-loathing. I don't know. What I do know is that today it is a mistake to see liberal foreign policy as deriving from anti-Americanism or lack of patriotism or a late efflorescence of 1960s radicalism.

On the contrary. The liberal aversion to national interest stems from an idealism, a larger vision of country, a vision of some ambition and nobility—the ideal of a true international community. And that is: To transform the international system from the Hobbesian universe into a Lockean universe. To turn the state of nature into a norm-driven community. To turn the law of the jungle into the rule of law—of treaties and contracts and UN resolutions. In short, to remake the international system in the image of domestic civil society.

They dream of a new world, a world described in 1943 by Cordell Hull, FDR's secretary of state—a world in which "there will no longer be need for spheres of influence, for alliances, for balance of power, or any other of the special arrangements by which, in the unhappy past, the nations strove to safeguard their security or promote their interests."

And to create such a true international community, you have to temper, transcend and, in the end, abolish the very idea of state power and national interest. Hence the antipathy to American hegemony and American power. If you are going to break the international arena

THINGS THAT MATTER 341

to the mold of domestic society, you have to domesticate its single most powerful actor. You have to abolish American dominance, not only as an affront to fairness but also as the greatest obstacle on the whole planet to a democratized international system where all live under self-governing international institutions and self-enforcing international norms.

III. REALISM

This vision is all very nice. All very noble. And all very crazy. Which brings us to the third great foreign policy school: realism.

The realist looks at this great liberal project and sees a hopeless illusion. Because turning the Hobbesian world that has existed since long before the Peloponnesian Wars into a Lockean world, turning a jungle into a suburban subdivision, requires a revolution in human nature. Not just an erector set of new institutions, but a revolution in human nature. And realists do not believe in revolutions in human nature, much less stake their future, and the future of their nation, on them.

Realism recognizes the fundamental fallacy in the whole idea of the international system being modeled on domestic society.

First, what holds domestic society together is a supreme central authority wielding a monopoly of power and enforcing norms. In the international arena there is no such thing. Domestic society may look like a place of self-regulating norms, but if somebody breaks into your house, you call 911, and the police arrive with guns drawn. That's not exactly self enforcement. That's law enforcement.

Second, domestic society rests on the shared goodwill, civility and common values of its individual members. What values are shared by, say, Britain, Cuba, Yemen and Zimbabwe—all nominal members of this fiction we call the "international community"?

Of course, you can have smaller communities of shared interests— NAFTA, ANZUS or the European Union. But the European conceit that relations with all nations—regardless of ideology, regardless of culture, regardless even of open hostility—should be transacted on the EU model of suasion and norms and negotiations and solemn contractual agreements is an illusion. A fisheries treaty with Canada is something real. An Agreed Framework on plutonium processing with the likes of North Korea is not worth the paper it is written on.

The realist believes the definition of peace Ambrose Bierce offered in *The Devil's Dictionary:* "Peace: *noun,* in international affairs, a period of cheating between two periods of fighting."

Hence the realist axiom: The "international community" is a fiction. It is not a community, it is a cacophony—of straining ambitions, disparate values and contending power.

What does hold the international system together? What keeps it from degenerating into total anarchy? Not the phony security of treaties, not the best of goodwill among the nicer nations. In the unipolar world we inhabit, what stability we do enjoy today is owed to the overwhelming power and deterrent threat of the United States.

If someone invades your house, you call the cops. Who do you call if someone invades your country? You dial Washington. In the unipolar world, the closest thing to a centralized authority, to an enforcer of norms, is America—American power. And ironically, American power is precisely what liberal internationalism wants to constrain and tie down and subsume in pursuit of some brave new Lockean world.

Realists do not live just in America. I found one in Finland. During the 1997 negotiations in Oslo over the land mine treaty, one of the rare holdouts, interestingly enough, was Finland. The Finnish prime minister stoutly opposed the land mine ban. And for that he was scolded by his Scandinavian neighbors. To which he responded tartly that this was a "very convenient" pose for the "other Nordic countries"—after all, Finland is their land mine.

Finland is the land mine between Russia and Scandinavia. America is the land mine between barbarism and civilization.

Where would South Korea be without America and its land mines along the DMZ? Where would Europe—with its cozy, arrogant community—be had America not saved it from the Soviet colossus? Where would the Middle East be had American power not stopped Saddam in 1991?

The land mine that protects civilization from barbarism is not parchment but power, and in a unipolar world, American power—wielded, if necessary, unilaterally. If necessary, preemptively.

Now, those uneasy with American power have made these two means of wielding it—preemption and unilateralism—the focus of unrelenting criticism. The doctrine of preemption, in particular, has been widely attacked for violating international norms.

What international norm? The one under which Israel was universally condemned—even the Reagan administration joined the condemnation at the Security Council—for preemptively destroying Iraq's Osirak nuclear reactor in 1981? Does anyone today doubt that it was the right thing to do, both strategically and morally?

In a world of terrorists, terrorist states and weapons of mass destruction, the option of preemption is especially necessary. In the bipolar world of the Cold War, with a stable non-suicidal adversary, deterrence could work. Deterrence does not work against people who ache for heaven. It does not work against undeterrables. And it does not work against undetectables: non-suicidal enemy regimes that might attack through clandestine means—a suitcase nuke or anonymously delivered anthrax. Against both undeterrables and undetectables, preemption is the only possible strategy.

Moreover, the doctrine of preemption against openly hostile states pursuing weapons of mass destruction is an improvement on classical deterrence. Traditionally, we deterred the use of WMDs by the threat of retaliation after we'd been attacked—and that's too late; the point of preemption is to deter the very acquisition of WMDs in the first place.

Whether or not Iraq had large stockpiles of WMDs, the very fact that the United States overthrew a hostile regime that repeatedly refused to come clean on its weapons has had precisely this deterrent effect. We are safer today not just because Saddam is gone, but because Libya and any others contemplating trafficking WMDs have—for the first time—seen that it carries a cost, a very high cost.

Yes, of course, imperfect intelligence makes preemption problematic. But that is not an objection on principle, it is an objection in practice. Indeed, the objection concedes the principle. We need good intelligence. But we remain defenseless if we abjure the option of preemption.

The other great objection to the way American unipolar power has been wielded is its unilateralism. I would dispute how unilateralist we have in fact been. Constructing ad hoc "coalitions of the willing" hardly qualifies as unilateralism just because they do not have a secretariat in Brussels or on the East River.

Moreover, unilateralism is often the very road to multilateralism. As we learned from the Gulf War, it is the leadership of the United States—indeed, its willingness to act unilaterally if necessary—that galvanized the Gulf War coalition into existence. Without the president of the United States declaring, "This will not stand," about the invasion of Kuwait—and making it clear that America would go it alone if it had to—there never would have been the great wall-to-wall coalition that is now so retroactively applauded and held up as a model of multilateralism.

Of course one acts in concert with others if possible. It is nice when others join us in the breach. No one seeks to be unilateral. Unilateralism simply means that one does not allow oneself to be held hostage to the will of others.

Of course you build coalitions when possible. In 2003, we garnered a coalition of the willing for Iraq that included substantial allies like Britain, Australia, Spain, Italy and much of Eastern Europe. France and Germany made clear from the beginning that they would never join in the overthrow of Saddam. Therefore the choice was not a wide coalition versus a narrow one, but a narrow coalition versus none.

There were serious arguments against war in Iraq—but the fact that France did not approve was not one of them.

Irving Kristol once explained that he preferred the Organization of American States to the United Nations because in the OAS we can be voted down in only three languages, thereby saving translators' fees. Realists choose not to be Gulliver. In an international system with no sovereign, no police, no protection—where power is the ultimate arbiter and history has bequeathed us unprecedented power—we should be vigilant in preserving that power. And our freedom of action to use it.

But here we come up against the limits of realism: You cannot live by power alone. Realism is a valuable antidote to the woolly internationalism of the 1990s. But realism can only take you so far.

Its basic problem lies in its definition of national interest as classically offered by its great theorist Hans Morgenthau: interest defined as power. Morgenthau postulated that what drives nations, what motivates their foreign policy, is the will to power—to keep it and expand it.

For most Americans, will to power might be a correct description of the world—of what motivates other countries—but it cannot be a prescription for America. It cannot be our purpose. America cannot and will not live by realpolitik alone. Our foreign policy must be driven by something beyond power. Unless conservatives present ideals to challenge the liberal ideal of a domesticated international community, they will lose the debate.

Which is why among American conservatives, another, more idealistic, school has arisen that sees America's national interest as an expression of values.

IV. DEMOCRATIC GLOBALISM

It is this fourth school that has guided U.S. foreign policy in this decade. This conservative alternative to realism is often lazily and invidiously called neoconservatism, but that is a very odd name for a school whose major proponents in the world today are George W. Bush and Tony Blair—if they are neoconservatives, then Margaret Thatcher was a liberal. There's nothing neo about Bush, and there's nothing con about Blair.

Yet they are the principal proponents today of what might be called democratic globalism, a foreign policy that defines the national interest not as power but as values and that identifies one supreme value, what John Kennedy called "the success of liberty." As President Bush put it in his speech at Whitehall last November: "The United States and Great Britain share a mission in the world beyond the balance of power or the simple pursuit of interest. We seek the advance of freedom and the peace that freedom brings."

Beyond power. Beyond interest. Beyond interest defined as power. That is the credo of democratic globalism. Which explains its political appeal: America is a nation uniquely built not on blood, race or consanguinity, but on a proposition—to which its sacred honor has been pledged for two centuries. This American exceptionalism explains why non-Americans find this foreign policy so difficult to credit; why Blair has had more difficulty garnering support for it in his country; and why Europe, in particular, finds this kind of value-driven foreign policy hopelessly and irritatingly moralistic.

Democratic globalism sees as the engine of history not the will to power but the will to freedom. And while it has been attacked as a dreamy, idealistic innovation, its inspiration comes from the Truman Doctrine of 1947, the Kennedy inaugural of 1961, and Reagan's "evil empire" speech of 1983. They all sought to recast a struggle for power between two geopolitical titans into a struggle between freedom and unfreedom, and yes, good and evil.

Which is why the Truman Doctrine was heavily criticized by realists like Hans Morgenthau and George Kennan—and Reagan was vilified by the entire foreign policy establishment for the sin of ideologizing the Cold War by injecting a moral overlay.

That was then. Today, post-9/11, we find ourselves in a similar existential struggle but with a different enemy: not Soviet communism, but Arab-Islamic totalitarianism, both secular and religious. Bush and Blair are similarly attacked for naïvely and crudely casting this struggle as one of freedom versus unfreedom, good versus evil.

Now, given the way not just freedom but human decency were suppressed in both Afghanistan and Iraq, the two major battles of this new war, you would have to give Bush and Blair's moral claims the decided advantage of being obviously true.

Nonetheless, something can be true and still be dangerous. Many people are deeply uneasy with the Bush-Blair doctrine—many conservatives in particular. When Blair declares in his address to Congress: "The spread of freedom is . . . our last line of defense and our first line of attack," they see a dangerously expansive, aggressively utopian foreign policy. In short, they see Woodrow Wilson.

Now, to a conservative, Woodrow Wilson is fightin' words. Yes, this vision is expansive and perhaps utopian. But it ain't Wilsonian. Wilson envisioned the spread of democratic values through as-yet-to-be invented international institutions. He could be forgiven for that. In 1918, there was no way to know how utterly corrupt and useless those international institutions would turn out to be. Eight decades of bitter experience later—with Libya chairing the UN Commission on Human Rights—there is no way *not* to know.

Democratic globalism is not Wilsonian. Its attractiveness is precisely that it shares realism's insights about the centrality of power. Its attractiveness is precisely that it has appropriate contempt for the fictional legalisms of liberal internationalism.

Moreover, democratic globalism is an improvement over realism. What it can teach realism is that the spread of democracy is not just an end but a means, an indispensable means for securing American interests. The reason is simple. Democracies are inherently more friendly to the United States, less belligerent to their neighbors and generally more inclined to peace. Realists are right that to protect your interests you often have to go around the world bashing bad guys over the head. But that technique, no matter how satisfying, has its limits. At some point, you have to implant something, something organic and self-developing. And that something is democracy.

But where?

V. DEMOCRATIC REALISM

The danger of democratic globalism is its universalism, its open-ended commitment to human freedom, its temptation to plant the flag of democracy everywhere. It must learn to say no. And indeed, it does say no. But when it says no to Liberia, or Congo, or Burma, or countenances alliances with authoritarian rulers in places like Pakistan or, for that matter, Russia, it stands accused of hypocrisy. Which is why we must articulate criteria for saying yes.

Where to intervene? Where to bring democracy? Where to nation-build? I propose a single criterion: where it counts.

Call it democratic *realism*. And this is its axiom: *We will support democracy everywhere, but we will commit blood and treasure only in places where there is a strategic necessity—meaning, places central to the larger war against the existential enemy, the enemy that poses a global mortal threat to freedom.*

Where does it count? Fifty years ago, Germany and Japan counted. Why? Because they were the seeds of the greatest global threat to freedom in midcentury—fascism—and then were turned, by nation-building, into bulwarks against the next great threat to freedom, Soviet communism.

Where does it count today? Where the overthrow of radicalism and the beginnings of democracy can have a decisive effect in the war against the new global threat to freedom, the new existential enemy, the Arab-Islamic totalitarianism that has threatened us in both its secular and religious forms for the quarter-century since the Khomeini revolution of 1979.

Establishing civilized, decent, non-belligerent, pro-Western polities in Afghanistan and Iraq and ultimately their key neighbors would, like the flipping of Germany and Japan in the 1940s, change the strategic balance in the fight against Arab-Islamic radicalism.

Yes, it may be a bridge too far. Realists have been warning against the hubris of thinking we can transform an alien culture because of some postulated natural and universal human will to freedom. And they may yet be right. But how do they know in advance? Half a century ago, we heard the same confident warnings about the imperviousness to democracy of Confucian culture. That proved stunningly wrong. Where is it written that Arabs are incapable of democracy?

Yes, as in Germany and Japan, the undertaking is enormous, ambitious and arrogant. It may yet fail. But we cannot afford not to try. There is not a single, remotely plausible, alternative strategy for attacking the monster behind 9/11. It's not Osama bin Laden; it is the cauldron of political oppression, religious intolerance and social ruin in the Arab-Islamic world—oppression transmuted and deflected by regimes with no legitimacy into virulent, murderous anti-Americanism. It's not one man; it is a condition. It will be nice to find that man and hang him, but that's the cops-and-robbers law-enforcement model of fighting terrorism that we tried for twenty years and that gave us 9/11. This is war, and in war arresting murderers is nice. But you win by taking territory—and leaving something behind.

THE NEW CENTURY

We are the unipolar power and what do we do?

In August 1900, David Hilbert gave a speech to the International Congress of Mathematicians naming twenty-three still unsolved mathematical problems bequeathed by the 19th century to the 20th. Had he presented the great unsolved geopolitical problems bequeathed to the 20th century, one would have stood out above all—the rise of Germany and its accommodation within the European state system.

Similarly today, at the dawn of the 21st century, we can see clearly the two great geopolitical challenges on the horizon: the inexorable rise of China and the coming demographic collapse of Europe, both of which will irrevocably disequilibrate the international system.

But those problems come later. They are for midcentury. They are for the next generation. And that generation will not even get to these problems unless we first deal with our problem.

And our problem is 9/11 and the roots of Arab-Islamic nihilism. September 11 felt like a new problem, but for all its shock and surprise, it is an old problem with a new face. September 11 felt like the initiation of a new history, but it was a return to history, the 20th-century history of radical ideologies and existential enemies.

The anomaly is not the world of today. The anomaly was the 1990s, our holiday from history. It felt like peace, but it was an interval of dreaming between two periods of reality.

From which 9/11 awoke us. It startled us into thinking everything was new. It's not. What is new is what happened not on 9/11 but ten years earlier on December 26, 1991: the emergence of the United States as the world's unipolar power. What is unique is our advantage in this struggle, an advantage we did not have during the struggles of the 20th century. The question for our time is how to press this advantage, how to exploit our unipolar power, how to deploy it to win the old/new war that exploded upon us on 9/11.

What is the unipolar power to do?

Four schools, four answers.

The isolationists want simply to ignore unipolarity, pull up the drawbridge and defend Fortress America. Alas, the Fortress has no moat—not after the airplane, the submarine, the ballistic missile—and as for the drawbridge, it was blown up on 9/11.

Then there are the liberal internationalists. They like to dream, and to the extent that they are aware of our unipolar power, they don't like it. They see its use for anything other than humanitarianism or reflexive self-defense as an expression of national selfishness. And they don't just want us to ignore our unique power, they want us to yield it piece by piece, by subsuming ourselves in a new global architecture in which America becomes not the arbiter of international events but a good and tame international citizen.

Then there is realism, which has the clearest understanding of the new unipolarity and its uses—unilateral and preemptive if necessary. But in the end, it fails because it offers no vision. It is all means and no ends. It cannot adequately define our mission.

Hence, the fourth school: democratic globalism. It has, in this decade, rallied the American people to a struggle over values. It seeks to vindicate the American idea by making the spread of democracy, the success of liberty, the ends and means of American foreign policy.

I support that. I applaud that. But I believe it must be tempered in its universalistic aspirations and rhetoric from a democratic globalism to a democratic realism. It must be targeted, focused and limited. We are friends to all, but we come ashore only where it really counts. And where it counts today is that Islamic crescent stretching from North Africa to Afghanistan.

In October 1962, during the Cuban Missile Crisis, we came to the edge of the abyss. Then, accompanied by our equally shaken adversary, we both deliberately drew back. On September 11, 2001, we saw the face of Armageddon again, but this time with an enemy that does not draw back. This time the enemy knows no reason.

Were that the only difference between now and then, our situation would be hopeless. But there is a second difference between now and then: the uniqueness of our power, unrivaled, not just today but ever. That evens the odds. The rationality of the enemy is something beyond our control. But the use of our power is within our control. And if that power is used wisely, constrained not by illusions and fictions but only by the limits of our mission—which is to bring a modicum of freedom as an antidote to nihilism—we can prevail.

The AEI Press, 2004

Adapted from the author's Irving Kristol Lecture to the American Enterprise Institute, Washington, D.C., February 10, 2004.

DECLINE IS A CHOICE (2009)

The weather vanes of conventional wisdom are engaged in another round of angst about America in decline. New theories, old slogans: Imperial overstretch. The Asian awakening. The post-American world. Inexorable forces beyond our control bringing the inevitable humbling of the world hegemon.

On the other side of this debate are a few—notably Josef Joffe in a recent essay in *Foreign Affairs*—who resist the current fashion and insist that America remains the indispensable power. They note that declinist predictions are cyclical, that the rise of China and perhaps India are just the current version of the Japan panic of the late 1980s or of the earlier pessimism best captured by Jean-François Revel's *How Democracies Perish*.

The anti-declinists point out, for example, that the fear of China is overblown. It's based on the implausible assumption of indefinite, uninterrupted growth; ignores accumulating externalities like pollution (which can be ignored when growth starts from a very low baseline, but ends up making growth increasingly, chokingly difficult); and overlooks the unavoidable consequences of the one-child policy, which guarantees that China will get old before it gets rich.

And just as the rise of China is a straight-line projection of current economic trends, American decline is a straight-line projection of the fearful, pessimistic mood of a country war-weary and in the grip of a severe recession.

Among these crosscurrents, my thesis is simple: The question of whether America is in decline cannot be answered yes or no. There *is* no yes or no. Both answers are wrong because the assumption that somehow there exists some predetermined inevitable trajectory, the result of uncontrollable external forces, is wrong. Nothing is inevitable. Nothing is written. For America today, decline is not a condition. Decline is a choice. Two decades into the unipolar world that came about with the fall of the Soviet Union, America is in the position of deciding whether to abdicate or retain its dominance. Decline—or continued ascendancy—is in our hands.

Not that decline is always a choice. Britain's decline after World War II *was* foretold, as indeed was that of Europe, which had been the dominant global force of the preceding centuries. The civilizational suicide that was the two world wars, and the consequent physical and psychological exhaustion, made continued dominance impossible and decline inevitable.

The corollary to unchosen European collapse was unchosen American ascendancy. We—whom Lincoln once called God's "almost chosen people"—did not save Europe twice *in order* to emerge from the ashes as the world's co-hegemon. We went in to defend ourselves and save civilization. Our dominance after World War II was not sought. Nor was the even more remarkable dominance after the Soviet collapse. We are the rarest of geopolitical phenomena: the accidental hegemon and, given our history of isolationism and lack of instinctive imperial ambition, the reluctant hegemon—and now, after a near decade of strenuous post-9/11 exertion, more reluctant than ever.

Which leads to my second proposition: Facing the choice of whether to maintain our dominance or to gradually, deliberately, willingly and indeed relievedly give it up, we are currently on a course toward the latter. The current liberal ascendancy in the United States—controlling the executive and both houses of Congress, dominating the media and elite culture—has set us on a course for decline. And this is true for both foreign and domestic policies. Indeed, they work synergistically to ensure that outcome.

The current foreign policy of the United States is an exercise in contraction. It begins with the demolition of the moral foundation of American dominance. In Strasbourg, President Obama was asked about American exceptionalism. His answer? "I believe in American exceptionalism, just as I suspect that the Brits believe in British exceptionalism and the Greeks believe in Greek exceptionalism." Interesting response. Because if everyone is exceptional, no one is.

Indeed, as he made his *hajj* from Strasbourg to Prague to Ankara to Istanbul to Cairo and finally to the UN General Assembly, Obama drew the picture of an America quite exceptional—exceptional in moral culpability and heavy-handedness, exceptional in guilt for its treatment of other nations and peoples. With varying degrees of directness or obliqueness, Obama indicted his own country for arrogance, for dismissiveness and derisiveness (toward Europe), for maltreatment of natives, for torture, for Hiroshima, for Guantánamo, for unilateralism and for insufficient respect for the Muslim world.

Quite an indictment, the fundamental consequence of which is to effectively undermine any moral claim that America might have to world leadership, as well as the moral confidence that any nation needs to have in order to justify to itself and to others its position of leadership. According to the new dispensation, having forfeited the mandate of heaven—if it ever had one—a newly humbled America now seeks a more modest place among the nations, not above them.

But that leads to the question: How does this new world govern itself? How is the international system to function?

Henry Kissinger once said that the only way to achieve peace is through hegemony or balance of power. Well, hegemony is out. As Obama said in his General Assembly address, "No one nation can or should try to dominate another nation." (The "can" in that declaration is priceless.) And if hegemony is out, so is balance of power: "No balance of power among nations will hold."

The president then denounced the idea of elevating any group of nations above others—which takes care, I suppose, of the Security Council, the G-20 and the Western alliance. And just to make the point unmistakable, he denounced "alignments of nations rooted in the cleavages of a long-gone Cold War" as making "no sense in an interconnected world." What does that say about NATO? Of our alliances with Japan and South Korea? Or even of the European Union?

This is nonsense. But it is not harmless nonsense. It's nonsense with a point. It reflects a fundamental view that the only legitimate authority in the international system is that which emanates from "the community of nations" as a whole. Which means, I suppose, acting through its most universal organs such as, again I suppose, the UN and its various agencies. Which is why when Obama said that those who doubt "the character and cause" of his own country should see what this new America—the America of the liberal ascendancy—had done in the last nine months, he listed among these restorative and relegitimizing initiatives paying up UN dues, renewing actions on various wholly vacuous universalist declarations and agreements, and joining such Orwellian UN bodies as the Human Rights Council.

These gestures have not gone unnoticed abroad. The Nobel Committee effused about Obama's radical reorientation of U.S. foreign policy. Its citation awarding him the Nobel Peace Prize lauded him for having "created a new climate" in international relations in which "multilateral diplomacy has regained a central position, with emphasis on the role that the United Nations and other institutions can play."

Of course, the idea of the "international community" acting through the UN—a fiction and a farce, respectively—to enforce norms and maintain stability is absurd. So absurd that I suspect it's really just a metaphor for a world run by a kind of multipolar arrangement not of nation-states but of groups of states acting through multilateral bodies, whether institutional (like the International Atomic Energy Agency) or ad hoc (like the P5+1 Iran negotiators).

But whatever bizarre form of multilateral or universal structures is envisioned for keeping world order, certainly hegemony—and specifically American hegemony—is to be retired.

This renunciation of primacy is not entirely new. Liberal internationalism as practiced by the center-left Clinton administrations of the 1990s—the beginning of the unipolar era—was somewhat ambivalent about American hegemony, although it did allow America to be characterized as "the indispensable nation," to use Madeleine Albright's phrase. Clintonian center-left liberal internationalism did seek to restrain American power by tying Gulliver down with a myriad of treaties and agreements and international conventions. That conscious constraining of America within international bureaucratic and normative structures was rooted in the notion that power corrupts and that external restraints would curb arrogance and over-reaching and break a willful America to the role of good international citizen.

But the liberal internationalism of today is different. It is not center-left but left-liberal. And the new left-liberal internationalism goes far beyond its earlier Clintonian incarnation in its distrust of and distaste for American dominance. For what might be called the New Liberalism, the renunciation of power is rooted not in the fear that we are essentially good but subject to the corruptions of power—the old Clintonian view—but rooted in the conviction that America is so intrinsically flawed, so inherently and congenitally sinful that it cannot be trusted with, and does not merit, the possession of overarching world power.

For the New Liberalism, it is not just that power corrupts. It is that America itself is corrupt—in the sense of being deeply flawed, and with the history to prove it. An imperfect union, the theme of Obama's famous Philadelphia race speech, has been carried to and amplified in his every major foreign-policy address, particularly those delivered on foreign soil. (Not surprisingly, since it earns greater applause over there.)

And because we remain so imperfect a nation, we are in no position to dictate our professed values to others around the world. Demonstrators are shot in the streets of Tehran seeking nothing but freedom, but our president holds his tongue because, he says openly, of our own alleged transgressions toward Iran (presumably involvement in the 1953 coup). Our shortcomings are so grave, and our offenses both domestic and international so serious, that we lack the moral ground on which to justify hegemony.

These fundamental tenets of the New Liberalism are not just theory. They have strategic consequences. If we have been illegitimately playing the role of world hegemon, then for us to regain a legitimate place in the international system we must regain our moral authority. And recovering moral space means renouncing ill-gotten or ill-conceived strategic space.

Operationally, this manifests itself in various kinds of strategic retreat, most particularly in reversing policies stained by even the hint of American unilateralism or exceptionalism. Thus, for example, there is no more "Global War on Terror." It's not just that the term has been abolished or that the secretary of homeland security refers to terrorism as "man-caused disasters." It is that the very idea of our nation and civilization being engaged in a global mortal struggle with jihadism has been retired as well.

The operational consequences of that new view are already manifest. In our reversion to pre-9/11 normalcy—the pretense of pre-9/11 normalcy—anti-terrorism has reverted from war fighting to law enforcement. High-level al-Qaeda prisoners, for example, will henceforth be interrogated not by the CIA but by the FBI, just as our response to the attack on the USS *Cole* pre-9/11—an act of war—was to send FBI agents to Yemen.

The operational consequences of voluntary contraction are already evident:

- Unilateral abrogation of our missile-defense arrangements with Poland and the Czech Republic—a retreat being felt all through Eastern Europe to Ukraine and Georgia as a signal of U.S. concession of strategic space to Russia in its old sphere of influence.
- Indecision on Afghanistan—a widely expressed ambivalence about the mission and a serious contemplation of minimalist strategies that our commanders on the ground have reported to the president have no chance of success. In short, a serious contemplation of strategic retreat in Afghanistan (only two months ago it was declared by the president to be a "war of necessity") with possibly catastrophic consequences for Pakistan.
- In Iraq, a determination to end the war according to rigid

timetables, with almost no interest in garnering the fruits of a very costly and very bloody success—namely, using our Strategic Framework Agreement to turn the new Iraq into a strategic partner and anchor for U.S. influence in the most volatile area of the world. Iraq is a prize—we can debate endlessly whether it was worth the cost—of great strategic significance that the administration seems to have no intention of exploiting in its determination to execute a full and final exit.

- In Honduras, where again because of our allegedly sinful imperial history, we back a Chávista caudillo seeking illegal extension of his presidency who was removed from power by the legitimate organs of state—from the supreme court to the national congress—for grave constitutional violations.

The New Liberalism will protest that despite its rhetoric, it is not engaging in moral reparations, but seeking real strategic advantage for the United States on the assumption that the reason we have not gotten cooperation from, say, the Russians, Iranians, North Koreans or even our European allies on various urgent agendas is American arrogance, unilateralism and dismissiveness. And therefore, if we constrict and rebrand and diminish ourselves deliberately—try to make ourselves equal partners with obviously unequal powers abroad—we will gain the moral high ground and rally the world to our causes.

Well, being a strategic argument, the hypothesis is testable. Let's tally up the empirical evidence of what nine months of self-abasement has brought.

With all the bowing and scraping and apologizing and renouncing, we couldn't even sway the International Olympic Committee. Given the humiliation incurred there in pursuit of a trinket, it is no surprise how little our new international posture has yielded in the coin of real strategic goods. Unilateral American concessions and offers of unconditional engagement have moved neither Iran nor Russia nor North Korea to accommodate us. Nor have the Arab states—or even the powerless Palestinian Authority—offered so much as a gesture of accommodation in response to heavy and gratuitous American pressure on Israel. Nor have even our European allies responded: They have anted up essentially nothing in response to our pleas for more assistance in Afghanistan.

The very expectation that these concessions would yield results is puzzling. Thus, for example, the president is proposing radical reductions in nuclear weapons and presided over a Security Council meeting passing a resolution whose goal is universal nuclear disarmament, on the theory that unless the existing nuclear powers reduce their weaponry, they can never have the moral standing to demand that other states not go nuclear.

But whatever the merits of unilateral or even bilateral U.S.-Russian disarmament, the notion that it will lead to reciprocal gestures from the likes of Iran and North Korea is simply childish. They are seeking the bomb for reasons of power, prestige, intimidation, blackmail and regime preservation. They don't give a whit about the level of nuclear arms among the great powers. Indeed, both Iran and North Korea launched their nuclear weapons ambitions in the 1980s and the 1990s—precisely when the United States and Russia were radically reducing their arsenals.

This deliberate choice of strategic retreats to engender good feeling is based on the naïve hope of exchanges of reciprocal goodwill with rogue states. It comes as no surprise, therefore, that the theory—as policy—has demonstrably produced no strategic advances. But that will not deter the New Liberalism because the ultimate purpose of its foreign policy is to make America less hegemonic, less arrogant, less dominant.

In a word, it is a foreign policy designed to produce American decline—to make America essentially one nation among many. And for that purpose, its domestic policies are perfectly complementary.

Domestic policy, of course, is not *designed* to curb our power abroad. But what it lacks in intent, it makes up in effect. Decline will be an unintended, but powerful, side effect of the New Liberalism's ambition of moving America from its traditional dynamic individualism to the more equitable but static model of European social democracy.

This is not the place to debate the intrinsic merits of the social democratic versus the Anglo-Saxon model of capitalism. There's much to be said for the decency and relative equity of social democracy. But it comes at a cost: diminished social mobility, higher unemployment, less innovation, less dynamism and creative destruction, less overall economic growth.

This affects the ability to project power. Growth provides the sinews of dominance—the ability to maintain a large military establishment capable of projecting power to all corners of the earth. The Europeans, rich and developed, have almost no such capacity. They made the choice long ago to devote their resources to a vast welfare state. Their expenditures on defense are minimal, as are their consequent military capacities. They rely on the U.S. Navy for open seas and on the U.S. Air Force for airlift. It's the U.S. Marines who go ashore, not just in battle but for such global social services as tsunami relief. The United States can do all of this because we spend infinitely more on defense—more than the next nine countries combined.

Those are the conditions today. But they are not static or permanent. They require constant renewal. The express agenda of the New Liberalism is a vast expansion of social services—massive intervention and expenditures in energy, health care and education—that will necessarily, as in Europe, take away from defense spending.

This shift in resources is not hypothetical. It has already begun. At a time when hundreds of billions of dollars are being lavished on stimulus and other appropriations in an endless array of domestic programs, the defense budget is practically frozen. Almost every other department is expanding, and the Defense Department is singled out for making "hard choices"—forced to look everywhere for cuts, to abandon highly advanced weapons systems, to choose between readiness and research, between today's urgencies and tomorrow's looming threats.

Take, for example, missile defense, in which the United States has a great technological edge and one perfectly designed to maintain American preeminence in a century that will be dominated by the ballistic missile. Missile defense is actually being cut. The number of interceptors in Alaska to defend against a North Korean attack has been reduced, and the airborne laser program (the most promising technology for a boost-phase antiballistic missile) has been cut back—at the same time that the federal education budget has been increased 100% in one year.

This preference for social goods over security needs is not just evident in budgetary allocations and priorities. It is seen, for example, in the liberal preference for environmental goods. By prohibiting the drilling of offshore and Arctic deposits, the United States is voluntarily denying itself access to vast amounts of oil that would relieve dependency on—and help curb the wealth and power of—various petro-dollar challengers, from Iran to Venezuela to Russia. Again, we can argue whether the environment versus security trade-off is warranted. But there is no denying that there is a trade-off.

Nor are these the only trade-offs. Primacy in space—a galvanizing symbol of American greatness, so deeply understood and openly championed by John Kennedy—is gradually being relinquished. In the current reconsideration of all things Bush, the idea of returning to the moon in the next decade is being jettisoned. After next September, the space shuttle will never fly again, and its replacement is being reconsidered and delayed. That will leave the United States totally incapable of returning even to near-Earth orbit, let alone to the moon. Instead, for years to come, we shall be entirely dependent on the Russians, or perhaps eventually even the Chinese.

Of symbolic but also more concrete importance is the status of the dollar. The social democratic vision necessarily involves huge increases in domestic expenditures, most immediately for expanded health care. The plans currently under consideration will cost in the range of $1 trillion. And once the budget gimmicks are discounted (such as promises of $500 billion cuts in Medicare that will never eventuate), that means hundreds of billions of dollars *added* to the monstrous budgetary deficits that the Congressional Budget Office projects conservatively at $7 trillion over the next decade.

The effect on the dollar is already being felt and could ultimately lead to a catastrophic collapse and/or hyperinflation. Having control of the world's reserve currency is an irreplaceable national asset. Yet with every new and growing estimate of the explosion of the national debt, there are more voices calling for replacement of the dollar as the world currency—not just adversaries like Russia and China, Iran and Venezuela, which one would expect, but just last month the head of the World Bank.

There is no free lunch. Social democracy and its attendant goods may be highly desirable, but they have their price—a price that will be exacted on the dollar, on our primacy in space, on missile defense, on energy security and on our military capacities and future power projection.

But, of course, if one's foreign policy is to reject the very notion of international primacy in the first place, a domestic agenda that takes away the resources to maintain such primacy is perfectly complementary. Indeed, the two are synergistic. Renunciation of primacy abroad provides the added resources for more social goods at home. To put it in the language of the 1990s, the expanded domestic agenda is fed by a peace dividend—except that in the absence of peace, it is a *retreat* dividend.

And there's the rub. For the Europeans there really is a peace dividend, because we provide the peace. They can afford social democracy without the capacity to defend themselves because they can always depend on the United States.

So why not us as well? Because what for Europe is decadence—decline, in both comfort and relative safety—is for us mere denial. Europe can eat, drink and be merry for America protects her. But for America it's different. If we choose the life of ease, who stands guard for us?

The temptation to abdicate has always been strong in America. Our interventionist tradition is recent. Our isolationist tradition goes far deeper. When the era of maximum dominance began 20 years ago—when to general surprise a unipolar world emerged rather than a post–Cold War multipolar one—there was hesitation about accepting the mantle. The liberal internationalism of the 1990s, the center-left Clintonian version, was reluctant to fully embrace American hegemony and did try to rein it in by creating external restraints. Nonetheless, in practice, it did boldly intervene in the Balkan wars (without the sanction of the Security Council, mind you) and openly accepted a kind of intermediate status as "the indispensable nation."

Not today. The ascendant New Liberalism goes much further, actively seeking to subsume America within the international community—*inter pares,* not even *primus*—and to enact a domestic social agenda to suit.

So why not? Why not choose ease and bask in the adulation of the world as we serially renounce, withdraw and concede?

Because, while globalization has produced in some the illusion that human nature has changed, it has not. The international arena remains a Hobbesian state of nature in which countries naturally strive for power. If we voluntarily renounce much of ours, others will not follow suit. They will fill the vacuum. Inevitably, an inversion of power relations will occur.

Do we really want to live under unknown, untested, shifting multipolarity? Or even worse, under the gauzy internationalism of the New Liberalism with its magically self-enforcing norms? This is sometimes passed off as "realism." In fact, it is the worst of utopianisms, a fiction that can lead only to chaos. Indeed, in an age on the threshold of hyperproliferation, it is a prescription for catastrophe.

Heavy are the burdens of the hegemon. After the blood and treasure expended in the post-9/11 wars, America is quite ready to ease its burden with a gentle descent into abdication and decline.

Decline is a choice. More than a choice, a temptation. How to resist it?

First, accept our role as hegemon. And reject those who deny its essential benignity. There is a reason that we are the only hegemon in modern history to have not immediately catalyzed the creation of a massive counter-hegemonic alliance—as occurred, for example, against Napoleonic France and Nazi Germany. There is a reason so many countries of the Pacific Rim and the Middle East and Eastern Europe and Latin America welcome our presence as balancer of power and guarantor of their freedom.

And that reason is simple: We are as benign a hegemon as the world has ever seen.

So, resistance to decline begins with moral self-confidence and will. But maintaining dominance is a matter not just of will but of wallet. We are not inherently in economic decline. We have the most dynamic, innovative, technologically advanced economy in the world. We enjoy the highest productivity. It is true that in the natural and often painful global division of labor wrought by globalization, less skilled endeavors like factory work migrate abroad, but America more than compensates by pioneering the newer technologies and industries of the information age.

There are, of course, major threats to the American economy. But there is nothing inevitable and inexorable about them. Take, for example, the threat to the dollar (as the world's reserve currency) that comes from our massive trade deficits. Here again, the China threat is vastly exaggerated. In fact, fully two-thirds of our trade imbalance comes from imported oil. This is not a fixed fact of life. We have a choice. We have it in our power, for example, to reverse the absurd de facto 30-year ban on new nuclear power plants. We have it in our power to release huge domestic petroleum reserves by dropping the ban on offshore and Arctic drilling. We have it in our power to institute a serious gasoline tax (refunded immediately through a payroll tax reduction) to curb consumption and induce conservation.

Nothing is written. Nothing is predetermined. We can reverse the slide, we can undo dependence if we will it.

The other looming threat to our economy—and to the dollar—comes from our fiscal deficits. They are not out of our control. There is no reason we should be structurally perpetuating the massive deficits incurred as temporary crisis measures during the financial panic of 2008. A crisis is a terrible thing to exploit when it is taken by the New Liberalism as a mandate for massive expansion of the state and of national debt—threatening the dollar, the entire economy and consequently our superpower status abroad.

There are things to be done. Resist retreat as a matter of strategy and principle. And provide the means to continue our dominant role in the world by keeping our economic house in order. And finally, we can follow the advice of Demosthenes when asked what was to be done about the decline of Athens. His reply? "I will give what I believe is the fairest and truest answer: Don't do what you are doing now."

The Weekly Standard, October 19, 2009

Adapted from the author's Wriston Lecture to the Manhattan Institute for Policy Research, New York, October 5, 2009.

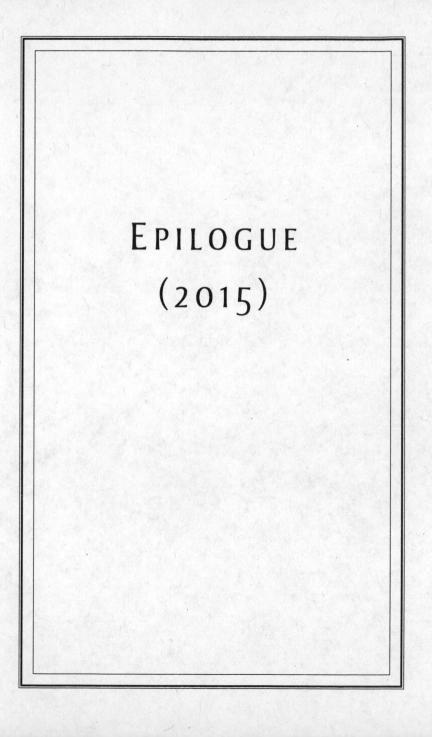

EPILOGUE
(2015)

CHAPTER 17

THE AGE OF OBAMA

UNCERTAIN TRUMPET

We shall fight in the air, we shall fight on the landing grounds, we shall fight in the fields, we shall fight in the hills—for 18 months. Then we start packing for home.

We shall never surrender—unless the war gets too expensive, in which case we shall quote Eisenhower on "the need to maintain balance in and among national programs" and then insist that "we can't simply afford to ignore the price of these wars."

The quotes are from President Obama's West Point speech announcing the Afghanistan troop surge. What a strange speech it was—a call to arms so ambivalent, so tentative, so defensive.

Which made his last-minute assertion of "resolve unwavering" so hollow. It was meant to be stirring. It fell flat. In August, he called Afghanistan "a war of necessity." On Tuesday night, he defined "what's at stake" as "the common security of the world." The world, no less. Yet we begin leaving in July 2011?

Does he think that such ambivalence is not heard by the Taliban, by Afghan peasants deciding which side to choose, by Pakistani generals hedging their bets, by NATO allies already with one foot out of Afghanistan?

Nonetheless, most supporters of the Afghanistan war were satisfied. They got the policy; the liberals got the speech. The hawks got three-quarters of what Gen. Stanley McChrystal wanted—30,000 additional U.S. troops. And the doves got a few soothing words. Big deal, say the hawks.

But it is a big deal. Words matter because *will* matters. Success in war depends on three things: a brave and highly skilled soldiery, such as the 2009 U.S. military, the finest counterinsurgency force in history; brilliant, battle-tested commanders such as Gens. David Petraeus and McChrystal, fresh from the success of the surge in Iraq; and the will to prevail as personified by the commander in chief.

There's the rub. And that is why at such crucial moments presidents don't issue a policy paper. They give a speech. It gives tone and texture. It allows their policy to be imbued with purpose and feeling. This one was festooned with hedges, caveats and one giant exit ramp.

No one expected Obama to do a Henry V or a Churchill. But Obama could not even manage a George W. Bush, who, at an infinitely lower ebb in power and popularity, opposed by the political and foreign policy establishments and dealing with a war effort in far more dire straits, announced his surge—Iraq 2007—with outright rejection of withdrawal or retreat. His implacability was widely decried at home as stubbornness but heard loudly in Iraq by those fighting for and against us as unflinching—and salutary—determination.

Obama's surge speech wasn't that of a commander in chief but of a politician, perfectly splitting the difference. Two messages for two audiences. Placate the right—you get the troops; placate the left—we are on our way out.

And apart from Obama's personal commitment is the question of his ability as a wartime leader. If he feels compelled to placate his left with an exit date today—while he is still personally popular, with large majorities in both houses of Congress, and even before the surge begins—how will he stand up to the left when the going gets tough and the casualties mount and he really has to choose between support from his party and success on the battlefield?

Despite my personal misgivings about the possibility of lasting success against Taliban insurgencies in both Afghanistan and the borderlands of Pakistan, I have deep confidence that Petraeus and McChrystal would not recommend a strategy that will be costly in lives without their having a firm belief in the possibility of success.

I would therefore defer to their judgment and support their recommended policy. But the fate of this war depends not just on them. It depends also on the president. We cannot prevail without a commander in chief committed to success.

And this commander in chief defended his exit date (versus the straw man alternative of "open-ended" nation-building) thusly: "because the nation that I'm most interested in building is our own."

Remarkable. Go and fight, he tells his cadets—some of whom may not return alive—but I may have to cut your mission short because my real priorities are domestic.

Has there ever been a call to arms more dispiriting, a trumpet more uncertain?

The Washington Post, December 4, 2009

THE REAGAN OF THE LEFT?

The media herd is stunned to discover that Barack Obama is a man of the left. After 699 teleprompted presidential speeches, the commentariat was apparently still oblivious. Until Obama's second inaugural address, that is.

Where has everyone been these four years? The only surprise is that Obama chose his second inaugural, generally an occasion for "malice toward none" ecumenism, to unveil so uncompromising a left-liberal manifesto.

But the substance was no surprise. After all, Obama had unveiled his transformational agenda in his first address to Congress, four years ago (Feb. 24, 2009). It was, I wrote at the time, "the boldest social democratic manifesto ever issued by a U.S. president."

Nor was it mere talk. Obama went on to essentially nationalize health care, 18 percent of the U.S. economy—after passing an $833 billion stimulus that precipitated an unprecedented expansion of government spending. By the White House's own reckoning, Washington now spends 24 percent of GDP, fully one-fifth higher than the postwar norm of 20 percent.

Obama's ambitions were derailed by the 2010 midterm shellacking that cost him the House. But now that he's won again, the revolution is back, as announced in Monday's inaugural.

It was a paean to big government. At its heart was Obama's pledge to (1) defend unyieldingly the 20th-century welfare state and (2) expand it unrelentingly for the 21st.

The first part of that agenda—clinging zealously to the increasingly obsolete structures of Social Security, Medicare and Medicaid—is the very definition of reactionary liberalism. Social Security was created when life expectancy was 62. Medicare was created when modern medical technology was in its infancy. Today's radically different demographics and technology have rendered these programs, as structured, unsustainable. Everyone knows that unless reformed, they will swallow up the rest of the budget.

As for the second part—enlargement—Obama had already begun that in his first term with Obamacare. Monday's inaugural address reinstated yet another grand Obama project—healing the planet. It promised a state-created green-energy sector, massively subsidized, even as the state's regulatory apparatus systematically squeezes fossil fuels, killing coal today, shale gas tomorrow.

The playbook is well known. As Czech president (and economist) Vaclav Klaus once explained, environmentalism is the successor to failed socialism as justification for all-pervasive rule by a politburo of experts. Only now it acts in the name of not the proletariat but the planet.

Monday's address also served to disabuse the fantasists of any Obama interest in fiscal reform or debt reduction. This speech was spectacularly devoid of any acknowledgment of the central threat to the postindustrial democracies (as already seen in Europe): the crisis of an increasingly insolvent entitlement state.

On the contrary. Obama is the apostle of the ever-expanding state. His speech was an ode to the collectivity. But by that he means only government, not the myriad of voluntary associations—religious, cultural, charitable, artistic, advocacy, etc.—that are the glory of the American system.

For Obama, nothing lies between citizen and state. It is a desert within which the isolated citizen finds protection only in the shadow of Leviathan. Put another way, this speech is the perfect homily for the marriage of Julia—the Obama campaign's atomized citizen, coddled from cradle to grave—and the state.

In the eye of history, Obama's second inaugural is a direct response to Ronald Reagan's first. On Jan. 20, 1981, Reagan had proclaimed: "Government is not the solution to our problem, government *is* the problem." And then succeeded in bending the national consensus to his ideology—as confirmed 15 years later when the next Democratic president declared, "The era of big government is over." So said Bill Clinton, who then proceeded to abolish welfare.

Obama is no Clinton. He doesn't abolish entitlements; he preserves the old ones and creates new ones in pursuit of a vision of a more just social order where fighting inequality and leveling social differences are the great task of government.

Obama said in 2008 that Reagan "changed the trajectory of America" in a way that Clinton did not. He meant that Reagan had transformed the political zeitgeist, while Clinton accepted and thus validated the new Reaganite norm.

Not Obama. His mission is to redeem and resurrect the 50-year pre-Reagan liberal ascendancy. Accordingly, his second inaugural address, ideologically unapologetic and aggressive, is his historical marker, his self-proclamation as the Reagan of the left. If he succeeds in these next four years, he will have earned the title.

The Washington Post, January 25, 2013

THE LAWLESS PRESIDENCY

As a reaction to the crack epidemic of the 1980s, many federal drug laws carry strict mandatory sentences. This has stirred unease in Congress and sparked a bipartisan effort to revise and relax some of the more draconian laws.

Traditionally—meaning before Barack Obama—that's how laws were changed: We have a problem, we hold hearings, we find some new arrangement ratified by Congress and signed by the president.

That was then. On Monday, Attorney General Eric Holder, a liberal in a hurry, ordered all U.S. attorneys to simply stop charging nonviolent, non-gang-related drug defendants with crimes that, while fitting the offense, carry mandatory sentences. Find some lesser, nontriggering charge. How might you do that? Withhold evidence—for example, the amount of dope involved.

In other words, evade the law, by deceiving the court if necessary. "If the companies that I represent in federal criminal cases" did that, said former deputy attorney general George Terwilliger, "they could be charged with a felony."

But such niceties must not stand in the way of an administration's agenda. Indeed, the very next day it was revealed that the administration had unilaterally waived Obamacare's cap on a patient's annual out-of-pocket expenses—a one-year exemption for selected health insurers that is nowhere permitted in the law. It was simply decreed by an obscure Labor Department regulation.

Which followed a presidentially directed 70-plus-percent subsidy for the insurance premiums paid by congressmen and their personal staffs—under a law that denies subsidies for anyone that well off.

Which came just a month after the administration's equally lawless suspension of one of the cornerstones of Obamacare: the employer mandate.

Which followed hundreds of Obamacare waivers granted by

Health and Human Services Secretary Kathleen Sebelius to selected businesses, unions and other well-lobbied, very special interests.

Nor is this kind of rule by decree restricted to health care. In 2012, the immigration service was ordered to cease proceedings against young illegal immigrants brought here as children. Congress had refused to pass such a law (the DREAM Act) just 18 months earlier. Obama himself had repeatedly said that the Constitution forbade him from enacting it without Congress. But with the fast approach of an election that could hinge on the Hispanic vote, Obama did exactly that. Unilaterally.

The point is not what you think about the merits of the DREAM Act. Or of mandatory drug sentences. Or of subsidizing health care premiums for $175,000-a-year members of Congress. Or even whether you think governors should be allowed to weaken the work requirements for welfare recipients—an authority the administration granted last year in clear violation of section 407 of the landmark Clinton-Gingrich welfare reform of 1996.

The point is whether a president, charged with faithfully executing the laws that Congress enacts, may create, ignore, suspend and/or amend the law at will. Presidents are arguably permitted to refuse to enforce laws they consider unconstitutional (the basis for so many of George W. Bush's so-called signing statements). But presidents are forbidden from doing so for reasons of mere policy—the reason for every Obama violation listed above.

Such gross executive usurpation disdains the Constitution. It mocks the separation of powers. And most consequentially, it introduces a fatal instability into law itself. If the law is not what is plainly written but is whatever the president and his agents decide, what's left of the law?

The problem is not just uncertain enforcement but the undermining of the very creation of new law. What's the point of the whole legislative process—of crafting various provisions through give-and-take negotiation—if you cannot rely on the fixity of the final product, on the assurance that the provisions bargained for by both sides will be carried out?

Consider immigration reform, now in gestation. The essence of any deal would be legalization in return for strict border enforcement. If some such legislative compromise is struck, what confidence can anyone have in it—if the president can unilaterally alter whatever (enforcement) provisions he never liked in the first place?

Yet this president is not only untroubled by what he's doing but open and rather proud. As he tells cheering crowds on his never-ending campaign-style tours: I am going to do such-and-such and I'm not going to wait for Congress.

That's caudillo talk. That's banana republic stuff. In this country, the president is required to win the consent of Congress first.

At stake is not some constitutional curlicue. At stake is whether the laws are the law. And whether presidents get to write their own.

The Washington Post, August 16, 2013

OBAMA AND THE ARC OF HISTORY

The president's demeanor is worrying a lot of people. From the immigration crisis on the Mexican border to the Islamic State rising in Mesopotamia, Barack Obama seems totally detached from the world's convulsions. When he does interrupt his endless rounds of golf, fund-raising and photo ops, it's for some affectless, mechanical, almost forced public statement.

Regarding Ukraine, his detachment—the rote, impassive voice—borders on dissociation. His U.N. ambassador, Samantha Power, delivers an impassioned denunciation of Russia. Obama cautions that we not "get out ahead of the facts," as if the facts of this case—Vladimir Putin's proxies shooting down a civilian airliner—are in doubt.

The preferred explanation for the president's detachment is psychological. He's checked out. Given up. Let down and disappointed by the world, he is in withdrawal.

Perhaps.

But I'd propose an alternative theory, less psychological than intellectual, that gives him more credit: Obama's passivity stems from an idea. When Obama says Putin has placed himself on the wrong side of history in Ukraine, *he actually believes it.* He disdains realpolitik because he believes that in the end such primitive 19th-century notions as conquest are self-defeating. History sees to their defeat.

"The arc of the moral universe is long, but it bends toward justice," said Obama in June 2009 (and many times since) regarding the Green Revolution in Iran.

Ultimately, injustice and aggression don't pay. The Soviets saw their 20th-century empire dissolve. More proximally, U.S. gains in Iraq and Afghanistan were, in time, liquidated. Ozymandias lies forever buried and forgotten in desert sands.

Remember when, at the beginning of the Ukraine crisis, Obama tried to construct for Putin "an off-ramp" from Crimea? Absurd as this idea was, I think Obama was sincere. He actually imagined that he'd be saving Putin from himself, that Crimea could only redound against Russia in the long run.

If you really believe this, then there is no need for forceful, potentially risky U.S. counteractions. Which explains everything since: Obama's pinprick sanctions, his failure to rally a craven Europe, his refusal to supply Ukraine with the weapons it has been begging for.

The shooting down of a civilian airliner seemed to validate Obama's passivity. "Violence and conflict inevitably lead to unforeseen consequences," explained Obama. See. You play with fire, it will blow up in your face. Just as I warned. Now world opinion will turn against Putin.

To which I say: So what? World opinion, by itself, is useless: malleable, ephemeral and, unless mobilized by leadership, powerless. History doesn't act autonomously. It needs agency.

Germany's Angela Merkel still doesn't want to jeopardize trade with Russia. France's François Hollande will proceed with delivery of a Mistral-class attack-helicopter carrier to Russia. And Obama speaks of future "costs" if Russia persists—a broken record since Crimea, carrying zero credibility.

Or did Obama think Putin—a KGB thug who rose to power by turning Chechnya to rubble—would be shamed into regret and restraint by the blood of 298 innocents? On the contrary. Putin's response has been brazen defiance: denying everything and unleashing a massive campaign of lies, fabrications and conspiracy theories blaming it all on Ukraine and the United States.

Putin doesn't give a damn about world opinion. He cares about domestic opinion, which has soared to more than 80 percent approval since Crimea. If anything, he's been emboldened. On Wednesday, his proxies shot down two more jets—a finger to the world and a declaration that his campaign continues.

A real U.S. president would give Kiev the weapons it needs, impose devastating sectoral sanctions on Moscow, reinstate our

Central European missile-defense system and make a Reaganesque
speech explaining why.

Obama has done none of these things. Why should he? He's on
the right side of history.

Of course, in the long run nothing lasts. But history is lived in the
here and now. The Soviets had only 70 years, Hitler a mere 12. Yet
it was enough to murder millions and rain ruin on entire continents.
Bashar al-Assad, too, will one day go. But not before having killed at
least 100,000 people.

All domination must end. But after how much devastation? And
if you leave it to the forces of history to repel aggression and redeem
injustice, what's the point of politics, of leadership, in the first place?

The world is aflame, and our leader is on the 14th green. The arc
of history may indeed bend toward justice, Mr. President. But as you
say, the arc is long. The job of a leader is to shorten it, to intervene on
behalf of "the fierce urgency of now." Otherwise, why do we need a
president? And why did you seek to become ours?

The Washington Post, July 25, 2014

BEWILDERED BYSTANDER

The president is upset. Very upset. Frustrated and angry. Seething about the government's handling of Ebola, said the front-page headline in the *New York Times* last Saturday.

There's only one problem with this pose, so obligingly transcribed for him by the *Times*. It's *his* government. He's president. Has been for six years. Yet Barack Obama reflexively insists on playing the shocked outsider when something goes wrong within his own administration.

The IRS? "It's inexcusable, and Americans are right to be angry about it, and I am angry about it," he thundered in May 2013 when the story broke of the agency targeting conservative groups. "I will not tolerate this kind of behavior in any agency, but especially in the IRS."

Except that within nine months Obama had grown far more tolerant, retroactively declaring this to be a phony scandal without "a smidgen of corruption."

Obamacare rollout? "Nobody is more frustrated by that than I am," said an aggrieved Obama about the botching of the central element of his signature legislative achievement. "Nobody is madder than me."

Veterans Affairs scandal? Presidential chief of staff Denis McDonough explained: "Secretary [Eric] Shinseki said yesterday . . . that he's mad as hell and the president is madder than hell." A nice touch—taking anger to the next level.

The president himself declared: "I will not stand for it." But since the administration itself said the problem was long-standing, indeed predating Obama, this means he had stood for it for five and a half years.

The one scandal where you could credit the president with genuine anger and obliviousness involves the recent breaches of White House Secret Service protection. The *Washington Post* described the first lady and president as "angry and upset," and no doubt they were. But the first Secret Service scandal—the hookers of Cartagena—evinced this from the president: "If it turns out that some of the allegations that have been made in the press are confirmed, then of course I'll be angry." An innovation in ostentatious distancing: future conditional indignation.

These shows of calculated outrage—and thus distance—are becoming not just unconvincing but unamusing. In our system, the president is both head of state and head of government. Obama seems to enjoy the monarchial parts, but when it comes to the actual business of running government, he shows little interest and even less aptitude.

His principal job, after all, is to administer the government and to get the right people to do it. (That's why we typically send governors rather than senators to the White House.) That's called management. Obama had never managed anything before running for the biggest management job on earth. It shows.

What makes the problem even more acute is that Obama represents not just the party of government but a grandiose conception of government as the prime mover of social and economic life. The very theme of his presidency is that government can and should be trusted to do great things. And therefore society should be prepared to hand over large chunks of its operations—from health care (one-sixth of the economy) to carbon regulation down to free contraception—to the central administrative state.

But this presupposes a Leviathan not just benign but competent. When it then turns out that vast, faceless bureaucracies tend to be incapable, inadequate, hopelessly inefficient and often corrupt, Obama resorts to expressions of angry surprise.

He must. He's not simply protecting his own political fortunes. He's trying to protect faith in the entitlement state by portraying its repeated failures as shocking anomalies.

Unfortunately, the pretense has the opposite effect. It produces not reassurance but anxiety. Obama's determined detachment conveys the feeling that nobody's home. No one leading. Not even from behind.

A poll conducted two weeks ago showed that 64 percent of likely voters (in competitive races) think that "things in the U.S. feel like they are out of control." This is one degree of anxiety beyond thinking the country is on the wrong track. That's been negative for years, and it's a reflection of failed policies that in principle can be changed. Regaining control, on the other hand, is a far dicier proposition.

With events in the saddle and a sense of disorder growing—the summer border crisis, Ferguson, the rise of the Islamic State, Ebola—the nation expects from the White House not miracles but competence. At a minimum, mere presence. An observer presidency with its bewildered-bystander pose only adds to the unease.

The Washington Post, October 24, 2014

ACKNOWLEDGMENTS

Given that the writings in this book span three decades, I should be thanking everyone who has ever helped me, a list longer than the Boston phone book. I shall therefore be ruthlessly and ungraciously selective.

My first thanks belong to those publishers and editors who took a chance on a young unknown: Marty Peretz, who hired me to my first journalism job at *The New Republic* in 1981; the late Henry Grunwald, who offered me a column in *Time* magazine two years later; and Meg Greenfield, who invited me to write the column I still write today for the *Washington Post*.

"I tried to be nice to people on the way up," said Walter Winchell, "because I knew I would see them all on the way down." I remain grateful to this day to those colleagues who were more than welcoming to me throughout my career, and most especially when I was starting out: Mort Kondracke, Mike Kinsley and Rick Hertzberg at *The New Republic;* Gordon Peterson, Jim Snyder and the late Tina Gulland on *Inside Washington*.

For the finest psychotherapy imaginable—the opportunity to vent nightly to an audience of several million—I am indebted to Roger Ailes and Rupert Murdoch, the geniuses who created Fox News. And to Brit Hume and Bret Baier, the talented and gracious anchors of Fox News' *Special Report*, who make everything look easy.

Special thanks to my editors at the *Washington Post*, Meg Greenfield and Fred Hiatt, the most admirable, fair-minded journalists one could possibly know, who have given me liberty for decades to write what I want. And to the Grahams, Katherine and Don, for their generous friendship and unwavering support.

In 28 years of writing for the *Post*, only once did I receive a call about something I was about to publish. Sometime in the '90s, in a fit of linguistic provocation, I used the adjective *gay* as a synonym for "happy." Meg called me the night before publication. I knew exactly why.

"So I couldn't slip it by you, could I?" I said before she could get past "Hello."

"Nope," she laughed. "You're about ten years late."

Having no particular enthusiasm for reviving this anachronism beyond making mischief, I put up no argument. Nor were there any ever after.

There is one more joy about writing for the *Post*. My column is syndicated by the Washington Post Writers Group. They edit my column before sending it out to now 400 newspapers. Alan Shearer and Richard Aldacushion are the best editors I've ever had, by about Secretariat's margin in the Belmont. Not a week has passed in all these years that they have not improved my copy—and brightened my Thursdays.

As to my own staff, I have had too many research assistants to thank individually, but I want to particularly acknowledge the contributions of Hillel Ofek, Peter NeCastro and Mike Watson. Mike was particularly helpful in putting together this manuscript, as were my fine and discerning editors at Crown, Sean Desmond and Mary Choteborsky. Tina Constable has been wonderfully encouraging in first suggesting and then carrying through this project, as has been the indefatigable Dana Perino in promoting it. Many thanks to my longtime attorney, Bob Barnett, for his guidance and wisdom in navigating me through the thickets. And special thanks to my personal assistant, Jean Junta, who keeps the trains, my office and my life running on time. And my gratitude to those who have kept me going all these years: Dr. William Davis, Bob Kitts, Jason Smith and Nancy Paul.

I have benefited immensely, both personally and intellectually, from the friendship and fellowship of George Will, Irwin and Cita Stelzer, Bea Kristol and the late Irving Kristol. The regular Sunday brunch we shared over so many years enriched not just my thinking but my life. And I'm deeply indebted to Pete Wehner for his great generosity in reviewing the manuscript of this book and offering very perceptive suggestions.

A special thanks is due to Win and Sarah Brown for a lifetime of deepest friendship and wisest counsel. And to my parents, Thea and the late Shulim Krauthammer, for a constancy of encouragement and support that has sustained me throughout.

Finally, this book is dedicated to my son, Daniel, whose incisive, brilliant mind has kept me intellectually honest and at my keenest since he was about 10 years old. And, to my wife, Robyn, who urged me 35 years ago to follow my calling without looking back. With extraordinary intelligence, humor, grace and lovingkindness, she has co-authored my life, of which this book is but a reflection.

INDEX

CHARLES KRAUTHAMMER is a syndicated columnist, political commentator and physician. His *Washington Post* column is syndicated in 400 newspapers worldwide. He appears nightly on Fox News' flagship evening-news broadcast *Special Report with Bret Baier*. As for doctoring, as a retired but still board-certified psychiatrist, he is best considered a psychiatrist in remission.

Krauthammer was born in New York City but moved to Montreal when he was five, prudently bringing his parents with him. He graduated McGill University with First Class Honors in political science and economics, was a Commonwealth Scholar in politics at Balliol College, Oxford, and received his M.D. from Harvard Medical School in 1975.

He served as a resident and then chief resident in psychiatry at the Massachusetts General Hospital from 1975–78. During his residency, he discovered an unusual form of manic-depressive disease ("Secondary Mania," *Archives of General Psychiatry,* November 1978) that continues to be cited in the medical literature.

In 1978, he quit the practice of psychiatry and came to Washington to work in the Carter administration on planning psychiatric research. During that time, he began contributing articles to *The New Republic*. In 1980, he served as a speechwriter for Vice President Walter Mondale.

In 1981, he joined *The New Republic* as a writer and an editor. Three years later, his *New Republic* essays won the National Magazine Award for essays and criticism. In 1983, he started writing a monthly back-page essay for *Time*. In 1985, he began his syndicated column for the *Washington Post*, which won the Pulitzer Prize two years later.

Krauthammer is a former member of the President's Council on Bioethics. He is also cofounder, with his wife, Robyn, and chairman of Pro Musica Hebraica, a nonprofit dedicated to the recovery and performance of classical Jewish music.

He lives with Robyn, an artist and sculptor, in Chevy Chase, Maryland. Their front yard, however, is in Washington, D.C.